FASTING FOR SPIRITUAL BREAKTHROUGH

ELMER L. TOWNS

In **Fasting for Spiritual Breakthrough**, Elmer Towns not only unravels the mystery of fasting, but provides a very clear biblical understanding of the value of fasting.

H. B. LONDON JR.
Vice President, Ministry Outreach/Pastoral Ministries
Focus on the Family

No one has given us the broad picture of what this means more convincingly than Elmer Towns in his stimulating new book, **Fasting for Spiritual Breakthrough**. This is truly a tract for the times!

C. PETER WAGNER
Fuller Theological Seminary

Regal

A Division of Gospel Light
Ventura, California, U.S.A.

Regal Books
A Division of Gospel Light
Ventura, California, U.S.A.
Printed in U.S.A.

Regal Books is a ministry of Gospel Light, an evangelical Christian publisher dedicated to serving the local church. We believe God's vision for Gospel Light is to provide
church leaders with biblical, user-friendly materials that will help them evangelize,
disciple and minister to children, youth and families.

It is our prayer that this Regal book will help you discover biblical truth for your own
life and help you meet the needs of others. May God richly bless you.

For a free catalog of resources from Regal Books/Gospel Light please contact your Christian sup-
plier or call 1-800-4-GOSPEL.

Library of Congress Cataloging-in-Publication Data
Towns, Elmer L.
    Fasting for spiritual breakthrough / Elmer L. Towns.
        p. cm.
    Includes bibliographical references.
    ISBN 0-8307-1839-7
    1. Fasting. 2. Fasting—Biblical teaching. I. Title.
BV5055.T69 1996   96-4988
248.4'7—dc20   CIP

15   16   17   18   19   20   /   05   04   03   02

Rights for publishing this book in other languages are contracted by Gospel Light Worldwide, the
international nonprofit ministry of Gospel Light. Gospel Light Worldwide also provides publishing
and technical assistance to international publishers dedicated to producing Sunday School and
Vacation Bible School curricula and books in the languages of the world. For additional information,
visit www.gospellightworldwide.org; write to Gospel Light Worldwide, P.O. Box 3875, Ventura, CA
93006; or send an e-mail to info@gospellightworldwide.org.

WARNING:

The fasts suggested in this book are not for everyone. Consult your physician before beginning. Expectant mothers, diabetics, and others with a history of medical problems can enter the spirit of fasting while remaining on essential diets. While fasting is healthful to many, the nature of God would not command a physical exercise that would harm people physically or emotionally.

/||\

\\\\\//

CONTENTS

FOREWORD

I HAVE LONG BELIEVED IN THE BIBLICAL PRINCIPLE OF FASTING. During the past 50 years I have fasted on numerous occasions and for different purposes. However, it was in 1994 that the Lord really began to deal with me about fasting in a fresh and powerful way, and to give me new insights into the subject.

On July 5th of that year, God led me to begin a 40-day fast for a great spiritual awakening in America and for the fulfillment of the Great Commission throughout the world. Before and during the fast, the Lord strongly impressed upon my heart that fasting, though not specifically mentioned, is the best way to help meet the conditions of humility and seeking God's face as set forth in 2 Chronicles 7:14.

> If My people, who are called by My name will humble themselves, and pray and seek My face, and turn from their wicked ways, then I will hear from heaven, and will forgive their sin and heal their land.

Also, on the 29th day of my fast, as I was reading God's Word, I was impressed to send letters to Christian leaders throughout America and to invite them to Orlando, Florida, to fast and pray together for revival and the fulfillment of the Great Commission. Invitations were soon in the mail. I was praying and hoping for at least "Gideon's 300" to respond positively and to join me at the planned December event.

More than 600 came! They represented a significant part of the Christian leadership of America from many different denominations, churches and ministries. It was three wonderful days of fasting, prayer, confession and unity. Many of the leaders gave testimony that it was one of the greatest spiritual experiences of their lives. I believe the incredible timing was no accident, because the very next month, January 1995, there were reports of major revival breaking out on campuses and in churches throughout the nation for which we had prayed. Of course, many others have prayed for revival for a long time, and our prayers only added to theirs; however, I am convinced that our December 1994 fasting and prayer event pleased God and helped move His hand to accomplish His purposes.

I strongly believe that America and much of the world will, before the end of the year A.D. 2000, experience a great spiritual awakening. This divine visit of the Holy Spirit of heaven will kindle the greatest spiritual harvest in the history of the Church. But before God comes in revival power, the Holy Spirit will call millions of Christians to repent, fast and pray in the spirit of 2 Chronicles 7:14. I have been impressed to pray that God will call at least 2 million Christians to fast and pray for 40 days for the coming great revival.

This timely, needed and excellent book, *Fasting for Spiritual Breakthrough*, by my dear friend Dr. Elmer L. Towns, is no doubt inspired by the Holy Spirit to instruct the Body of Christ. His insights will give us greater understanding of the discipline of fasting, and inspire us to use this biblical principle to humble ourselves and to seek God's face. I strongly commend Dr. Towns for being obedient to our Lord and for his labors in putting together this valuable biblical information on the absolute importance of fasting with prayer.

DR. WILLIAM R. BRIGHT
Founder and President
Campus Crusade for Christ International

ACKNOWLEDGMENTS

THE MATERIAL IN THIS BOOK WAS TAUGHT IN THE PASTOR'S BIBLE CLASS at Thomas Road Baptist Church, Lynchburg, Virginia, during the summer of 1995. Thank you, class, for listening to my lessons and sharing with me the things you have learned about fasting. I wrote each chapter as I taught a lesson. For the most part, it was not the older Christians but the younger people who talked to me about this series and tried the things I taught. I have learned much about fasting by looking at it through the eyes of my students.

I am indebted to my pastor, Jerry Falwell, for the insights he has given me about fasting, especially from his book *Fasting: What the Bible Teaches* (Wheaton, Ill.: Tyndale House, 1981); to Mrs. Shelly Seager, who typed the manuscript; and to Dr. Douglas Porter, who did the library research for the glossary and appendices.

Rex Russell, M.D., made a great medical contribution to this book.

Except for those who are physically unable, I require every student who takes my course "EVAN 610/910, Spiritual Factors of Church Growth" to fast. Students must discipline themselves to fast one day, keep a prayer list, attempt a faith-event and keep a spiritual journal. As I've read their papers, these students have taught me much about how to fast and what to avoid during a fast.

Every manuscript is the product of many experiences. I have listened

ACKNOWLEDGMENTS

to sermons about fasting, read many books and talked to many who have fasted. All of these have influenced me, and I give credit to everyone; not the least, the Holy Spirit, who has guided me, and the Lord Jesus Christ who has been my example. Remember, He fasted 40 days before beginning His ministry. In the final analysis, for all of the omissions and mistakes in this text, I take final responsibility. May God use this book for His intended purpose.

ELMER L. TOWNS
Summer 1995

10

INTRODUCTION

IF YOU SEEK A CLOSER WALK WITH GOD, THIS BOOK IS FOR YOU. AT FIRST glance you may not think so, because the discipline of *fasting* has fallen into such widespread disuse that people do not know its power. But let me tell you about an experience that occurred to my secretary, Shelly Seager, and her husband, Dave, as Shelly was typing this manuscript.

Dave had been asked to interview for a job in Harrisburg, Pennsylvania. Shelly described this position as "an opportunity of a lifetime." Dave really wanted the position. So they agreed to do something they had never tried. They fasted 24 hours and spent much time in prayer. (Biblically, prayer and fasting go together.)

The morning after Dave had spent extra time in prayer, the long-distance call came.

It was from Harrisburg. They offered him the position.

Of course, I am not going to guarantee that every circumstance in your life can be "fixed" by fasting. I do, however, insist that modern Christians need to take another look at why this classic spiritual discipline has been neglected in our day.

Richard Foster, the author who has awakened so many people to the spiritual disciplines, has said that there has not been a major book on fasting for a hundred years.

Why?

Perhaps we are currently so into "feel-good religion" that we don't want to be bothered with any thought of hunger or self-denial. Perhaps our confidence in activism, such as splashy evangelistic programs, to virtually bring in the kingdom of God has made us forget the spiritual factors in church growth. Perhaps the widespread promise that "You can have it all" has blocked all thought of sacrifice from our minds.

As Foster also suggests, some Christians may have been turned off to fasting because of the way a few monks and ascetics in the past fasted. They fasted in ways that fell into the old gnostic trap of declaring that matter (such as food, and the body) is evil and only the spiritual is good. Thus we may think fasting is a part of the outlook that maintains any enjoyment of God's good earthly gifts is tantamount to sin. This trap, of course, is not an argument against the actual practice of fasting, but against its abuse.

The disciples of John the Baptist (noted for their practice of fasting) once asked Jesus why His disciples did not fast. "Jesus answered them, 'How can the guests of the bridegroom mourn while he is with them?'" (Matt. 9:15, *NIV*). The answer was obvious. As long as Jesus was present with His disciples, they didn't fast. Jesus then said, "The time will come when the bridegroom will be taken from them; then they will fast" (v. 15).

Obviously, the bridegroom is no longer present on earth in His physical body; He was taken up to heaven at the ascension (see Acts 1:9). *Jesus assumed that after He ascended into heaven, those who believed in Him would fast:* "Then shall they fast in those days" (Mark 2:20, *KJV*); "Moreover when ye fast" (Matt. 6:16, *KJV*). Now that the bridegroom has been taken from us, we should be engaged in disciplines of self-denial enabling us to enjoy something of the closeness to Him enjoyed by the original disciples when they walked and talked daily with their Lord.

I know fasting can not only draw us closer to the bridegroom, but it can also accomplish beneficial results in the lives of others who have deep needs. Fasting has transpersonal or social benefits.

My pastor fasts, and I have seen him raise enormous amounts of money through fasting. My church fasts, and I have seen God intervene in a time of a national crisis. The students fast at the university where I teach. In 1985 almost every one of the 5,000 students fasted for physical healing for Dean of Students Vernon Brewer from cancer, and 10 years later he remains alive and effectively ministering in foreign missions. I know God honors prayers and fasts.

Because so many people are unfamiliar with the variety of ways to fast, you will find suggestions at the end of each chapter about how to undertake each of the nine fasts suggested in this book. These sections should be considered as general guidelines only. Fasting is not a legalistic discipline, but should be adapted to each worshiper's individual purpose. Ultimately, you yourself must determine the length of your fast, what if anything you should eat or drink and other aspects related to your particular fast. The bibliography at the end of this book has valuable resources that will help you in this area. Appendix 4, "How to Keep a Fasting Journal," will help you keep track of what God does in your life through fasting.

Primarily, however, this book is intended to describe the *purposes* and show you the *results* of fasting. It is written to show how fasting can enable you to become an overcomer, to increase your faith and to accomplish great things in the lives of others.

Although I do not think fasting is mandatory for believers today, I do believe the discipline is available to strengthen you spiritually and to help you overcome barriers that might keep you from living the victorious Christian life.

At such a time as this, a major book on the spiritual discipline of fasting is needed. Why?

- Because more than ever before, believers are in bondage to demonic powers and need strength to stand against sin (see The Disciple's Fast).
- Because believers throughout the world need solutions to many complex problems and threatening situations they are facing (see The Ezra Fast).
- Because the Church is in desperate need of revival, and every tribe and tongue and nation is in desperate need of evangelization (see The Samuel Fast).
- Because the world in general and the Church in particular are crying out for people of character and integrity—people who have found in Christ the emotional healing and strength to overcome sinful and destructive habits (see The Elijah Fast).
- Because the abundance of food has insulated North American believers from the realities of starvation and malnutrition in the two-thirds world (see The Widow's Fast).

- Because the media has so captured the national attention that even believers are operating according to principles completely alien to God's will for their lives (see The Saint Paul Fast).
- Because even with the abundance of food and medical technology in North America, people are not necessarily healthier (see The Daniel Fast).
- Because a great many believers have become so entangled in economic and social pursuits that they need to be set free to establish their testimonies and to influence others for Christ (see The John the Baptist Fast).
- Because of the growing influence of demonic forces and the waning influence of biblical Christianity in North America, and the fact that believers need protection from the evil one (see The Esther Fast).

In addition to this last point, the time is long past when Christians could bask in the warmth of an evangelical Protestant consensus in North America. Our culture has become post-Christian and militantly pluralistic. Our culture is little by little losing the influence of the Bridegroom. We need to fast to reestablish contact with Him.

If you are serious enough about the personal and social tasks before you as a Christian to take up the discipline of fasting, you can expect resistance, interference and opposition. Plan for it, insofar as you are able. Do not be caught unawares. Remember that you are attempting to advance in your spiritual journey and to gain ground for the Kingdom. That necessitates taking ground away from the enemy—and no great movement of the Holy Spirit goes unchallenged by the enemy.

I encourage you to find a prayer partner who will stand with you when you fast—to offer intercession for you as you endeavor to seek the Lord through this spiritual discipline.

It is important to remember that fasting is a physical discipline. Consult your physician before beginning to fast. Not everyone should fast. Not everyone should fast for more than one day at a time. Not everyone should attempt all nine fasts suggested in this book. The fast is simply a tool that may be used to glorify God and realize answers to prayer. You can get the same results without fasting if your heart is perfectly prepared. If not, and you are physically healthy, a fast may be God's answer.

My Hope for You

I have great visions for this book. Like a parent giving birth to a new baby, every author sees his new volume as something so special that it will change the world. I want every Christian in the world to learn to fast—to fast properly—to fast for results.

If every Christian fasted, the results could shake our society like a windstorm bending a sapling. Christians would demonstrate that they live differently, that their faith is imperative, that the Almighty works in their daily lives.

If all our churches fasted, they would move forward in evangelism and reach out in feeding and helping others. God would then pour His presence upon His people.

≡ I ≡

THE FASTS GOD CHOOSES

FROM THE BEGINNING, PEOPLE HAVE PURSUED GOD. THEY WRONGLY built the Ziggurat (tower) of Babel to reach Him (see Gen. 11:1-9). They rebelliously carved images to please God. They arrogantly conceived and lived by legalistic laws to impress God. They constructed monasteries and isolated themselves to please God. As we shall see, they even fasted wrongly in an attempt to divert His attention from other things they should have been doing, but were neglecting.

It's important to note that religious practices such as fasting are less important than doing God's will. As Micah 6:8 points out, what the Lord truly requires of us is devotion to Himself: "To do justly, to love mercy, and to walk humbly with your God." Fasting is not an end in itself; it is a means by which we can worship the Lord and submit ourselves in humility to Him. We don't make God love us any more than He already does if we fast, or if we fast longer. As Galatians states, "Stand fast therefore in the liberty by which Christ has made us free, and do not be entangled again with a yoke of bondage" (5:1). The goal of any discipline is freedom. If the result is not greater freedom, something is wrong.

Even if we wanted to, we could not manipulate God. We fast and pray for results, but the results are in God's hands. One of the greatest spiritual benefits of fasting is becoming more attentive to God—becoming more aware of our own inadequacies and His adequacy, our own contingencies and His self-sufficiency—and listening to what He wants us to be and do.

Christian fasting, therefore, is totally antithetical to, say, Hindu fasting. Both seek results; however, Hindu fasting focuses on the self and tries to get something for a perceived sacrifice. Christian fasting focuses on God. The results are spiritual results that glorify God—both in the person who fasts and others for whom we fast and pray.

GOD'S PURPOSE FOR FASTING

In this book I have focused on the well-known and often quoted passage of Scripture in Isaiah 58:6-8, which gives a veritable laundry list of warnings as well as positive results that can occur when we submit ourselves to the discipline of fasting.

It is as important to learn from this passage the kinds of fasts that do *not* please God as it is to understand those fasts He desires. God's people in Isaiah's day had been fasting, but without results. The reason, God says, is that *they ignored the way fasting should change their lives*, treating it as an empty ritual:

> On the day of your fasting, you do as you please and exploit all your workers. Your fasting ends in quarreling and strife, and in striking each other with wicked fists. You cannot fast as you do today and expect your voice to be heard on high (Isa. 58:3,4, *NIV*).

Like so many Christians today, God's people considered worship to be merely a private, inward act. All of the focus on fasting was on the personal dimension. Listen to God's rebuke of this concept:

> Is this the kind of fast I have chosen, only a day for a man to humble himself? Is it only for bowing one's head like a reed and for lying on sackcloth and ashes? Is that what you call a fast, a day acceptable to the Lord? (v. 5, *NIV*).

The purpose of all worship, including fasting, is to change the worshiper in ways that have social and interpersonal impact. We worship not just to gratify ourselves, but also to become empowered to change the world! God goes on to specify the kind of fast He chooses:

> Is not this the fast that I have chosen? to loose the bands of wickedness, to undo the heavy burdens, and to let the oppressed go free, and that ye break every yoke? Is it not to deal thy bread to the hungry, and that thou bring the poor that are cast out to thy house? when thou seest the naked, that thou cover him; and that thou hide not thyself from thine own flesh? Then shall thy light break forth as the morning, and thine health shall spring forth speedily: and thy right-eousness shall go before thee; the glory of the Lord shall be thy rereward (vv. 6-8, *KJV*).

We must not interpret the earlier verses in this passage as a call to a "social gospel" in the sense that would deny the importance of personal, heartfelt worship. God was not asking His people to stop fasting so they might instead bring in the Kingdom through social change. Far from it— He wanted the people to continue fasting, but to expand fasting through their actions into their everyday lives. Through the prophet Joel, God called His people to "Turn to Me with all your heart, *with fasting*" (Joel 2:12, emphasis mine). We may assume that Isaiah is communicating God's desire that fasting be continued, and that its effects be evidenced beyond the mere private and personal.

I find in Isaiah 58, therefore, a model for the fruits God expects to see from genuine faith and devotion. Rightly used, fasting can help us present Him with those fruits. Thus, the passage prompted me to find in other places in Scripture nine kinds of fasting I think Christians should rediscover today—not just for their own benefit, but for the benefit of others as well. Let's look at the passage again, listing the aspects that will be the basis for the rest of this book.

In Isaiah 58, God says He has chosen fasts that (1) loosen the bonds of wickedness, (2) undo heavy burdens, (3) let the oppressed go free, (4) break every yoke, (5) give bread to the hungry and provide the poor with housing, (6) allow the people's light to break forth like the morning, (7) cause their health to spring forth speedily, (8) cause their righteous-ness to go before them and (9) cause the glory of the Lord to be their reward (or "rear guard").

Rightly practiced, we see in Isaiah's day a privileged son of Judah bowing before God and pleading with his people to turn from their sin, abandon their idolatry and worship the Lord through fasting and service to the poor and afflicted.

There are indications that Israelites even pressed fellow Jews into slavery, perhaps in response to their failure to pay debts (see Neh. 5:8). Even though debt-servitude was allowed in some cases, those pressed into this kind of service were not to be treated as mere slaves (see Lev. 25:39-42). This law was apparently being widely violated in Isaiah's day.

We must admit that we will not find all of these social conditions present in our own situations. But if we read the passage with biblical imaginations, we can see a modern and often personal application of each aspect of the kind of fast that pleases God.

For example, even if literal slavery is not a widespread problem in our own society, what of the servitude of the soul? Just as an Israelite might fast in protest of the literal enslavement of others, so we might fast in resistance against selling ourselves to Satan. In each of these social sins a personal parallel can be seen. So in the description of the nine fasts, I invite you as a serious disciple of Christ to find a contemporary application of the original intention of this great passage on fasting.

NINE FASTS GOD CAN USE

To better illustrate and reveal the significance of these nine reasons for fasting, I have chosen nine biblical characters whose lives personified the literal or figurative theme of each of the nine aspects highlighted in Isaiah 58:6-8. Each fast has a different name, accomplishes a different purpose and follows a different prescription.

I do not want to suggest that the nine fasts we are about to explore are the only kinds of fasts available to the believer, or that they are totally separate from each other. Nor do I want to suggest that there is only one type of fast for a particular problem. These suggested fasts are models to use and adjust to your own particular needs and desires as you seek to grow closer to God. What follows is a brief overview of the nine fasts that will comprise the rest of this book:

1. The Disciple's Fast
Purpose: "To loose the bands of wickedness" (Isa. 58:6)—freeing ourselves and others from addictions to sin.

Key Verse: "This kind goeth not out but by prayer and fasting" (Matt. 17:21, *KJV*).

Background: Jesus cast out a demon from a boy whom the disciples had failed to help. Apparently they had not taken seriously enough the way Satan had his claws set in the youth. The implication is that Jesus' disciples could have performed this exorcism had they been willing to undergo the discipline of fasting. Modern disciples also often make light of "besetting sins" that could be cast out if we were serious enough to take part in such a self-denying practice as fasting—hence the term "Disciple's Fast."

2. The Ezra Fast

Purpose: To "undo the heavy burdens" (Isa. 58:6)—to solve problems, inviting the Holy Spirit's aid in lifting loads and overcoming barriers that keep ourselves and our loved ones from walking joyfully with the Lord.

Key Verse: "So we fasted and entreated our God for this, and He answered our prayer" (Ezra 8:23).

Background: Ezra the priest was charged with restoring the Law of Moses among the Jews as they rebuilt the city of Jerusalem by permission of Artaxerxes, king of Persia, where God's people had been held captive. Despite this permission, Israel's enemies opposed them. Burdened with embarrassment about having to ask the Persian king for an army to protect them, Ezra fasted and prayed for an answer.

3. The Samuel Fast

Purpose: "To let the oppressed (physically and spiritually) go free" (Isa. 58:6)—for revival and soul winning, to identify with people everywhere enslaved literally or by sin and to pray to be used of God to bring people out of the kingdom of darkness and into God's marvelous light.

Key Verse: "So they gathered together at Mizpah, drew water, and poured it out before the Lord. And they fasted that day, and said there, 'We have sinned against the Lord'" (1 Sam. 7:6).

Background: Samuel led God's people in a fast to celebrate the return of the Ark of the Covenant from its captivity by the Philistines, and to pray that Israel might be delivered from the sin that allowed the Ark to be captured in the first place.

4. The Elijah Fast

Purpose: "To break every yoke" (Isa. 58:6)—conquering the mental and emotional problems that would control our lives, and returning the control to the Lord.

Key Verse: "He himself went a day's journey into the wilderness....He arose and ate and drank; and he went in the strength of that food forty days and forty nights" (1 Kings 19:4,8).

Background: Although Scripture does not call this a formal "fast," Elijah deliberately went without food when he fled from Queen Jezebel's threat to kill him. After this self-imposed deprivation, God sent an angel to minister to Elijah in the wilderness.

5. The Widow's Fast

Purpose: "To share [our] bread with the hungry" and to care for the poor (Isa. 58:7)—to meet the humanitarian needs of others.

Key Verse: "The jar of flour was not used up and the jug of oil did not run dry, in keeping with the word of the Lord spoken by Elijah" (1 Kings 17:16, *NIV*).

Background: God sent the prophet Elijah to a poor, starving widow— ironically, so the widow could provide food for Elijah. Just as Elijah's presence resulted in food for the widow of Zarephath, so presenting ourselves before God in prayer and fasting can relieve hunger today.

6. The Saint Paul Fast

Purpose: To allow God's "light [to] break forth like the morning" (Isa. 58:8), bringing clearer perspective and insight as we make crucial decisions.

Key Verse: "And he [Saul, or Paul] was three days without sight, and neither ate nor drank" (Acts 9:9).

Background: Saul of Tarsus, who became known as Paul after his conversion to Christ, was struck blind by the Lord in the act of persecuting Christians. He not only was without literal sight, but he also had no clue about what direction his life was to take. After going without food and praying for three days, Paul was visited by the Christian Ananias, and both his eyesight and his vision of the future were restored.

7. The Daniel Fast

Purpose: So "thine health shall spring forth" (Isa. 58:8, *KJV*)—to gain a healthier life or for healing.

Key Verse: "Daniel purposed in his heart that he would not defile himself with the portion of the king's delicacies, nor with the wine which he drank" (Dan. 1:8).

Background: Daniel and his three fellow Hebrew captives demonstrated in Babylonian captivity that keeping themselves from pagan foods God had guided them not to eat made them more healthful than others in the king's court.

8. The John the Baptist Fast

Purpose: That "your righteousness shall go before you" (Isa. 58:8)—that our testimonies and influence for Jesus will be enhanced before others.

Key Verse: "He shall be great in the sight of the Lord, and shall drink neither wine nor strong drink" (Luke 1:15, *KJV*).

Background: Because John the Baptist was the forerunner of Jesus, he took the "Nazirite" vow that required him to "fast" from or avoid wine and strong drink. This was part of John's purposefully adopted lifestyle that designated him as one set apart for a special mission.

9. The Esther Fast

Purpose: That "the glory of the Lord" will protect us from the evil one (see Isa. 58:8).

Key Verses: "Fast for me...[and] my maids and I will fast...[and] I will go to the king...[and] she found favor in his sight" (Esther 4:16; 5:2).

Background: Queen Esther, a Jewess in a pagan court, risked her life to save her people from threatened destruction by Ahasuerus (Xerxes), king of Persia. Prior to appearing before the king to petition him to save the Jews, Esther, her attendants and her cousin Mordecai all fasted to appeal to God for His protection.

FOUR KINDS OF FASTING

The nine fasts described in this book are merely suggestive of a variety of ways to practice this helpful discipline. There are probably as many ways to fast as there are ways to pray—obviously, there is no set number in either case. The following four kinds of fasts, however, taken from Dr. Rex Russell's book *What the Bible Says About Healthy Living* (Regal Books, 1996; see Appendix 1), are good guidelines for you to follow or modify as God directs.

1. The *normal fast* is going without food for a definite period during

which you ingest only liquids (water and/or juice). The duration can be 1 day, 3 days, 1 week, 1 month or 40 days. Extreme care should be taken with longer fasts, which should only be attempted after medical advice from your physician.

2. The *absolute fast* allows no food or water at all, and should be short. Moses fasted for 40 days; but this would kill anyone without supernatural intervention, and should never be attempted today. Be sure to test the spirit that tries to talk you into a 40-day fast, even if it includes liquids.

3. The *partial fast* is one that omits certain foods or is on a schedule that includes limited eating. It may consist of omitting one meal a day. Eating only fresh vegetables for several days is also a good partial fast. John Wesley ate only bread (whole grain) and water for many days. Elijah practiced partial fasts at least twice. John the Baptist and Daniel with his three friends are other examples of those who participated in partial fasts. People who have hypoglycemia or other diseases might consider this kind of fast.

4. A *rotational fast* consists of eating or omitting certain families of foods for designated periods. For example, grains may be eaten only every fourth day. The various food families are rotated so that some food is available each day.

PHYSICAL BENEFITS OF FASTING

The spirit and the body are so interrelated in God's creative design that fasting has both spiritual and physical benefits. Russell's book describes several tangible benefits to fasting that are good to know before we begin.

Russell notes that just as the seventh day was designated as a day of rest at Creation, so the very cells of our bodies may need a rest from food. One of the main benefits of a night's sleep includes rest for our digestive systems. We call, appropriately enough, the first meal of the day *break-fast*.

Dr. Russell notes that our bodies were designed to respond to sickness by fasting and fever! When we are sick we usually don't want to think about eating, but to snuggle down in the covers and be left alone. We work hard to lower a high temperature because it causes us to ache, motivating us to seek the bed, rather than the table. Rest, fever and fasting are parts of God's design to fight infection.

God designed our bodies to heal themselves at the level of the cells,

Dr. Russell observes. These healing processes use proteins, carbohydrates and fats to gain calories and nutrients, yet each of the ways these substances are utilized produces waste products. The cells have built-in ways to clear this waste, and apparently they can be overloaded. Fasting helps unclog the system and eliminate poisons. It is encouraging to know that the same God who designed the discipline of fasting designed our bodies to be benefited by periods of abstinence from food (see appendix 1).

A BRIEF HISTORY OF FASTING

Christians who accept the invitation to fast have the unique privilege of identifying with some of the great heroes of faith throughout the ages. Fasting has a varied and interesting past.

Fasting in the Old Testament
The word "fast" is derived from the Hebrew term *tsom*, which refers to the practice of self-denial. The New Testament using the Greek word *nesteia* for the fast, also refers to self-denial.

Most scholars believe that the practice of fasting began with the loss of appetite during times of great distress and duress. Hannah, who would later become the mother of Samuel, was so distressed about her barrenness that "she wept and did not eat" (1 Sam. 1:7). Also, when King Ahab failed in his attempt to purchase Naboth's vineyard, he "would eat no food" (1 Kings 21:4).

Fasting apparently began as a natural expression of grief; however, after time it became customary to reflect or prove one's grief to others by abstaining from food and/or showing sorrow. David fasted to demonstrate his grief at Abner's death (see 2 Sam. 3:35). Many references in Scripture describe fasting as "afflicting" one's soul or body (see Isa. 58:3,5, *KJV*). Fasting came to be practiced as an external means of demonstrating and later encouraging an internal feeling of remorse for sin.

Fasting was a perfectly natural human expression of human grief; therefore, it became a religious custom to placate the anger of God. People began fasting to turn away God's anger from destroying them. Eventually, fasting became a basis for making one's petition effective to God. David defended his fasting before the death of his son by Bathsheba, indicating his hope that while the child lived David's prayer might be answered. When the child died, David promptly ended his fast, denoting that he knew then that neither fasting nor praying could any longer avail (see 2 Sam. 12:15-23).

When God vented His wrath against a nation for its wickedness, fasting became a national mode of seeking divine favor and protection. Therefore, it was only natural that a group of people should associate themselves in confession, fasting, sorrow for sin and intercession to God.

Fasting in the New Testament

In the New Testament, fasting was a widely practiced discipline, especially among the Pharisees and the disciples of John the Baptist. Jesus began His public ministry with an extended fast of 40 days (see Matt. 4:1,2). As we have noted, when the apostles of Jesus were criticized by both the Pharisees and John the Baptist's disciples for not fasting, Jesus defended their not fasting while He was present, but implied that they would fast after He was taken from them (see Matt. 9:14,15).

Jesus gave His disciples no specific guidelines concerning the frequency of fasting. He taught that their fasting should differ from that of the Pharisees in that they should fast to God rather than to impress others with their supposed spirituality (see Matt. 6:16-18).

Fasting was later practiced in the New Testament Church, especially when ordaining elders and/or designating people for special ministry projects (see Acts 13:1-3). Fasting was apparently practiced by Paul and other Christian leaders fairly regularly (see 1 Cor. 7:5; 2 Cor. 6:5).

Fasting in the Early Church

Epiphanius, bishop of Salamis, born in A.D. 315, asked, "Who does not know that the fast of the fourth and sixth days of the week are observed by the Christians throughout the world?" Early in the history of the Church, Christians began fasting twice weekly, choosing Wednesdays and Fridays to prevent being confused with the Pharisees, who fasted Tuesdays and Thursdays.

The practice of fasting for several days before Easter to prepare spiritually for the celebration of Christ's resurrection was also commonly practiced. Later, this fast took the form of a series of 1-day fasts each week for several weeks prior to Easter. Remnants of these Early Church fasts are seen in the Catholic traditions of shunning meats other than fish on Fridays, and the observation of Lent during the 40-day period prior to Easter. It was also customary for Christians in the post-apostolic period to fast in preparation for their baptisms.

Fasting in Revival Movements

The discipline of fasting has long been associated with reform and revivalistic movements in Christianity. The founders of the monastic movement practiced fasting as a regular discipline in their spiritual lives. Although later monasticism grew to practice fasting and other forms of asceticism in a vain attempt to achieve salvation, it is probable that the earliest monks fasted in their desire for the Church to experience revival and reform.

Each of the sixteenth-century reformers also practiced fasting, as did the leaders of the evangelical revivals in the centuries to follow. Jonathan Edwards fasted for 22 hours prior to preaching his famous sermon, "Sinners in the Hands of an Angry God." During the Laymen's Prayer Revival in America in 1859, Christians fasted during their lunch hours and attended prayer meetings in churches near their places of employment. This prayer revival broke out in the large industrial cities of the northeastern United States.

Prayer was often accompanied by fasting as people sought the Lord for spiritual blessing during the worldwide awakening in 1906. Billy Graham reports fasting and praying during his voyage to England to conduct his first British crusades in the early '50s. The response in his meetings at that time has been described as one of the greatest revivals of our time. Many revival movements have advocated a return to the early Christian practice of fasting two days each week.

Fasting for Divine Intervention

Periodically, political leaders have declared a national day of prayer and fasting for divine intervention in crisis situations. In 1588, the victory of Sir Francis Drake over the Spanish Armada was widely recognized by the English as an act of divine intervention.

The pilgrims fasted the day before disembarking from the Mayflower in 1620, as they prepared to establish a mission colony to reach the native peoples of North America. It was common for political leaders in many New England villages to call for a fast when they faced a crisis.

Friday, February 6, 1756, was designated a day of solemn fasting and prayer in England over war with France in the Americas. Lincoln also called for a national day of prayer and fasting during the Civil War. On both occasions, military victories by England and the northern states of the United States were viewed as divine interventions by those who fasted and prayed for those successes.

Similar days of prayer and fasting have been proclaimed by political leaders as recently as World War II. In the midst of the Battle of Britain, George VI designated Sunday, September 8, 1940, as a day of prayer and fasting. In a radio broadcast made days after the day of prayer, British Prime Minister Winston Churchill compared Britain's state with the earlier threats of the Spanish Armada and Napoleon. In his memoirs, Churchill identified September 15 (the Sunday following the day of prayer) as "the crux of the Battle of Britain." After the war, it was learned that Hitler decided to postpone his planned invasion of Britain for two days (September 17). Similar calls for a day of prayer also accompanied the D day invasion of Europe by the allies on June 6, 1944.

In short, fasting has a long and impressive history as a discipline adopted by believers for a variety of reasons, but all of them are connected by the principle of self-denial. We may deny the self to emphasize the needs of the nation, of others who need God's blessing or of our own spiritual needs.

I invite you to find, in the chapters that follow, an approach to fasting that will accomplish such holy purposes in your own life and in the lives of those you love.

⇉ 2 ⇇

THE
DISCIPLE'S FAST

"I HAVE A SEXUAL ADDICTION," A PERSON TOLD ME AT THE CHURCH altar. This person had been to several counselors, had come to the altar several times and had tried everything suggested. This person was serious about being released from the problem.

"Have you tried fasting?" I asked.

"No."

I explained the steps described in this chapter for breaking bondage, introducing the Disciple's Fast: "This kind goeth not out but by prayer and fasting" (Matt. 17:21, *KJV*).

When I later saw the contented smile on this person's face, I knew God had answered the prayers and honored the self-discipline of the Disciple's Fast.

THE PROBLEM OF "BESETTING SINS"

A significant reason to fast is that it releases people from the bondage of sin. "Is not this the fast that I have chosen? to loose the bands of wickedness" (Isa. 58:6, *KJV*).

Many Christians are helpless victims to "besetting sins" (see Heb. 12:1, *KJV*). Besetting sins are not common sins of neglect or momentary lapse. Nor are they sins of rebellion, in which God says, "Thou shalt not," and the person says "I will" in His face. Besetting sins are habitual sinful behaviors or attutides that victimize and enslave people.

When you are a victim of a besetting sin, you do not clench your fist in the face of God and transgress His purpose; you are helpless and broken before Him because of your sin. A besetting sin makes you a slave and takes away your will. You cry out, "I can't help myself!" As one person said, "I am forced to play a game where I always lose, and I can't quit playing. I hate the game...I hate playing...I hate life."

The apostles tried unsuccessfully to deal with such a sin involving a demonized boy. Jesus said the problem was so severe that it couldn't be treated by ordinary means. "This kind goeth not out but by prayer and fasting," He said (Matt. 17:21, *KJV*).

Are you, as a disciple of Christ, besieged by a besetting sin that calls for such measures? Jesus died on the cross for all sin, including your besetting sin. The substitutionary blood atonement of Jesus Christ is the most powerful thing on earth because it destroys sin, and delivers from death and hell. Christians sing "There is power in the blood," and believe in the accomplishments of calvary.

Yet some Christians are in bondage to alcohol, drug, sex and tobacco addictions. Others struggle with compulsive eating, extramarital affairs and lying. Any sin that can't be broken with ordinary "willpower" can be termed a besetting sin.

Scripture promises, "No temptation has overtaken you except such as is common to man" (1 Cor. 10:13). Your temptation to sin is not unique; others face it as well. You, however, are chained to it like a compulsive slave. Yet Scripture promises "a way out" (see 1 Cor. 10:13). The Disciple's Fast can be that very way of escape for you, as a disciple.

Why Are We in Bondage?
Besetting sins beset us because we believe Satan's lie. "He is a liar," Jesus said (John 8:44). Satan lies to us about sin and we believe him instead of God. In besetting sins, Satan gets us to believe one of the following three lies (otherwise called "compulsions"):

1. I tried before, and can't break it.
2. I don't want to do this, but can't help it.
3. I need an answer, but can't find it.

Because we believe Satan's lie, we cannot see that there *is* a way of escape. Although we can change our desires and find the answers, we believe we are powerless because we have surrendered our wills to Satan rather than to God.

Satan's lie convinces us that we have no power against sin. Fortunately, Paul testified for our encouragement, "For the good that I will to do, I do not do; but the evil I will not to do, that I practice" (Rom. 7:19).

When Satan controls our thoughts, he controls our lives. When he lies to us about our lives, we are in bondage.

We ask the questions: How can we break external bondages in our lives? How can we regain control of our lives?

When you take control of your physical appetite, you develop strength to take control of your emotional appetite.

THE POWER OF THE DISCIPLE'S FAST

The demon-possessed boy's father did not understand his son's problem. He said, "Lord, have mercy on my son: for he is a lunatic, and sore vexed: for ofttimes, he falleth into the fire, and oft into the water" (Matt. 17:15, *KJV*). The father thought his son was sick or had some internal retardation, not understanding that his son was controlled by an external spirit. But Jesus knew that a demon had entered into the boy and had taken control of his life.

The father brought his boy to the disciples for deliverance, but "they could not cure him" (Matt. 17:16). The disciples were unable to break the boy's bondage.

Some people are unable to quit smoking or break their homosexual relationships. Although they weep, pray sincerely and seek deliverance, they remain in bondage. The Disciple's Fast deals with these kinds of bondages.

You are wrestling for control of your life when you enter the Disciple's Fast. By controlling what you eat, you determine that you will control your life for God's purpose. When you make a vow and reinforce it with the Disciple's Fast, you move into the strength of decision making. You give up necessary or enjoyable food as a demonstration of the commitment of your will. When you make a choice to fast, you strengthen yourself to stand against a force that has enslaved your spiritual appetite. In the Disciple's Fast you control your physical appetite to strengthen your spiritual appetite. Look at what happens in this fast.

You make a life-freeing choice to be delivered. One who came to Jesus asking for healing was confronted with the Lord's question, "Do you want to be made well?" (John 5:6). Jesus knew the man wanted to be cured, so why did He ask the question? He was not asking for information, because Jesus knew all things. He was asking to build anticipation or "willpower" in the patient. Jesus wanted the man to *desire* the power that He could give him.

Some people will go to their church altars to ask God to take away bondages. "Lord, please take cigarettes from me," they beg. These people are often expecting God to do it all. They want God to "zap" them and instantaneously take away their appetites for tobacco. That is not the way God works. He wants us to look within, so *we* make the decision to follow Him. God does not want people to be robots controlled by switches He presses to force them to give up their sins.

God wants people to love Him voluntarily and to quit sinning voluntarily. He wants us to demonstrate our commitment to Him, not in one big "quick change," as Clark Kent into Superman, but by making choices and acting on those choices.

You recognize that an external power is responsible for your bondage. The boy's father in Matthew 17 did not recognize that a demon held his son in bondage. Apparently the disciples did not recognize the cause of the problem either. Yet Jesus immediately "rebuked the demon, and it came out of the boy" (v. 18, *NIV*).

One of the first steps in the Disciple's Fast is to recognize the external power of our bondages. This does not necessarily mean we have demons, but it does mean we are controlled externally, not internally. Some believe they are alcoholics because their fathers were alcoholics. Others have convinced themselves that they were born as homosexuals. Although the causes of these problems are external, these people suffer internal depression. "I'm worthless," they inwardly confess, and give up—when in fact, if they regained control of their bodies through fasting, they could reach into their spirits to take control of their inner humanities. Recognizing that an external power has made us weak is the first step in recovering control of ourselves.

You confess your previous lack of faith. Before you can be strong, you have to confess your weakness. Before running the marathon, the runner must realize the physical need to practice, exercise and build up the physical body. The disciples did not realize their need in the face of the demonic power in the boy, therefore they could not cast out the demon. They asked, "Why couldn't we force out the demon?" (Matt. 17:19, *CEV*). Jesus answered, "It is because you don't have enough faith!" (v. 20).

It is a statement of faith to recognize what God can do. It is also a statement of faith to recognize what a person cannot do. Faith is recognizing God's strategy and submitting to it.

You specifically state your besetting sin. As you will see in the next section, the Disciple's Fast involves stating its faith-purpose specifically. When you are fasting to break bondage, you must write out the specific bondage you want to break. Notice what happens when you start writing:

- You strengthen your will by stating what you want.
- You focus your energies on the problem.
- You build up anticipation to break the problem.
- You build up your faith in God to expect an answer.

Jesus said to the disciples, "If ye have faith as a grain of mustard seed, ye shall say unto this mountain, Remove hence" (v. 20, *KJV*).

Faith is never blind faith, such as walking to the end of the diving board and jumping into a pool, hoping there will be water in it. Faith is confidence. When you say "I believe," you are saying "I know." When Jesus said "If you have faith," He was saying, "If you know you can break this bondage, it will happen to you."

The old farmer said, "Faith is believing what you know ain't so"—but that is not New Testament faith. New Testament faith is believing what you know *is* so.

When you write out a faith-purpose statement, you begin to exercise the faith that is required for deliverance from your problem. Your faith experience leads to a faith expression (what you say) that leads to the faith event (fasting).

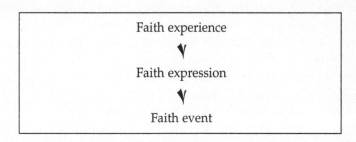

Faith experience
▼
Faith expression
▼
Faith event

Although it is important to *fast specifically for a specific sin(s)*, it is not necessary to list specific acts. Identify the bondage by its principle, but do not write out the gory details. (Reliving the details can rekindle the tire of lust rather than producing power to overcome it.)

You fast repeatedly until you get a breakthrough. When Jesus said, "This kind goeth not out but by prayer and fasting" (v. 21, *KJV*), the verb action in the original language is continuous. Jesus meant we should continuously fast to get power over besetting sins. This may involve fasting for a longer time or more often (once a week for several weeks) than we might have expected.

Fasting for an answer is similar to prayer. Sometimes you can pray once in an act of faith, and God hears and answers. You don't have to keep it up like a child begging for something a parent doesn't want to give. On other occasions you must continually ask in faith before an answer will come. "Ask, and it will be given to you; seek, and you will find; knock, and it will be opened to you" (7:7). Why does God sometimes make us wait? Frequently He tests us to determine if we mean business. Often it takes time for conditions to answer our prayers. For example, we pray for rain, but it takes time for rain clouds to form.

Look at it from God's perspective. He could answer immediately. He knows beforehand that we will pray in faith, so God could prepare the rain clouds ahead of time. But God sees our perspective. We need to pray often and fast continually to build up our faith and our "spiritual character."

The longer we fast, the more we obey God. The longer we abstain from food, the more determined we become. After a time, our faith grows to trust God for greater miracles in our lives.

PRESCRIPTION FOR DELIVERANCE

Those unable to break bad habits experience an overwhelming sense of frustration. They can't break free of the bondages associated with their habits. They want to change, but something inside refuses to let them take control of their lives. Whether physically addicted to a substance or not, people experience psychological addictions to sin that prevent them from making the significant changes they desperately desire.

For those who struggle with a sin that has a grip that just won't let go, the Disciple's Fast offers hope. Choose the kind and duration of fast that is right for you. Write down the specific foods to be avoided (see "Preparing for the Disciple's Fast" at the end of the chapter).

Specific spiritual steps need to be taken, too. Spiritual bondage grows from seeds that are planted in our minds. The seeds send their roots into our subconscious minds, influencing our emotions, physical capacities and desires. Those of us in bondage would affirm our belief in God's omnipotence, yet would also describe ourselves as helpless victims unable to break the power of sin, our old natures, Satan or our addictive habits.

This is why Scripture so often links fasting with prayer. If we attempt to break an addictive sin without taking into account the spiritual steps necessary to break that sin, we will experience the frustrations and discouragement of persistent failure. To break spiritual bondage, we must follow the steps God has provided for spiritual warfare.

"(For the weapons of our warfare are not carnal, but mighty through God to the pulling down of strong holds;) casting down imaginations, and every high thing that exalteth itself against the knowledge of God, and bringing into captivity every thought to the obedience of Christ" (2 Cor. 10:4,5, *KJV*).[1]

Step 1: Renounce Counterfeit Control
The first step in breaking spiritual bondage involves *discerning reality from that which is counterfeit*. This requires recognizing and renouncing any control over your mind that is not from Christ. "As the serpent beguiled Eve through his subtlety, so your minds should be corrupted from the simplicity that is in Christ" (2 Cor. 11:3, *KJV*).

Counterfeit control may come from one of several sources. The anti-Christian values learned in an ungodly home can impact a family for generations. We have all been exposed to the godless influence of the mass media in the books, movies and music we experience. Have you ever been involved innocently or actively in the occult, New Age, spiritism, black or white magic, cults or other religions? These sources represent an external power that would influence our lives. Satanic rituals and bonding oneself to alien spirits also place people in spiritual bondage.

Jesus contrasted His ministry with that of the devil when He stated, "The thief does not come except to steal, and to kill, and to destroy. I have come that they may have life, and that they may have it more abundantly" (John 10:10). To experience the abundant life Jesus promised and be free of spiritual bondage, we must renounce the counterfeit influences in our lives.

Pray audibly, "I renounce (*insert here those counterfeit influences that are holding you in spiritual bondage*)."

Praying audibly is the first important step on the road to experiencing your liberty in Christ. Take time to examine your history. Note all external and internal influences, and denounce them audibly when you pray.

Step 2: Acknowledge Self-Deception

The second step on the road to Christian liberty involves *discerning truth from that which is deceptive.* For many people, this step is very difficult. It involves acknowledging our own efforts to deceive ourselves, and choosing to embrace the truth of God. God wants to begin the process of liberating us from the spiritual bondage internally. David wrote, "You desire truth in the inward parts; and in the hidden part You will make me to know wisdom" (Ps. 51:6).

The problem with self-deception is that we are so successful at it that we don't know we are successful and don't realize the damage it does to us. Many people have deceived themselves for so long that they have difficulty believing they are deceived.

Several biblical principles may be applied to discern areas where we have deceived ourselves. First, we deceive ourselves when we hear and fail to apply the Word of God in our lives (see Jas. 1:22). Second, "If we say that we have no sin, we deceive ourselves, and the truth is not in us" (1 John 1:8). Also, "If anyone thinks himself to be something, when he is nothing, he deceives himself" (Gal. 6:3).

Another way we deceive ourselves is in evaluating our wisdom by the standard of age rather than by the wisdom of God (see 1 Cor. 3:18). Finally, we deceive ourselves when we think we can sin and then escape the consequences (see 1 Cor. 6:9). Some ministers who have fallen into sexual sins probably began as men of God, but committed "minor" sins and thought they got away with them. As one thing leads to another, their sins became more severe and they thought they were above the consequences of sin.

As long as we continue to deceive ourselves, we will remain in spiritual bondage. In contrast, Jesus said, "You shall know the truth, and the truth shall make you free" (John 8:32). To move out of the realm of self-deception into the liberating truth of the gospel, we must admit we are deceived.

Pray audibly, "I acknowledge (*insert here those areas where you have deceived yourself*)."

When you are honest with God and yourself, you allow God's truth to free you from deception.

Step 3: Forgive to Overcome Bitterness

The third step on the path to liberty involves *forgiving others so you can overcome bitterness and gain freedom.* If you refuse to forgive anyone, you place yourself in spiritual bondage to them and to sin. Paul reminded the Corinthians:

> If you forgive anyone, I also forgive him. And what I have forgiven—if there was anything to forgive—I have forgiven in the sight of Christ for your sake, in order that Satan might not outwit us. For we are not unaware of his schemes" (2 Cor. 2:10,11, *NIV*).

As you work through your bondage to sin and others, you should list the names of those you need to forgive. This is a list of names, not a list of sins or other violations they may have committed against you or someone to whom you are close. Continually bringing up past sins is evidence that you have not forgiven them.

Forgiveness is a choice. Because God requires us to forgive others, it is something we can do. Our natural inclination is to seek revenge when we have suffered. When we don't want to let others "off the hook," however, it means they still have their hooks in us. That places us in bondage to them. If we don't forgive others for their sakes, we should forgive them for our own sakes.

Forgiveness is not merely a conflict between yourself and the offender, but a matter between you and God. When you forgive, you choose to live with the consequences of wrongs committed against you. If you do not forgive, you will live with bitter consequences anyway. The choice is yours. You choose whether to live in the freedom of forgiveness or in the bitterness of bondage.

Pray audibly, "I forgive (*insert here the names of those who have wronged you in some way*)." As you forgive others, you experience God's forgiveness in your life.

Step 4: Submit to God's Authority

The fourth step involves *overcoming rebellion in your life by submitting to the authority of God and those He has placed over you.* Jesus compared being under authority to a manifestation of great faith (see Matt. 8:8-10). This involves trusting not only God directly, but also the line of authority He has appointed to provide leadership in your life.

God has placed all of us "under authority." We are called to submit to the authority of (1) civil government (see Rom. 13:1-7); (2) church leadership (see Heb. 13:17); (3) parents (see Eph. 6:1-3); (4) husbands (see 1 Pet. 3:1-4); (5) employers (see 1 Pet. 2:13-23); and (6) God (see Dan. 9:5,9). Each of these authorities has a sphere of influence in our lives. Dealing with a rebellious spirit or attitude and placing ourselves under authority is another step toward breaking bondage in our lives.

Pray audibly, "I submit to (*insert here the specific authority in your life*)."

Submitting to the authorities God has placed in your life is an important element in the Disciple's Fast because it is evidence of your submission to God Himself.

Step 5: Take Personal Responsibility

To break your bondage, *confront the problem of pride with a spirit of humility.* This is the only way you can accept your share of the responsibility for your problem. You can overcome bondage in your life by following the example of Jesus Christ. When you give in to the sin of pride and self-exaltation, you are in bondage. Jesus Christ wants you to be free. He promised, "Therefore if the Son makes you free, you shall be free indeed" (John 8:36).

Freedom is not being passive. You submit to Christ to become active. You are free to actively do what God wants you to do. The key to experiencing full freedom in Christ is to take responsibility for your actions. When you confess your sins, God promises both cleansing and forgiveness (see 1 John 1:9).

Each time you confess the same sin, God forgives; however, even though God forgives, the inner "you" becomes progressively weaker in esteem or acceptance. Many Protestants suffer from a condition I call "confessionitis," which is the same "confession box" cycle of Roman Catholics. They repeatedly confess their sins, but then immediately return to their sins after confession because they are in bondage to them.

The cure for confessionitis is found in the way we confess our sins. We should not just say, "I'm sorry for (*insert specific sin here*)." This leaves us with excuses for our actions such as "I couldn't help it" or "The devil made me do it."

You are responsible for the sin that has habitual control over your body (see Rom. 6:13). To pray, "I'm sorry" doesn't mean you take responsibility for it. You are called upon to renounce (repent) every sin done in your body. This involves praying audibly.

Fast and pray, "I am responsible for (*insert specific sin here*). "When you take responsibility for yourself and your sin, you humble yourself before God and enable Him to bless you with the freedom He desires to give you.

Step 6: Disown Sinful Influences
The final step to spiritual freedom involves *disowning sinful influences that come from friends and acquaintances*. Each of us is predisposed to certain behavior from several sources, including (a) emotional/psychological problems, (b) genetics, (c) direct sinful stimulation, (d) wrong heroes or role models and (e) direct satanic or demonic activity.

For many people, these things are part of their family heritage. To gain spiritual liberty over the bondage associated with these influences, we must disown the sins of others and their influence on our lives (see Exod. 20:4,5; Gal. 5:24).

This may appear easier said than done. Actually, a few simple steps can help you through this process. First, recognize that you have been crucified, buried and raised with Jesus Christ and you now sit in the heavenlies (see 2 Cor. 4:14). Second, publicly state that you belong to the Lord Jesus Christ (see Gal. 5:24). Then verbally claim the blood of Jesus over the evil one (1 Cor. 6:20; 1 John 1:7).

Pray audibly, "I disown (*insert specific negative influence in your life*)."

These six steps can help you break the influence of things that might otherwise keep you and your family in bondage for generations to come. To summarize:

Six Steps to Freedom
1. I renounce...
2. I acknowledge...
3. I forgive...
4. I submit...
5. I take responsibility...
6. I disown...

PRINCIPLES TO REMEMBER

Practicing the Disciple's Fast successfully will not be accomplished by slavishly following the preceding six steps. You must be actively and purposely involved in determining how, and whether, each step is to be applied to your own unique situation. The following are some principles to consider.

Take inventory of all six principles. Some people will need to work through all six steps, praying audibly each of the six prayers. You may think you have no problem with one of these items until you make it a matter of prayer. Be especially aware of your tendency to delude yourself. Make each step a matter of honest reflection and prayer before you follow it.

Focus on your problem. If, after honest reflection and earnest prayer, you sincerely believe that you do not need all six of these steps, select those that do apply to your individual needs. Only one or two may be adequate to deal with your problem. Spend your time on your major problem.

The purpose principle. The more specific and purposeful you are, the more specific your results. If you are vague in dealing with your sin, you will have defused any possible results. When you fast to break a specific sin, you focus all of your energies onto that sin. Then God can give you the ability to overcome it.

The prescription principle. When you deal with sins, you must learn to pray the exact prescribed words that deal with why you were in bondage. Only when you audibly remind yourself of the causes of your sins will you be able to break the result. It is not enough to pray "Forgive me, Lord," and let it go at that. You must also fast and pray; for example, "I take responsibility for having allowed myself to become addicted to alcohol." Naming your sin and affirming your accountability for your actions is a step toward overcoming the "besetting sin."

The inner journey principle. You never gain an outward victory over sin until you take inner responsibility for your actions. You cannot journey without until you have journeyed within. Just as the rings of a tree tell us it grows from the inner to the outer, so Christians must develop inner character before they can deal with the outer problems. The roots must grow before there is fruit.

The public principle. Obviously you will have to deal with your sin to break its bondage over you. The question arises: How public should your confession be? Basically, sin is an internal act or attitude. It is something that usually begins in the heart long before it reaches the hand. Given time, however, sin eventually becomes public. Those things done in darkness ultimately work into the glare of camera lights and public scrutiny.

Fasting is a private vow made to God. Therefore you must begin dealing with sin in your private fast before it becomes public. You begin with your confession to God. "If we confess our sins, He is faithful and just to forgive us our sins" (1 John 1:9). Sometimes, however, sin must be confessed to another person, or to a church—that is, the public.

How public should your confession be?

You should include in your circle of confession all those who were included in your circle of sin. If it was a private sin, keep your confession private. If only a few people know about your sin, then only those people should hear your confession. If you have sinned against the Church and the world, your confession should be open and in public.

PREPARING FOR THE DISCIPLE'S FAST

Aim: Achieving freedom from addiction, or from a besetting sin.

Affirmation: I believe there is no earthly temptation that can enslave me, but that God has a way of escape for me (see 1 Cor. 10:13). I believe in the power of the blood of Christ and in the strength of the name of Christ (see Acts 3:16; 16:18). Therefore, I am fasting because I want the Son of God to make me free indeed (see John 8:36).

Vow: God being my strength, and grace being my basis, I commit myself to the Disciple's Fast outlined here.

Fast: Foods from which I shall abstain_____

Beginning: Date and time I will start fasting_____

End: Date and time I will stop_____

Purpose: I am fasting to_____

Bible Basis: "To loose the bands of wickedness" (Isa. 58:6, *KJV*).

Resources Needed:

_____

Signed_____ Date_____

Note
1. The basic outline for this section is from Neil Anderson's *Victory over the Darkness* (Ventura, Calif.: Regal Books, 1990); *The Bondage Breaker* (Eugene, Oreg.: Harvest House, 1988); and *Setting Your Church Free* (Ventura, Calif.: Regal Books, 1994). See Appendix C.

≣ 3 ≣

THE EZRA FAST

MY WIFE AND I ONCE FOUND OURSELVES OWNING TWO HOUSES. WE HAD moved to Lynchburg, Virginia, because God led me to help found Liberty University there. We bought a house in Lynchburg, and put the sale of our previous house in God's hands. It didn't sell for two years. We fasted together to solve the problem. I never doubted the leadership of God, and I prayed daily for its sale. My wife and I agreed together (see Matt. 18:18) and fasted, but it still didn't sell. We didn't give up; consequently, after we had fasted for the third time, God sold our house.

"Life is like a football game," says Sam Rutigliano, former NFL coach of the Cleveland Browns. "And he who makes the fewest errors...wins." I don't think my wife and I made an error buying a house in Lynchburg; however, our decision did raise an unforeseen problem.

Everyone has problems and hard times. Job, in the oldest book of the Bible, said, "Man who is born of woman is of few days and full of trouble" (Job 14:1). According to natural laws, everything that is made will break. Every person will eventually get old and feeble. Every business will collapse if not attended. Houses must be painted, cars must be tuned up, fields must be replanted every spring and everyone must face problems that need to be solved. Again, Job understood this: "Man is born to trouble as surely as sparks fly upward" (Job 5:7, *NIV*).

Most people, however, are surprised when they have problems. Recently I was rushing home from church to be in time to receive an important telephone call. While driving rapidly up Thomas Road, my right front tire blew out. I exclaimed with a pound on my steering wheel, what I always say when trouble comes.

> **TOWNS'S FRUSTRATION**
> Why me?
> Why now?
> Why this?

I expect a perfect world, so I am surprised when I have problems. Yet, reading the Scriptures should convince me that there are problems—serious problems—life threatening problems—problems that will be difficult to solve.

If you are like me, expectations of a perfect life result in three wrong attitudes toward problems. When problems come we think:

> **THREE WRONG ATTITUDES**
> **TOWARD PROBLEMS**
> You are unusual.
> You are unspiritual.
> God has forsaken you.

A secretary in my office was complaining because a check bounced. She was absolutely sure that her husband had done it or that the bank had made an error. I heard her on the telephone with the bank, then a long silent pause...

"Oh...I forgot to stub that check!"

We all make mistakes that cause us problems. We all forget about things, and our forgetfulness creates more stress. We are all human, and that means we can't think of everything.

Three attitudes will galvanize your thinking as you prepare to solve problems.

> **THREE PROBLEM-SOLVING ATTITUDES**
> You cannot run from problems.
> You cannot keep problems from happening.
> You can solve your problems.

EZRA FACED A PROBLEM

The book of Ezra tells the story of the Jews traveling back from captivity in Persia. King Cyrus of Persia gave them permission to return in 538 B.C., and to rebuild the Temple in Jerusalem. First, Zerubbabel led the people back to begin work on the Temple. The surrounding nations caused trouble, so the work went slowly, even stopping for several years. The Temple was finally finished in 515 B.C.

Then Ezra, a priest, attempted to lead a second group of people back to Jerusalem. He gathered them on the banks of the Ahava River, but then realized he had a major problem.

Put on the Spot

Ezra needed protection as he led a multitude of defenseless people across the wilderness to return to the Promised Land. The "badlands" were inhabited with gangs of thieves who attacked caravans. Ezra said, "I was ashamed to request of the king an escort of soldiers and horsemen to help us against the enemy on the road" (Ezra 8:22).

It was similar to the American homesteaders traveling West, who needed the U.S. Cavalry when they crossed Indian territory. Ezra's problem, however, was different. He found himself on the spot. "After all, we had told the king that our God takes care of everyone who truly worships him, but that he gets very angry and punishes anyone who refuses to obey" (v. 22, *CEV*).

The Risk of Theft

Not only were the Jews returning home, but they were also bringing all of their household goods and treasures with them. Do not think of Israel as prisoners released from prison. They were not like Jewish escapees from the holocaust during World War II. Many Jews had settled down in Babylon, built houses and established businesses. Archaeologists have discovered that the Jews—who previously were a nation of farmers—became a people who thrived as shopkeepers in Babylon.

Many Jews had grown wealthy in captivity. Those who remained in captivity sent treasures with Ezra to rebuild the Temple. These Jews did not want to settle in the primitive conditions of the Promised Land. They didn't want to suffer privations to rebuild their nation. They wanted to enjoy the luxury of Babylon. These Jews were required to send along gold and silver for rebuilding the Temple. Ezra was transporting their money and many of their possessions. "In all there were: 25 tons of silver; 100 silver articles weighing 150 pounds; 7,500 pounds of gold" (v. 26, *CEV*). Ezra was fearful that this treasure might be stolen.

Fasting About the Problem
Faced with this significant problem, Ezra called a fast: "So we fasted and entreated our God for this, and He answered our prayer" (v. 23).

Notice that the problem was more than a personal matter. It involved all of God's people who were traveling across the wilderness, plus all of the thousands remaining in Babylon who had given gold and other treasures to him. Ezra's problem was also their problem. This was a problem of national proportion. How could he get the people, gold and silver back to the Promised Land? He could call the people to what we are calling an Ezra's Fast.

PRESCRIPTION FOR THE EZRA FAST

A private problem requires a private fast. A group problem requires the group to fast with you. Even when the circle of concern becomes national, the circle of fasting should be as large as the circle of concern.

Step 1: Choose Those to Be Involved
My church faced a financial problem in the late '70s, so we called a fast for the entire church. We asked everyone to fast according to the formula given in Israel for the day of atonement: "Everyone must go without eating from the evening of the ninth to the evening of the tenth" (Lev. 23:32, *CEV*). The congregation was asked to fast for one day—from sundown to sundown.

My pastor asked everyone to prepare to fast from Sunday night until Monday night. When the congregation came to church on Sunday morning, they were reminded to fast beginning that evening. Because the fast was fresh in their minds, everyone could join as one. Also, they were instructed how to fast—eat a light snack before Sunday evening church; then after church they would only drink liquids until Monday evening. After sundown on Monday evening, they could break their fasts. Once the people were informed about the problem and acquainted with the reasons and the procedures for the fast, the pastor asked for a commitment.

"I want all those who will fast with us this evening to stand."

The entire church stood with the pastor. The congregation gathered that Sunday evening with a great spirit of anticipation. We believed God was going to perform a great financial miracle for us. I asked the pastor's wife if her husband really believed that God was going to answer our prayer.

"He really believes God will do it" was her answer.

Obviously, we fasted for a specific answer, but the answer came from prayer as well. There were times of individual prayer, and people also assembled at the church for prayer. In separate groups, the women, the pastors and the youth gathered to pray.

The results? The people trusted God for more than $1 million, and the work of God was accomplished.

Step 2: Share the Problem

Not only must people be asked to fast, but they must also be involved in the problem. Ezra said, "I proclaimed a fast...that we might humble ourselves before our God, to seek from Him the right way for us" (Ezra 8:21). The people following Ezra fasted because they were scared. They wanted safety for themselves and their children. The greater the problem, the more likely people will fast with intensity and pray with sincerity.

Step 3: Fast Seriously

For a meaningful fast, people must not only withhold food, but they must also agonize in prayer. Fasting is more than diet adjustment; it involves spiritual agony and intercession. Ezra's fast was "that we might afflict ourselves before our God" (v. 21, *KJV*). Originally, when people faced a life-threatening situation, they were too frightened or distressed to eat. They adjusted their diets out of agony and deep struggle of soul.

The *cause* was the problem; the *effect* was diet adjustment. Eventually, people began to see that they needed this deep spiritual exercise to pray properly. Thus they reversed the effect—fasting, so everyone might enter into the cause—spiritual travail in intercession.

Fasting communicated to all people the seriousness of their journey. To get from Babylon back to the Promised Land, Ezra and his fellow Israelites had to cross a threatening terrain. So Ezra communicated the seriousness of the threat to their lives.

> FASTING PRODUCES
> Spiritual introspection
> Spiritual examination
> Spiritual confession
> Spiritual intercession

Step 4: Fast Before Attempting a Solution

We often approach a problem with the traditional problem-solving strategy. We brainstorm all possible solutions, choosing a solution out of our own human wisdom. But Ezra did something before even discussing the problem with his elders: "I gathered them together to the river that runneth to Ahava; and there abode we in tents three days" (v. 15, *KJV*). During that time he waited for the Levites to join them (see vv. 15-20).

Notice the timing of the fast:

> He did not fast as he traveled.
> He did not fast before they all gathered.
> He did not try to solve the problem before fasting.

It is important that you recognize the spiritual nature of the problem before you try to solve it. Actually, we should live in the attitude of fasting because we should live with an attitude of dependence upon God. When facing a money problem, we usually try to cut financial corners, borrow money, arrange payments with our debtors; and when everything else fails, we may pray and even fast. Ezra, however, gathered the people and fasted first. The timing of the fast is just as important as its mechanics.

Step 5: Fast on Site with Insight

A new movement called "Prayerwalking" is sweeping America.[1] It's nothing more than following the Old Testament injunction where God told Abraham to walk throughout the land He was going to give him (see Gen. 13:17). Also, God instructed Joshua to walk around Jericho before the battle (see Josh. 6:3-5). Then as Joshua was going to conquer the Promised Land, God told him to walk by faith throughout the land he would conquer (see 1:3-9). Prayerwalking is "praying on site with insight." When we stand at the place of need, we pray with more heed.

Ezra implemented old-fashioned prayerwalking by bringing the people face to face with their problem—he brought them to the banks of the river before launching out into the wilderness. "Beside the Ahava River, I asked the people to go without eating and to pray" (Ezra 8:21, *CEV*).

Step 6: Fast for Step-by-Step Guidance

During the fast, not before, we seek solutions to our problems. Too often large problems frighten us, and we can't think accurately or productively about the problems. We need to break down large problems into increments. If we can solve the smaller problems one by one, we can solve the larger problems. We need to fast and pray not only for the final solutions, but also for step-by-step solutions to the problems.

There was more than one road for Ezra and the people to travel to Jerusalem, and more than one solution to their problem. The question was, Which is the right road? Apparently, some roads had more travelers than others. Many of these travelers were soldiers traveling on diplomatic and governmental business. As a result, people felt protected by their presence. Also, some roads were so well traveled that bands of robbers found alternate routes.

Ezra called a fast "to seek of [God] a right way" (v. 21, *KJV*). The Bible tells us that God sovereignly directs our steps, but we should use common sense along the way. "We draw our maps to the destination, but God directs each step on the road" (Prov. 16:9, paraphrased). A modern version says, "We make our own plans, but the Lord decides where we will go" (*CEV*).

Use your own ingenuity. Ezra fasted to solve his problem, but he did more than fast—he used his ingenuity. When you face a problem, don't limit yourself to prayer. Prayer is wonderful, but when you only pray, you haven't done enough. The Bible teaches both "faith and works." On our knees we pray as if everything depends on God, but we get up and work as if everything depends on us. Our work involves sweat work, planned work, intricate work, determined work and smart work.

So Ezra began, "We went without food and asked God himself to protect us" (Ezra 8:23, *CEV*). Then Ezra devised a plan for the tremendous amount of money that had been given to him. He realized that part of his caravan might be lost if they were attacked by a large band of thieves, so he divided up the treasure and distributed it among the 12 priests, so some of it might get through even though some might be lost (vv. 24,25).

49

By dividing the money, Ezra did more than protect it from thieves without. He also made each priest accountable for an exact amount of the treasure. Because the human heart is sinful, it might have been easy for one of the priests to keep a portion of the treasures entrusted to him. After all, if a family had a ton of silver, it might be tempting to keep a few earrings. So Ezra took specific measures to prevent this from happening.

Just because Ezra was a spiritual man didn't mean he was naive or stupid. He understood human nature. Everyone in business knows that people are more likely to be honest when they are made accountable.

PRINCIPLES TO CONSIDER

The problem-solving Ezra Fast is not an attempt to escape problems, but to enlist the Holy Spirit's aid in tackling them. As previously noted, we will never escape problems. This does not mean we fast for every problem. Fasting is a serious endeavor, so we fast primarily for serious problems.

In doing so, as Step 6 indicates, practical steps as well as fasting and prayer are required. In turn, the following are some practical principles for problem solving.

Three Causes of Problems
You can deal with your problem better when you understand its cause. There are three primary causes of problems.

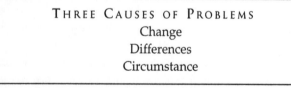

THREE CAUSES OF PROBLEMS
Change
Differences
Circumstance

Change causes problems. The Duke of Canterbury once said what many think: "Any change for any reason for any purpose should be deplored."

No one likes to change. Changes in the church's program especially invites problems. Therefore, when facing major changes such as a change of location, changing the doctrinal statement or even changing personnel, call those who are affected to a fast.

The church in Acts fasted when facing a major change in strategy— they planned to send a missionary team to evangelize the lost. Before they sent out Barnabas and Paul on the first missionary journey, the Bible mentions twice that they fasted. "As they ministered to the Lord and fasted, the Holy Spirit said, 'Now separate to Me Barnabas and Saul for the work to which I have called them'" (Acts 13:2).

This church's new strategy was the outcome of fasting, but referring to this once was not enough. Notice the second time the word is used: "Then, having fasted and prayed, and laid hands on them, they sent them away" (v. 3).

In the physical world, all motion causes friction. The friction from motion in human relationships leads to breakdown and more problems. When you go through major changes in life, whether marriage, a new job or the threat of losing your present job, friction and stress occur. Therefore, use the Ezra Fast.

Differences cause problems. When people from different ethnic, doctrinal or family backgrounds come into a church, they often want changes. The solution is to put all people on the same starting line with the Ezra Fast. Fast before any major change. Just as Ezra gathered the people at the river to look into the threatening wilderness, unite all church people in a fast so together they can see their problem, and together they can pray for an answer.

The question is not whether differences among people will cause problems in your church, but rather what you will do and how you will respond to problems that *will* arise because of people's differences. Although we do not call for the Ezra Fast to give the church a sense of unity, a sense of unified action is surely one of the byproducts of fasting.

Circumstances cause problems. Whether we are talking about your personal circumstances or those in your group, circumstances cause problems. These problems are not interpersonal or spiritual in nature. The church may want to buy land, relocate, face city zoning or institute a new program that is radically different from the existing program. A bank or business may fail with your money. When you face a problem you did nothing to initiate, call for an Ezra Fast.

When your community faces an extended union strike or a large layoff in an industry that affects your church, call for an Ezra Fast.

When your church doesn't have enough space for the people who want to worship, or the facilities are old or you face a money problem, call for an Ezra Fast.

Three Questions to Ask

When you enter the Ezra Fast, do more than just ask God to solve the problem. Begin applying problem-solving strategy to the issue at hand. In attempting to solve your problem, you must first assess it. It is helpful to ask three questions to determine the size of your crisis.

THREE QUESTIONS TO ASK

How big is the problem?

Who is involved in the problem?

What does the larger group think about the problem?

How big is the problem? Problems often seem much larger than they actually are. During the Ezra Fast, take time to think through the problem and its ramifications. Sometimes in the Ezra Fast the problem will shrink because you realize it is not as large as it appears. You gradually see it objectively. At other times in the Ezra Fast, a problem will loom larger than you thought because you understand its magnitude.

When you are fasting, determine the basic issues involved in the problem. Write these issues down. As you pray through the problem, you must first define it. Remember: A well-defined problem is a half-solved problem.

Who is involved in the problem? When you define the problem, ask who has explained the problem to you or to the group. In any church, certain people always seem to alert the pastor to minor problems. The way these people describe the problem suggests that it is much larger than it actually is. Make sure that you see the problem through objective eyes, through God's eyes and then through your church's eyes. Never limit yourself to the eyes of the person who brings the problem to you.

Pray through motives. During the Ezra Fast, you need to ask *why* this is a problem. Sometimes the problem is rooted in the motives of the people involved. Sometimes it stems from motives of people outside the church. Most problems are really a conflict of attitudes between people rather than a conflict of circumstances or schedules. When people get their attitudes right, most problems will solve themselves.

As you pray during the Ezra Fast, determine the best time to address the problem. Many problems will solve themselves without your involvement, if given time. Even as you are fasting, therefore, you may be giving your problem time to solve itself. The Ezra Fast may be the moratorium that is needed to solve the problem. Also, time allows emotions to cool and issues to come into focus.

What does the larger group think about the problem? When you get everyone in the church involved in the Ezra Fast, you focus the attention of everyone in the church on the problem.

Sometimes you need to consult people individually to gather data. At other times, a pastor will gather information from the board, a fact-finding committee or even the whole congregation. Sometimes you must interview many people, but do so individually to determine facts, discover attitudes and gain insight into the nature and/or timing of the problem. When you consult those most directly involved in the problem and encourage their input, you strengthen your ability to lead people to resolution.

Calling for an Ezra Fast accomplishes two purposes. You are inviting God into the problem and asking for His solution, and you are inviting everyone involved to be a part of the solution.

A problem may affect only one segment of people directly, but its implications may touch other people. This is true in a family, a congregation or a work setting. Therefore, seek to involve the larger group in the Ezra Fast because the larger group should take responsibility for the problem, develop a solution and solve the problem.

People ask advice from those they respect. When you invite people to the Ezra Fast, you show them respect and appreciation for their contributions; hence, you will gain their support. You not only gain their wisdom to solve the problem, but you also gain their respect. They will look up to your spiritual leadership.

Three Attitudes Toward Problems

A Christian usually adopts three attitudes when approaching a problem. I first heard this formula from a southern preacher who was describing how the church should react to a threat.

THREE ATTITUDES TOWARD PROBLEMS
1. *Fuss*—preach against a sin.
2. *Fight*—organize the church to resist the sin.
3. *Die*—fight sin to the death.

Although these three common attitudes toward problems are broad-based, ultimately it is best to apply a strategy to solve your problem. The Ezra Fast may not result in a total solution to your problem, but by fasting you may learn the seriousness of the problem, and thus discover a strategy for dealing with it.

Good leaders pick their own battles. Be careful not to let someone else choose your battle for you. There will always be a cause that will motivate Christians or your church to action (e.g., abortion, civil rights violations, the sale of alcohol or pornography, etc.). But you cannot spend all of your life fighting battles. Although the Christian life is both battling and building, the majority of your life should be spent building up the Church, building up the saints and building up yourself. Those who fight every alleged dragon eventually loose their credibility. Dr. Adrian Rogers, former president of the Southern Baptist Convention, advised, "Some hills are not worth fighting for."

Three Problem-Solving Eyes

The greatest benefit of the Ezra Fast is that God gives you "eyes" to see the problem. As you fast to God, you see the problem through His eyes. But you must also see the problem through the eyes of your family/congregation. It is important to see the problem through the eyes of those who created the problem, such as your opponent.

THREE PROBLEM-SOLVING EYES
Eyes to see the positive.
Eyes to see the people.
Eyes to see the facts.

Eyes to see the positive. When you call for the Ezra Fast, you should first pray for victory. Know what you want the outcome to be, and ask God to give it to you. Don't enter the fast "problem centered," because this will make you a pessimist and render you unable to pray in faith. Pray as the disciples did, who asked the Lord, "increase our faith" (Luke 17:5). Keep looking to God, and He will make you positive.

"We must get rid of everything that slows us down, especially the sin that just won't let go. And we must be determined to run the race that is ahead of us. We must keep our eyes on Jesus" (Heb. 12:1,2, *CEV*).

When we are mentally, emotionally or spiritually blinded, we don't see properly.

BLIND EYES
Emotional eyes are blinded with tears.
Fearful eyes are blinded with terror.

The Ezra Fast produces a new vision of what God can do. Blinded eyes surrender their values, but the Ezra Fast helps refocus your priorities in the Word of God. Blinded eyes blame other people, but during the Ezra Fast you see the cause of the problem. Blinded eyes make us guilty, but during the Ezra Fast we confess our sins and stand forgiven in Christ.

Problems grow when you lose perspective. The Ezra Fast can build up a positive perspective both toward the problem and toward God's plan for your life. Do not give in to your problem, nor to the people around you. Above all, do not give up your values.

Eyes to see the people. During the Ezra Fast, focus not only on the problem, but also on those who are fasting with you. Those who are wholeheartedly with you are usually not the problem. Those who criticize the fast, resist it or do something to undermine it may be part of the problem—although they are probably not its instigators.

The Ezra Fast may give you an opportunity to pray with others. "If two of you on earth agree about anything you ask for, it will be done for you by my Father in heaven" (Matt. 18:19, *NIV*). During the Ezra Fast, therefore, gather people together for corporate prayer meetings. Ask for (1) requests from the group, (2) testimonies from the group and (3) prayer by members of the group.

Eyes to see the facts. When you enter into the Ezra Fast, you may be embarking on a strategy to handle or solve your problems. Begin by looking for scriptural solutions to the problem. Take time to write out the scriptural principles involved in the problem. Ask, "How have people in the Bible solved a problem similar to this?" Ask, "How have others in the Church solved a problem similar to this?" Answering these questions will compel you to read the Bible, and to understand passages that speak to the problem. All the while, you are attempting to discover biblical solutions that may be applicable to your situation.

Throughout the Ezra Fast, strive to keep a balance between "head knowledge" of the Word and the "heart expression" of the Spirit as you address your problem. Too much Spirit without the Word will lead you to an emotional *blow up*. Too much Word without the Spirit will cause you to *dry up*. The right balance between the Word and the Spirit will lead you to *grow up*.

Step-by-Step Problem Solving

When people participate in the Ezra Fast, they need to make sure they have a step-by-step strategy for problem solving. Some people think that during the Ezra Fast they should only meditate and pray. They expect God to give them answers out of a vacuum. Although God may speak in the dark of the night, He usually does not. Actually, following a step-by-step strategy to solve a problem could be successfully used by those outside of Christ. Because it involves truth, and all truth comes from God, the same strategy could be used by those who are in Christ. Problem solving is not a key that is hidden in the Bible for only the redeemed. Everyone faces problems, and God has given to all people a sound mind. He therefore expects all of us to use our total resources to solve our problems. A step-by-step approach to problems is available to all.

PROBLEM SOLVING
- Get the facts.
- Establish biblical principles.
- Evaluate the facts.
- Determine the various solutions.
- Choose a solution.

Step 1: Get the Facts

You need more than a Bible and a concordance as you approach the Ezra Fast. Although these are essential, you must also include all the facts and information you can gather. This involves files, records, charts, lists and any other pertinent information.

If you are planning the Ezra Fast while away from home, begin packing for the trip a few days in advance. Make sure that all file folders, records and books are in a briefcase/box. Once you get to the place for the Ezra Fast, you will want to review all the facts before formulating an opinion. Sorting through all the reports, minutes and files will refresh your mind by bringing the information into your awareness. You are already beginning to move toward an understanding of the problem.

Write out your problem, then write down any sub-points it may have. This may involve listing the primary and secondary people involved, as well as all the events involved in the consequences. Sometimes writing out the problem involves listing times of events related to the problem, money, assets and/or issues. As you begin to write out the problem, don't be satisfied with a single declaration. A reexamination of the files may give you a different perspective. Then you will need to rewrite the problem. You need as much information as possible to make a good decision and determine your plan of action.

THE TOWNS RULE FOR PROBLEM SOLVING
You make good decisions on good information.
You make bad decisions on bad information.
Without any information, you make lucky decisions.

Step 2: Establish Biblical Principles
After you have clearly defined the problem, search the Word of God to determine biblical principles for the solution to the problem. The Bible speaks to all issues without naming every issue. Just as a new car has an "operator's manual," so God has given us the Bible as our operator's manual containing principles for all of life. Although every issue is not discussed in the Bible, the basic principles of life still apply to every issue. If at all possible, have available Christian and secular books dealing with the topic. (Consult your local Christian bookstores for books about the topic.) Also, find information by consulting concordances, Bible dictionaries and encyclopedias, commentaries and topical handbooks.

Step 3: Evaluate the Facts
During the Ezra Fast, you will have time to think through your problem. First, write out the problem from the top of your head. Then as you pray, attempt to rewrite the problem from the bottom of your heart. There can be a difference between the top of your head and the bottom of your heart, just as there is a difference between your objective analysis and your emotional commitment. Your problem and its stifling influences may exist somewhere between the two.

During the Ezra Fast, spend time in prayer, and when God reveals new insight, redefine the problem. Each time you spend extended time in the presence of God, come back to your pencil and paper to define the problem again. It is said that the steps to solving a problem are taken in the steps to defining the problem.

STEPS TO SOLVING A PROBLEM
- Find the problem.
- Define the problem.
- Refine the problem.
- Redefine the problem.

Step 4: Determine the Various Solutions to the Problem

Too often Christians expect an answer in an environment of sublime contentment. They think problem solving occurs without effort. They expect God to speak out of a vacuum, and that is not His usual way. God speaks through information found in the Word and from other sources. You may go into a quiet place for prayer; however, there are more steps to solving a problem than just prayer and contemplation.

Follow the problem-solving steps to find a solution. As you enter into the Ezra Fast, every time a solution to your problem comes to mind, write it down. Obviously, not all of the ideas that come into your head will be good ones. Even so, write them down. Through the discipline of writing down even a ridiculous solution, the correct solution may "pop" into your mind. One solution may trigger another. Therefore, do not attempt to solve your problem until you have exhausted your list of solutions.

Even then, your exhaustive list of solutions may not be *the* exhaustive list. Share your list with others, especially those who are on the Ezra Fast with you. Maybe they have a thought or idea you have missed, and vice versa.

On rare occasions, you may want to ask everyone participating in the Ezra Fast for solutions. About 150 years ago, the Independent Presbyterian Church of Savannah, Georgia, was contemplating building a new sanctuary. The building was to be set toward the rear of the property, resulting in a large front yard. Everyone voted unanimously for the project except one lady, who withheld her vote. It is said that she prayed (we do not know if she fasted), then went to the chairman of the session and shared her idea.

She suggested building the new sanctuary toward the front of the property, to allow room for a garden between the sanctuary and an educational building toward the rear. The garden could be used for weddings and social gatherings. It would be a garden where the beautiful camellias and azaleas of the area could grow.

Furthermore, beautiful windows on either side of the pulpit could face the lovely garden. Because there were no electric lights in those days, the windows would shed light on the pulpit. When brought to vote by the congregation, again there was a unanimous vote—this time to move the sanctuary forward and allow for the garden. It is possible for one small voice in a congregation to offer a solution to a problem that no one else has seen.

Step 5: Choose the Best Solution

As long as we live in this life, nothing is perfect except the Son of God and the Word of God. No human is perfect, nor is anything perfect that is done by humans. Therefore, we will never have a "perfect" solution to a problem. We can only have a "best" solution.

And what is a best solution to a problem? One that is agreed on by everyone who has participated in the Ezra Fast. It is the best solution when it brings about the resolution of the problem and resolves tensions. It is the best solution when God is honored and Christians grow in grace.

Finally, yield your problem to God. In His sovereignty, God may have given you the problem to draw you closer to Himself. Usually people want to be free of problems. The problem you long to be free from, however, may actually be the circumstance that allows you to become what you long to be.

	PREPARING FOR THE EZRA FAST
Aim:	Solving a problem through the Ezra Fast.
Vow:	I will examine all facts to understand the problem and will ask God to give me insight into its causes and solution. After I have followed all the principles God has shown me, and have done everything I can do to solve the problem, I will accept the results within the providence of God (see Rom. 8:28).
Fast:	Foods from which I shall abstain _____

Beginning:	Date and time I will start fasting _____
End:	Date and time I will stop fasting _____
Purpose:	I am fasting to _____

Problem Solving Strategy

Statement of the Problem:	_____
Bible Basis:	To fast and petition our God about the problem, asking Him to answer our prayer (see Ezra 8:23).
Resources Needed:	_____

Signed _____ Date _____

Note

1. Graham Kendrick and Steve Hawthorne, *Prayerwalking* (Altamonte Springs, Fla.: Creation House, 1993).

⩳ 4 ⩴

THE SAMUEL FAST

ONE OF THE MOST REMARKABLE PERIODS OF REVIVAL CHURCH HISTORY grew out of a fast.

In the early eighteenth century, the great evangelist Jonathan Edwards fasted for 24 hours before preaching the sermon many claim sparked the revival in New England that grew into the First Great Awakening. The sermon was called "Sinners in the Hands of an Angry God."

A prayer revival swept throughout the nation in 1859, and some of it grew out of what might be called a type of fasting, because people did go without food. The revival began in the great metropolitan cities of the eastern United States. Christians left their work at noon, walked quickly to the nearest churches—not the churches of their memberships—and spent their lunch breaks in prayer.

Technically, they did not call their time with God and each other a fast; but because they gave up their lunchtimes to devote themselves to prayer, it can be called a type of fast.

ROOTS OF REVIVAL

Historians usually attribute the great revival of 1859 to three things. First, interdenominational unity, exemplifed by the fact that believers prayed at the nearest churches. People of different denominations were bonded together in intercession. Second, the revival came not through preaching, writing or any other source, but through prayer. Third, the revival was inspired by the laity rather than the clergy.

A great revival also swept throughout ancient Israel, when they were governed by the great judge, Samuel. Because this revival, too, involved fasting, we can draw inspiration for revival in our day by the Samuel Fast.

Revival has been defined as "God pouring Himself out on His people." There is corporate revival, sometimes called Atmospheric Revival, when people feel the presence of God. Then there is Individual Revival wherein believers are filled with the Holy Spirit. The Church has generally defined revival in the words of Scripture, as "times of refreshing...from the presence of the Lord" (Acts 3:19). Notice three truths about revival:

1. Revival is not an automatic experience. It is something to be desired, and prayed for.
2. God is the source of revival. It comes from His presence.
3. Refreshing results are experienced when revival comes.

Scripture ties fasting and revival together. As believers fast and pray, God sends revival to His people. As we have seen, God proclaimed through the prophet Isaiah, "Is this not the fast that I have chosen...to let the oppressed go free?" (Isa. 58:6). The word "oppressed" can also be translated "broken." Although we may not have oppression such as slavery to contend with in our society, we have masses who are broken in spirit and bound by sin. Furthermore, injustice throughout the world still results in oppressed people.

The Samuel Fast can be a tool for freeing those who are oppressed, and healing those who are broken by sin.

BACKGROUND OF THE SAMUEL FAST

The book of Judges tells how God's people kept rejecting Him and turning to idols. Each time, the Lord punished Israel by allowing the surrounding nations to attack and defeat them. And each time they were defeated, the Israelites turned back to the Lord and begged for His help. Finally, in answer to their prayers, God sent special leaders called judges, who restored the people to righteousness, enabling them to defeat their enemies. Typically, Israel would follow the Lord as long as the ruling judge lived. But when he died, they would again reject the Lord, repeating the cycle again and again. Each judge led a few tribes at the most; however, none of the judges brought the entire nation together. Israel was a confederation of loosely bound family tribes. They did not have a king, and "everyone did what they thought was right" (Judg. 21:25, CEV).

God called Samuel as a young boy to lead the nation of Israel. Before he grew into manhood, Israel sinned by using the Ark of the Covenant as a "good luck charm" to lead the people into battle. For this affront, God allowed the Philistines to defeat Israel. The enemy slaughtered many Israelite soldiers, and took the Ark of the Covenant as a captured prize. The Philistines used their position to oppress God's people, and each year they returned to extract heavy taxes from the defeated Israelites.

Samuel was a prophet, priest and the last judge to lead Israel before the nation chose a king and became a monarchy. Samuel united the nation by bringing revival to the people. He inspired Israel's army to fight against her enemies, who were raiding the nation.

Samuel initiated a nationwide revival through fasting, among other spiritual disciplines. Therefore, the Samuel Fast is portrayed here as a fast for revival and evangelism. It is described in a threefold perspective: pre-fast preparation, the actual fast itself and the post-fast results.

PRE-FAST PREPARATION

Samuel did not introduce the fast for revival to Israel without requiring serious preparation. He required that the people put away the foreign gods they had accumulated and commit themselves wholly to God. In the same way, the Samuel Fast today requires specific preparation.

Recognize Your Bondage

Before revival comes we must recognize the source of our bondage to sin that hinders revival. Some people are in bondage to sinful habits and specific sins. Others are under demonic influences, while some are in bondage to their memories and their pasts. Whatever the need for revival, we must first recognize our bondages and the debilitating influences those bondages have on our lives.

I tell my students preparing for ministry, "You can't get people saved until you get them lost." Until a person knows (1) he or she is a sinner, (2) sin will cast him or her into hell, (3) there is no salvation other than in Christ (see Acts 4:12) and (4) being saved is his or her greatest need, that person can't be motivated to be saved.

As the saying goes, "You can lead a horse to water, but you can't make it drink." But if you get the horse thirsty by putting salt on its tongue, when you lead it to water, it will drink.

The solution to any problem begins with the recognition of need. In 1978 I distributed food during a famine in Haiti, where I saw emaciated children who were too weak to eat. What perplexed me was that many children who were starving had no desire to eat. They were at the point of death. The very physical conditions that were killing them were also masking their needs. Until people know they need food, they will not eat to gain strength. In the same way, until people know they need revival, they will not seek the Lord of the harvest who will "pour Himself on His people."

Fortunately, when Samuel called Israel to revival, the people recognized their bondages. They cried out, "Do not stop crying out to the Lord our God for us, that he may rescue us" (1 Sam. 7:8, NIV). The people had come to a point of such frustration that they cried out for deliverance.

Pray for God's Presence Among His People

When we pray for revival, we have to invite God Himself to live among His people. Remember, the Church is more than a building and more than people. The Church is the presence of the Lord among His people. That is, the Church is the spiritual presence of Jesus Christ in the midst of His people. The apostle Paul referred to "the church, which is His body" (Eph. 1:22,23).

To prepare for revival, the Church must:

1. *Recognize its need for God's presence among its people.* Notice what initiated the revival when Samuel was leading the people. "The men...fetched up the ark of the Lord" (1 Sam. 7:1, KJV). Because the Ark of the Covenant was the symbolic place where the Lord dwelt among His people, when the people sought the Ark of the Lord, they were seeking for God to dwell among them.

Years earlier, the Ark had departed, symbolizing God's absence from the midst of His people. The Philistines had defeated the Israelites, and carried off the Ark as their battle prize. When the wife of Phinehas (one of the priests who was responsible for the spiritual debacle) delivered her child, she named him Ichabod, saying, "'The glory has departed from Israel!' because the ark of God had been captured" (4:21, *KJV*).

As you enter the Samuel Fast seeking revival in your life, you must confess, "Ichabod." You must confess, "I have lost the presence of God in my life."

Losing the presence of God is not what some call losing one's salvation. Even though you may be secure about your salvation, your day-by-day walk with the Lord may have dried up because you have not sought His daily presence. Therefore, just as Israel had to seek the Ark of the Covenant, the Samuel Fast is your opportunity to seek the reentry of the glory of God's presence into your life.

2. *Assemble the people at God's place.* Throughout history, God has had a place where He meets with His people. Although this place is not always riveted to one geographical spot, the place may be identified by assembling, fellowshiping and seeking His presence. Samuel wanted the people to experience revival, so he commanded, "Gather all Israel to Mizpah" (7:5).

Why were the people called to Mizpah? This was the city where God met Israel before the city of Jerusalem became the capital city. Mizpah had become the usual place for the people to go when they wanted to experience the presence of the Lord (see Judg. 10:17; 11:11; 20:3; 21:5).

Today we do not have to visit a geographical spot to find God. He dwells among His people, the Church. This is not a building, nor is it a denomination, nor a name such as Baptist, Presbyterian or Assembly of God. A church is an assembly of people where Jesus Christ dwells in their midst. "For where two or three are gathered together in My name, I am there in the midst of them" (Matt. 18:20). Therefore, when we seek revival—"God pouring Himself on His people"—we must assemble His seeking people.

Be Sure God's Leaders Are in Place

Everyone is equal before God, and each person stands on level ground at the foot of the Cross; however, the leaders of the congregation—its shepherds—have a special role in the Samuel Fast. They must lead the flock as examples to feed and protect the sheep (see Acts 20:28-31).

The Bible emphasizes the need for leaders. Common people, gifted people and royalty have all been effective leaders among God's people.

God does not overlook average people, because when God's spirit is poured upon them, they become "above average"; they become leaders of other people. All Bible history flows through leaders—their births, their lives, their works, their calls, their successes, their failures, the things they did, the things they taught and finally, their deaths.

When God wanted to birth a nation, he chose one leader to begin it— Abraham. In the days of famine in Egypt, Joseph became the governor who saved the world from starvation. When God wanted a deliverer for His people from Egypt, Moses was His leader. Moses died and God raised up Joshua. Throughout the period of the judges, God raised up leaders such as Deborah, Gideon, Jehud and Samson. After the judges, God raised up a shepherd boy to be His king—David. God called a bold prophet Elijah to give His message to a backslidden nation. Every time the nation of Israel lapsed into sin and deep spiritual need, God raised up a leader.

Revival required a priest-leader, so the people sanctified Eleazar, son of Abinadab, to guard the Ark of the Lord (1 Sam. 7:1). Then another leader, God's spokesman, stepped to the front: "Samuel spake unto all the house of Israel" (7:3, *KJV*).

You enter the Samuel Fast to pray for revival and evangelism. As you pray for God to "pour His spirit on His people," you must be "leadership conscious." This means you must be willing to be a leader, pray for God to raise up leaders and pray for God to use the leaders that are already in place.

CONDUCTING THE SAMUEL FAST

Step 1: Call the Body Together
The results of individual and corporate fasting are different from each other. Individual fasting makes a person individually responsible to God. Corporate fasting makes a person responsible for what God does to the corporate Body. There is a time for your church to fast, or for those in your Bible study to join together with a spiritual vow not to eat until God answers your corporate prayer.

Notice Samuel's command, "Gather all Israel" (v. 5). At the time, Israel was only a confederation that was divided into 12 tribes. Although they were united in worship and common ancestry, the nation had no internal political, military or social structure.

When Samuel called for a gathering of the people, he was doing more than getting them together for worship. It was more than a get-together for a sacred music concert or a citywide evangelistic meeting. Samuel was telling Israel to recognize its obligation one to another, and to fulfill its responsibility one to another. Samuel realized that to have revival, he needed oneness in mind, heart and vision. Fasting was one way to bring the people together in unity—and it can still serve that purpose today.

Step 2: Demonstrate True Repentance

If a public gathering of God's people were the only criteria for revival, then we should have revival every Sunday morning. But that doesn't happen. When you use the Samuel Fast to bring about revival, you must follow the example of Israel: "All the people of Israel mourned and sought after the Lord" (v. 2, *NIV*). They were truly sorry for their sins. Some might question the sincerity of their repentance, thinking it was only a "sorrow of punishment." They say this because the oppressive taxation by the Philistines and the constant warring raids on their land brought about physical suffering and political wars.

Sometimes when a mother punishes her son for disobedience, she is not sure whether he is sorry because of the punishment or because he violated her standard. Nevertheless, most mothers believe that a sorrowful spirit can build character. Whether the son is sorry for the primary reason or a secondary reason, he learns not to do it again.

When Israel lamented after the Lord, Samuel tested the people to determine their true repentance. He said, "If you return to the Lord with all your hearts, then put away the foreign gods and Ashtoreths" (v. 3). When you begin the Samuel Fast, God may convict you of a sin as you are praying. The evidence of your sincerity is seen when you stop sinning.

God gives the conditions for revival in 2 Chronicles 7:14. This verse is introduced with a conditional "if." *If* God's people meet the conditions, He will send revival. "If My people who are called by My name will humble themselves, and pray and seek My face, and turn from their wicked ways, then I will hear from heaven, and will forgive their sin and heal their land" (2 Chron. 7:14).

In the Samuel Fast, abstaining from food is an outward demonstration of inward sincerity. For this reason, fasting is sometimes called "affliction" in Scripture. When his prayers were not answered, David said, "I humbled [afflicted] myself with fasting" (Ps. 35:13). People feel weak and sometimes light-headed without food. Often the appetite begs for food. But the demonstration of sorrow for the sins committed is evidenced by continuing the fast to its end.

Step 3: Separate from Secret Sin

God's people must search for hidden sin within themselves and separate from it—and the Samuel Fast's temporary denial of the flesh in favor of the spirit can bring those sins to light.

Some people are convicted of sins as they sit praying in church or listening to a sermon. As a result they may have gone forward to the altar to confess their sins. Some may have remained in their seats, confessing their sins. Nevertheless, the confession of these "sins of remembrance" did not bring revival (God did not pour Himself upon His people). Why? Perhaps because other sins in their lives had not yet come to light. These are called "secret sins." Therefore we must pray with the psalmist, "Search me, O God, and know my heart...And see if there is any wicked way in me" (Ps. 139:23,24).

a. Backsliders are blinded to sin in their lives. The very presence of sin in our minds blinds us to that sin. Because sin is choosing to turn from God, or ignoring God so that we turn from God, we are willfully ignorant of our obligation to Him. For this cause, Paul prayed for the saints in Ephesus that "the eyes of your understanding [may be] enlightened" (Eph. 1:18).

b. Backsliders are careless about sin in their lives. Backsliders ignore the warning to the Hebrews, "We must pay more careful attention, therefore, to what we have heard" (Heb. 2:1, *NIV*). When a person has willfully sinned, that person becomes a backslider, whether taking 1 or 100 steps away from God. The fact that a person has apparently gotten away with a first step away from God, and "escaped" punishment, gives the person false confidence to take more steps away from God.

c. During fasting God can show hidden sin to the believer—the sin that is prohibiting God's blessing. The prodigal son demanded his inheritance, then went out to spend all of his money in riotous living. He is the classic backslider who left the riches of his father's house. "When he came to his senses, he said, 'How many of my father's hired men have food to spare, and here I am starving to death!'" (Luke 15:17, *NIV*). When he was hungry, he remembered the good things he had received in his father's house. So when we fast, bringing our physical bodies to a place of hunger, we then can feel the hunger of our spiritual souls. During the Samuel Fast God shows us our hidden sins. The psalmist noted, "You have set our iniquities before You, our secret sins in the light of Your countenance" (Ps. 90:8).

   d. *More sin is gradually revealed as we continue the Samuel Fast.* Fasting must be an ongoing process, meaning that we have to fast for more than one day. Sometimes we may fast for two or more separate days, separated by a time of partaking of food. Whereas a two-day fast may produce an intensive examination for sin, there are advantages of two separate days of fasting. The time we spend between our fasts provides opportunity to think through the ramifications of our needs, and our sins may become clearer to us. However it happens, fasting must be more than a one-time event. It must be an action we employ throughout our lives.

Step 4: Have Corporate Confession of Sin
Although some don't believe in corporate sin, maintaining that only individuals sin, the Bible does give illustrations of individuals who confess sin for the group as a whole. Daniel privately confessed Israel's corporate sin: "We have sinned and done wrong" (Dan. 9:5, *NIV*). Although each person must privately confess individual sin (see 1 John 1:8-10), each person must also confess the group's sin. Notice that in the original Samuel Fast there was a corporate confession of sin. The people confessed, "We have sinned against the Lord" (1 Sam. 7:6).

   When you confess "We have sinned" in private, you obviously include yourself in that sin. When the group prays corporately, "We have sinned," each individual must include himself or herself and his or her sin in the prayer.

   As an illustration, perhaps the Sunday School at your church is dead. No matter how well you teach the Bible, nothing seems to happen. Leadership is lethargic and pupils seem to care less that the Bible is being taught. Somewhere along the line, leadership made bad decisions that brought about the lethargy. The bad decisions influenced the attitudes of the students. To bring revival to a Sunday School in this condition, the leadership must pray, "We have sinned." Although they did not make the decisions, they now represent the institution where the bad decisions were made. The present leadership can't pray, "They sinned." That's a cop-out. The current leadership represents the institution where God is not working, and they must pray, "We have sinned."

Before Nehemiah could rebuild the walls of the city of Jerusalem, he also had to enter into corporate confession. Notice how his prayer began: "Lord God of Heaven, you are great and fearsome" (Neh. 1:5, *CEV*). Then he comes to his part of intercession:

> I am your servant, so please have mercy on me and answer the prayer that I make day and night for these people of Israel who serve you. I, my family, and the rest of your people have sinned by choosing to disobey you and the laws and teachings you gave to your servant Moses (vv. 6,7, *CEV*).

If you have been guilty of criticizing your church, or the spiritual life of the people where you fellowship, you are in bondage to their sin (see the Disciple's Fast). As you enter the Samuel Fast, first confess your sins, then the sins of all the people. The greatest spiritual power occurs when all the people confess their sins. Then God hears from heaven and revival can occur.

Step 5: Acknowledge the Power of the Word
No revival has ever occurred without the involvement of the Word of God as "the power of God for the salvation of everyone who believes" (Rom. 1:16, *NIV*).

During Samuel's early days, the Bible says in the *King James Version*, "The Word of God was precious in those days" (1 Sam. 3:1). But the word "precious" meant "rare" when the *King James Version* was translated. The verse actually means, "In those days the word of the Lord was rare; there were not many visions" (*NIV*). But when Samuel came to minister to Israel, he brought the Word of God to them. He was both judge and prophet, and one of the duties of the prophet was to interpret God's will to the people and to give them God's Word. Samuel was a prophet who was faithful to his calling as he ministered the Word to Israel. As a result, God sent revival.

As you enter the Samuel Fast, spend time studying the great revivals of Scripture, which show clearly the power of the Word of God.

- *Under Jacob.* On the return to Bethel, Jacob ordered his entire household to put away their false gods and to wash and change their garments. They did this as Jacob built an altar to the true God. The false gods were then buried under an oak in Shechem (see Gen. 35:1-4).

- *Under Samuel*. In response to the exhortation of Samuel, based on God's Word, the people put away their false gods and prepared their hearts to serve the only true God (see 1 Sam. 7:3-6).
- *Under Moses*. Revival occurred when complaining Israel saw the mighty hand of God in the parting of the Red Sea. On the safe (eastern) side of the sea, Moses led the people in a song of praise, while Miriam and the women furnished the special music (see Exod. 14:31—15:21).
- *Under David*. (a) When the Ark of the Covenant was brought into Jerusalem for the first time (see 1 Chron. 15:25-28; 16:1-43; 29:10-25). (b) At the dedication of the materials to be used in building the future Temple (see 1 Chron. 29).
- *Under Solomon*. This occurred at the actual dedication of the temple (see 1 Kings 6-8).
- *Under Asa*. King Asa removed the Sodomites and all false idols out of the land. He even deposed his own grandmother because of her idolatry (see 1 Kings 15:11-15).
- *Under Jehoshaphat*. The king led a revival when he ordered the cleansing of the Temple and the sanctification of the Levitical priests—all based on the Word of the Lord (see 2 Chron. 19).
- *Under Elijah*. This took place after the contest with the prophets of Baal on Mount Carmel (see 1 Kings 18:21-40).
- *Under Jehu*. He exterminated all Baal worshipers and their temples (see 2 Kings 10:15-28).
- *Under Jehoiada*. This godly high priest led the people in a covenant whereby they forsook their idols and worshiped God (see 2 Kings 11:17-20).
- *Under Hezekiah*. Like Jehoshaphat, King Hezekiah and God's people experienced revival when he cleansed the Temple of God (see 2 Chron. 29-31).
- *Under Manasseh*. When wicked King Manasseh became converted, he led his people in a revival by ordering the destruction of all idols (see 2 Chron. 33:11-20).
- *Under Josiah*. This revival began when the Book of the Law

was accidentally discovered during a Temple cleanup event. The public reading of God's Word had a profound effect upon both King Josiah and his people (see 2 Kings 22—23).

- *Under Ezra.* Through Ezra's preaching, God wanted His people to be separate from the pagans surrounding them, so the Jewish remnant ceased their ungodly marriage alliances with the heathen of the land (see Ezra 9—10).
- *Under Nehemiah.* After Nehemiah had rebuilt the walls around Jerusalem, Ezra stood by its gates and publicly read and taught from God's Word, causing a great revival (see Neh. 13).
- *Under Jonah.* The Ninevites, through Jonah's preaching of God's Word, repented and stayed the destructive hand of God (see Jonah 3).
- *Under Esther.* This time of repentance and rejoicing followed the salvation of the Jews from the plot of wicked Haman (see Esther 9:17-22).
- *Under John the Baptist.* John preached the imminent appearance of Israel's Messiah, warning the people to repent and submit to water baptism (see Luke 3:2-18).
- *Under Jesus.* The conversion of a sinful Samaritan woman instigated this revival in Samaria (see John 4:28-42).
- *Under Philip.* The strong preaching of Philip the evangelist concerning the Kingdom of God produced a great revival in Samaria (see Acts 8:5-12).
- *Under Peter.* (a) At Pentecost, after his great sermon (see Acts 2). (b) At Lydda, after he had healed Aeneas (see Acts 9).
- *Under Paul.* One of the greatest revivals occurred in Ephesus during Paul's third missionary journey. This account should be carefully read (Acts 19:11-20).[1]

Step 6: Get in Touch with the Symbolic

God communicates to His people through symbolic events (miracles), days (Passover), furniture (tabernacle) and ceremonies (baptism and the Lord's Table). The tabernacle was a tent that symbolically communicated God's holiness and presence. In the same way, the Sabbath was a symbol, as was circumcision.

The Samuel Fast will be more meaningful to you if you are aware of its symbolic significance. It is an outer symbol of an inner desire for God's presence in your life. When you enter the Samuel Fast, you make a statement to God, to others and to yourself. What symbols in the Samuel Fast will bring God's refreshing in your life?

a. Not eating. When Israel came to Mizpah, "On that same day they went without eating to show their sorrow, and they confessed they had been unfaithful to the Lord" (1 Sam. 7:6, *CEV*). Their heartfelt sorrow was evident because they afflicted themselves through fasting. We, too, must demonstrate to God our heart attitude.

A word of caution, however, is needed. Fasting can become legalistic. Some people enter into a fast thinking their "good works" become the basis for answered prayer. When they do not get an answer, they hypocritically blame the system God put into place. People are not saved by good works, and the power of fasting to bring people closer to God resides in God, not in the "work" of fasting. The outer work of fasting can reflect the inner heart's desire, but it is not a work of human effort that binds God to respond (see Isa. 58:1-5). In His sovereignty, God sees the heart and responds.

b. Sacrificing to God. From the first time man offended God through sin, he was required to bring a sacrifice to God to demonstrate his sorrow for sin and his request for forgiveness. The first children, Cain and Abel, were required to bring a sacrifice to God:

> Cain brought some of the fruits of the soil as an offering to the Lord. But Abel brought fat portions from some of the first-born of his flock. The Lord looked with favor on Abel and his offering, but on Cain and his offering He did not look with favor (Gen. 4:3-5, *NIV*).

Obviously, Abel's sacrifice was accepted because the blood of an animal substituted for his sin. Abel should have died, but the animal died in his place. The substitutionary blood sacrifice of Abel made him acceptable to God. Because there was no blood in the fruit sacrifice of Cain, it was rejected.

In the first Samuel Fast, two offerings were made by Samuel and Israel. The important one was the blood sacrifice. "Samuel took a suckling lamb and offered it as a whole burnt offering to the Lord. Then

Samuel cried to the Lord for Israel, and the Lord answered him" (1 Sam. 7:9). Clearly, the blood of the lamb was a substitute, an atonement for the life of the sinful people.

There was also another sacrifice. "They [the people] drew water from the well and poured it out as an offering to the Lord" (v. 6, *CEV*). Water was often scarce in the land of Palestine. Pouring water out to God was a symbol of the people's devotion to Him. At other times, pouring out water symbolized cleansing, satisfaction and life itself. All of these symbols were probably present in the people's expression of sacrifice to the Lord.

POST-FAST EVENTS

Post-Fasting Attacks

When you enter into the Samuel Fast, your fast is not an isolated event. All of heaven's forces are poised because God knows you have come into the secret place for prayer and fasting. Your spiritual enemy, however, also knows, and hates that you have entered into a fast to pray for revival and soul winning. "When the Philistine rulers found out about the meeting at Mizpah, they sent an army there to attack the people of Israel" (v. 7, *CEV*).

Even as you enter into your Samuel Fast, Satan may tempt you to abandon your goal. He hates revival because he never wants God to pour Himself on His people. Therefore, Satan will try to (1) make you too hungry, (2) put other thoughts in your mind, (3) tempt you to quit, (4) interrupt your schedule, (5) discourage you and (6) generally attack your fast.

The fast of Israel must have been effective. Samuel had begun praying and Israel had begun fasting. But because Israel gathered at Mizpah to fast, confess her sins and sacrifice to the Lord, the Philistines were quick to attack. There is another principle here. You may not get complete victory just because you fast and pray. Rather than entering into a time of peace and prosperity, you may find yourself under even more attacks from the enemy.

Fasting as a Process

Too often people think they gain complete victory over their sins by going to the church altar. They think they can fast and pray for revival and God will pour out His spirit among His people. Yet spiritual revival does not flow as does turning on the bathroom faucet, nor does spiritual light come on as does the flick of a wall switch.

Because Christianity is a relationship, so is revival, and relationships take time to cultivate. First we must have a proper relationship with God. Relationships are intricate and complex, so we must spend time fasting to understand God. Second, Christianity involves relationships with others. We must pray for others, and pray with others. We cannot waltz into the throne room of almighty God and immediately get His wholehearted support for our "get spiritually rich quick" plans. Just as a sales presentation at a multinational organization leading to a large contract involves a process of time, so a Samuel Fast leading to revival involves time.

After Israel fasted, they should have been secure in the presence of God—but they weren't. Instead, "The Israelites were afraid when they heard that the Philistines were coming. 'Don't stop praying!' They told Samuel. 'Ask the Lord our God to rescue us'" (v. 7, *CEV*). To attain revival, we must desire it wholeheartedly, seek it sincerely and be willing to repent from every known sin; and we must be willing to give up every intrusion into our schedules for the process of relationship building to mature. When we achieve revival, we will have put God first with our time, our talents, our money and our bodies.

Post-Fasting Action

We usually set many spiritual forces into motion when we begin to fast. Although we may be unaware of what is happening, we have seen that fasting puts the power of God to work, and that it may agitate the power of Satan. Several things can be done after your Samuel Fast to encourage the work of God and discourage the work of Satan.

You may have to ask forgiveness of someone, make restitution or start a new Christian service. Also, you may have to tithe, share the gospel or spend lengthy times at the church where the presence of God is manifesting itself. When you enter the Samuel Fast, be prepared for God to work. You cannot put God in a box called a sanctuary and tell Him when He can start manifesting Himself—nor can you stop Him when you've had enough.

Look for Signs of Victory

As Samuel was praying for Israel, they went out to attack the Philistines.

But God saw the hearts of the people, and He began answering even as they prepared to fight. "The Lord answered [Samuel's] prayer and made thunder crash all around [the enemy]. The Philistines panicked and ran away" (v. 10, *CEV*).

Israel probably did not expect victory in this manner. As the army gathered into assault lines, and as soldiers strapped on their helmets or checked their equipment, God planned victory in another way. *The Living Bible* describes the scene in this way: "The Lord spoke with a mighty voice of thunder from heaven, and they were thrown into confusion, and the Israelis routed them, and chased them...killing them all along the way" (v. 10, *TLB*).

Victory as a Process

The thunder from heaven was only the beginning of the battle. What Israel experienced at the battle of Mizpah was similar to the first British victory over the Germans at Alemein during World War II. Following the battle, Winston Churchill stood to speak in Parliament with cautious optimism: "This is not the end. This is not the beginning of the end. This is the end of the beginning."

The thunderous sound of victory over the Philistines was not the final victory. As the Philistines ran away, "The men of Israel rushed out of Mizpah and pursued the Philistines, slaughtering them along the way to a point below Beth Car" (v. 11, *NIV*).

When God gave victory to Israel, the nation might have thought peace had finally arrived, but Israel's dream of peace was only partially realized. "The Philistines were so badly beaten that it was quite a while before they attacked Israel again" (v. 12, *CEV*). Notice that the Philistines were badly beaten, and that it was a long time before they were again attacked. But there *was* another attack and another battle. You will have battles with sin and attacks from the evil one as long as you live, so continue to apply this principle to your life. The victory you achieve as a result of the Samuel Fast "Is the end of the beginning."

When you enter the Samuel Fast, you ask for revival—for God to pour Himself out on His people. This may happen in a one-time experience; for instance, at a Sunday morning service where God works in the midst of the church. That doesn't guarantee, however, that God will do the same work the following week. The Philistines were a lifelong problem to Israel: "For as long as Samuel lived, the Lord helped Israel fight the

Philistines" (1 Sam. 7:13, *CEV*). Because victory is not just a one-time event, but a continuous process, the Samuel Fast is something you will do for the rest of your life.

Celebrating with Symbols of Victory
Just as symbols were important during the Samuel Fast itself, they can be used to celebrate the victory. After the great battle at Mizpah, "Then Samuel took a stone and set it up between Mizpah and Shen, and called its name Ebenezer [which means "stone of help"], saying, 'Thus far the Lord has helped us'" (v. 12). Years later, as the children of these soldiers would walk by Mizpah, they could see a stone to remind them of a past victory.

a. Your victory stone should look to the past. We place plaques on our walls and mementos on our desks to remind us of the times we won a track meet. We have a special book dedicated to us because we met a sales quota. These "victory stones" help us remember past achievements, hence building up our anticipation for future achievements. When you think back to Ebenezer, remember that "the Lord helped us."

b. Your victory stone should look to the present. Next time you walk into the church sanctuary, notice the foundation stone of the building. It probably tells you the date when construction began or when the building was dedicated. Although it reminds you of a past event, you feel the present enjoyment of that church sanctuary weekly. That foundation stone is an "Ebenezer"—a stone of help.

c. Your victory stone should look to the future. When I go into the gymnasium where I teach, I look up into the rafters and see the banners that indicate where our various teams have previously won the Big South Conference. Looking at those banners motivates our team to win another victory. The phrase "thus far has the Lord helped us" implies the need for God's help in the future.

PRINCIPLES TO REMEMBER

The need for leadership to secure the blessing of God. Remember when you enter the Samuel Fast that God's people are sheep, and their basic need is for a shepherd. The Samuel Fast sometimes dictates that you not pray for revival, but for God's *instrument* of revival—a godly leader through whom God can work.

Israel had been in bondage for years before Samuel arrived on the scene. The old judge Eli was fat, lazy, blind and ineffective. Before him the judge Samson had broken his Nazirite vow and was addicted to sexual lust. Neither of them was able to give the nation the leadership it needed. Then God prepared a young man named Samuel, who was dedicated to Him from his birth. This was the young man through whom God brought revival and victory.

The need for unity among God's people. When you enter the Samuel Fast, you must pray not only for revival, but also for unity among God's people. You will never feel closer to the people of your church than when you fast together, sacrifice together, receive God's answer together and rejoice together.

The need for faith and works. There are two extremes in the Christian life, and it is easy to gravitate into either. Some go to the extreme of thinking that programs, meetings and other human activities will bring about revival. Although God works through organization, there is no way that we can do the work of God with efficient management. It requires spiritual power that is tapped only by faith, not works.

Some go to the other extreme of only praying for revival. Remember the principle:

> You can't bring about revival with prayer alone.
> You can't bring about revival without prayer.

We need a balance of faith and works. God and man must work together. "We are God's fellow workers" (1 Cor. 3:9).

The role of symbols in God's work. This principle is worth mentioning again. Although there is no power in a symbol, a symbol can represent great power. Some think that wearing a cross around one's neck or putting a cross on a building will bring about the blessing of God. That is not the case—the opposite is true: When we have the blessing of God upon our lives, we will want to show it by displaying the cross. The power is in the God of the cross. The same is true with our buildings. We pray for God to work in our buildings, then we put crosses on the buildings to tell the world that this is where God is living and where He works.

The Samuel Fast exemplifies fasting as a symbol not of our own power to move God by abstaining from food, but of our faith in His power to bring revival.

PREPARING FOR THE SAMUEL FAST

Aim: The Samuel Fast for revival and soul winning.

Affirmation: I believe in the power of God to revive individuals and people (see Ps. 85:6). I believe God will pour Himself out on His people (see Acts 2:17) and send times of refreshing from His presence (see Acts 3:19). I believe when people humble themselves, pray, seek God's renewal and turn from their wicked ways, God will respond (see 2 Chron. 7:14). Therefore I will fast and pray for revival and soul winning.

Vow: God being my strength, and grace being my basis, I commit myself to the Samuel fast for God's glory.

Fast: What I will withhold_____

Beginning: Date and time I will start _____

End: Date and time I will stop_____

Purpose: I am fasting to _____

Bible Basis: 1 Samuel 7:2-11.

Bible Promise: "If My people who are called by My name will humble themselves, and pray and seek My face, and turn from their wicked ways, then will I hear from heaven, and will forgive their sin and heal their land" (2 Chron. 7:14).

Resources Needed: _____

Prayer Partners: _____

Steps After Fast: _____

Signed_____ Date _____

Note

1. H. L. Willmington, *Willmington's Guide to the Bible*, (Wheaton, Ill.: Tyndale House Publishers, 1987), pp. 292-294.

≒ 5 ≒

THE ELIJAH FAST

THE ONLY TIME A REGULAR FAST WAS REQUIRED IN SCRIPTURE WAS ON the Old Testament's Day of Atonement (see "Fast, required" in Glossary). Fasting is not required in the New Testament, but is allowed as a tool that provides answers to prayer when correctly implemented. Jesus didn't command that we fast, but He recognized that we would use this tool. "When ye fast...fast unto my Father" (Matt. 6:18).

The Elijah Fast is taken from Isaiah 58:6, "Is this not the fast that I have chosen...that you break every yoke?" It is a fast to help break negative emotional habits.

ELIJAH'S NEGATIVE EMOTIONAL HABIT

Elijah was the bold prophet who stood alone on Mount Carmel to challenge 450 prophets of Baal. Many Israelites had begun to worship the false god Baal, but Elijah challenged: "How long will you waver between two opinions? If the Lord is God, follow him; but if Baal is God, then follow him" (1 Kings 18:21, NIV).

Elijah was not only bold before his opponents, but he also challenged God. To prove the reality of God versus Baal, Elijah defied the prophets of Baal to have their god light the fire on a sacrificial altar. When they could not, Elijah had his own altar drenched with water, then challenged God:

Lord God of Abraham, Isaac, and Israel, let it be known this day that You are God in Israel and I am Your servant, and that I have done all these things at Your word (v. 36).

God honored Elijah's challenge and fire fell from heaven, lighting the altar of the Lord. It was such a mighty display of power that the people arose at Elijah's command and killed the false prophets.

This so enraged wicked Queen Jezebel, who had sponsored Baal worship in Israel through her husband, King Ahab, that she swore to kill Elijah. And "Elijah was afraid and ran for his life" (19: 3, *NIV*). Fleeing to the wilderness, Elijah lapsed into terrible despondency, and perhaps became paranoid.

Those who saw Elijah's bold public display would never have thought he had mental or emotional problems, but there in the wilderness the prophet's negative habits emerged.

Elijah's problem was not Jezebel. He was like some of the extroverts who are the center of attention at an office conference—those who must be in total control—over meetings, over others and over themselves. During alone times, however, they suffer chronic depression or despondency. Elijah's problem was himself.

Jezebel's threat revealed to Elijah that he was certainly not in control. So he not only fled from her, but he also isolated himself from his people, the nation of Israel. Journeying to the south, he left his servant in Judah and went a day's journey into the desert (see v. 4), deliberately choosing to go where there was no food. There Elijah prayed that God would take his life. Elijah had an emotional problem. Like many today, his inability to remain in control and to know that his future was secure left him feeling abandoned and deeply depressed. Many in similar situations have committed suicide. Like Elijah, they are victims of their own negative emotional habits.

HABITS OF THE HEART

Everyone has certain habits of thought and feeling, some good and some bad. A good habit is saying "thank you" when someone does something nice for you. A family member may have a good habit of cleaning out the sink after using it.

Some people have superstitious habits. For example, a ball player must wear a lucky hat. For others, it's not stepping on the crack in the sidewalk. An instinctive habit could be stuttering or scratching an alleged wound after it has already healed. Some of these habits and behavioral responses are relatively harmless; however, others can be serious.

We are not born with these mental and emotional habits. They are acquired as we grow. My granddaughter refused to say "thank you" when I gave her a gift, so her mother withheld the gift until she said it. Gratitude is an acquired habit. A baby is born with clutched fists and must be taught appreciation.

A habit is defined as a behavior pattern acquired by frequent repetition that is reflected in regular or increased performance. The word "habit" comes from a root meaning "clothing that is usually worn"—such as a nun's habit. Habits may express themselves in simple outward traits, or in complex emotional responses and habitual attitudes toward life—in habits of the heart.

God promises that fasting can break self-destructive habits. "Is not this the fast that I have chosen?...that ye break every yoke?" (Isa. 58:6, KJV). The Elijah Fast is especially useful in breaking negative attitudes and bad emotional habits.

The Elijah Fast is not a common corrective device to be used for freeing yourself from minor habits. It is called for in severely negative cases of mental and emotional response. It often works because it is a discipline that builds self-discipline and self-esteem. But more important than psychological esteem, the Elijah Fast invites God into the problem. Then in the strength of God, victory is possible.

Habits reflect themselves differently. Because life is a choice, people who have bad attitudes have chosen to have bad attitudes. They get up in the morning grumpy and choose to be irritated at their spouses, children and coworkers. By frequent repetition, they have chosen a constant state of irritation or anger. They have chosen to have negative personalities.

These people won't be told to "cheer up" or "lighten up." Some habits have people in bondage—psychological, physical or social bondage. Bondage enslaves people to their habits. When people have spent their lifetimes becoming depressed, they cannot become optimists by listening to one sermon. Nor does one counseling session change a lifetime of bad decisions. The Elijah Fast involves a total response extending for several days, or a one-day fast repeated throughout a specified time frame.

Symptoms of Needing This Fast

People suffering from mental problems and emotional habits similar to those of Elijah often struggle with one of several kinds of self-image problems.

DESTRUCTIVE SELF-IMAGES
- Negative self-image.
- Low self-image.
- Threatening self-image.
- Self-rejection.

Because of his mental or emotional habits, when problems arose that threatened his control over circumstances, or his self-image, Elijah had a tendency to withdraw from people and run from his problems, slip into despondency and/or depression ("He prayed that he might die," 1 Kings 19:4) and become either emotionally burned out or suffer from self-pity.

How can God break the cycle of pessimistic despondency? The answer is found in the example of Elijah.

Lessons from Elijah's Response

What can we learn from Elijah's style of responding to difficulty?

Defeat Often Follows Victory

There was no doubt that "the hand of the Lord was on Elijah" (18:46, KJV). By prayer, he brought fire from heaven. He commanded the execution of the prophets of Baal, and completely thwarted evil King Ahab. Yet when Queen Jezebel threatened to kill him, he ran away and prayed that God would take his life.

Was Elijah's boldness at the contest with the prophets of Baal only a cover-up for his deeper insecurities and fears or habits of pessimistic withdrawal? Was his despondency a recurring phenomenon that only appeared when Jezebel threatened him, and not at other times?

Other men of God have had similar defeats following great victories. Noah preached against the drunkenness of an entire generation, yet his children were judged because of Noah's sin of drunkenness (see Gen.

9:24,25). Abraham trusted God by faith, yet lied about his wife (see 12:12). Moses was the meekest man on the face of the earth (see Num. 12:3); however, he was not allowed to enter the Promised Land because he selfishly struck the rock to bring forth water. The disciple Peter claimed he would never deny the Lord, but within 24 hours of that affirmation, denied Him with cursing (see John 13:37,38).

Be careful when you have a great success for God. You are a prime candidate for special satanic attacks. The Bible teaches, "If you think you are standing firm, be careful that you don't fall!" (1 Cor. 10:12, *NIV*).

God Knows the Heart and Its Habits

Elijah was known for his boldness. He boasted, "As the Lord of hosts lives, before whom I stand, I will surely present myself to [Ahab] today" (1 Kings 18:15). Apparently, Elijah meant what he said. He stood against the prophets of Baal, calling down fire out of heaven in a great victory over them.

Was he just "grandstanding?" If not, why did his boldness suddenly disappear when evil Queen Jezebel threatened to make his life "as the life of one of them"(19:2)? In the crisis of the moment, Elijah ran away. But God knew all along what was in his heart.

We Can Get Depressed Doing God's Work

It's obvious that God worked through Elijah. He was the only one to stand for God when others compromised by worshiping Baal. He even boasted, "I alone am left" (v. 10). He was wrong. God told him that there were 7,000 in Israel who had not bowed to Baal. Elijah's problem was his "self-centeredness." He was so focused on himself that he could not see what God was doing in the lives of others. He couldn't see the greater picture. God had to distance Elijah from the problem so Elijah could see the big picture. The Elijah Fast can enable you to see the big picture.

It is possible for you to be so chained to and focused on a habit of thought or emotional response that you cannot see what God wants to do for you or what He's done for others. Your habit has you blinded to the power of God.

Past Victory May Not Break Bad Habits

Having been used greatly of God in the past does not mean you are presently ready to serve God. In business you often hear, "What have you done for me lately?" The same can be said of your spiritual life. Yesterday's victories do not guarantee tomorrow's successes. After Elijah's victory over 450 prophets of Baal, he ran and sat under a weeping willow tree. Symbolically, Elijah himself was weeping under the weeping willow, lamenting, "Now they are trying to kill me, too" (v. 10, NIV).

Do any of Elijah's responses to difficult challenges in life sound familiar? If so, you may be a candidate for the following remedy.

Prescription for the Elijah Fast

Step 1: Prepare Physically and Emotionally

As you consider fasting, do not act prematurely or fly off on a tangent. Many people afflicted with habitual negative emotional responses are also impetuous. They do things on the spur of the moment rather than out of a carefully calculated purpose. Prior to a fast, take three measured steps: (1) vow to God that you will fast; (2) prepare for the fast; then (3) fulfill your resolution.

How did Elijah prepare for his inadvertent fast? He lay down and fell asleep! (see v. 5). Sometimes people are despondent or otherwise vulnerable to negative emotional habits because they are physically weak.

Without the physical stamina to resist the inclination of our inner person, we may fall into uncontrollable habits. Sleeping at least gave Elijah physical strength. Then he broke his fast and ate: "There by his head was a cake of bread baked over hot coals, and a jar of water. He ate and drank and then lay down again" (v. 6, NIV). "The food and water made him strong enough to walk forty more days" (v. 8, CEV).

Mental and emotional effort are needed to prepare for a fast, and these are aided by physical preparation. Look at the "checklist" at the end of this chapter to make adequate preparation for the Elijah Fast.

Step 2: Recognize Your Limitations

Elijah knew what he must do. He needed to go to the place where God had revealed Himself to His people—to Sinai—where God appeared to Moses in the burning bush. But he was not ready for the trip—"The journey is too great for you," the angel said (v. 7).

The initial steps in breaking a negative emotional response are: (a) admit you cannot break your habit alone and (b) let others help you defeat your habit. Alcoholics Anonymous teaches that people in the grip of alcoholism are "powerless" to break their habits themselves. They must depend on a "higher power," and on a "buddy" who will help them get through difficult times.

Step 3: Go Where You Can Meet God

Sometimes it is important to celebrate the Elijah Fast away from home and friends. You may have to go to a mountain cabin, a motel or some other private retreat. If there is a place where God has met you in the past—such as a church auditorium or a camp—that might be the place to fast and pray. Why? Because just as you may physically return to a geographical place, you spiritually return to God's anointed position.

Note that Elijah "strengthened by that food...traveled forty days and forty nights until he reached Horeb, the mountain of God" (v. 8, *NIV*). Technically, Horeb is a mountain range, and Sinai is a tall peak within that range. Mount Sinai is the place where God appeared to Moses in the flame of fire after the deliverance of Egypt, and where He issued the Ten Commandments.

Actually revisit the place. Sometimes we must go back to the very location where we had past spiritual victories. The world says, "You can never go home again." Maybe not to live, but you *can* go home to get something you've lost during the journey. As the environment reinforces our emotions, so we are strengthened to trust God for future victories.

Revisit the place symbolically. Sometimes you can't actually revisit the place geographically, but you can go there in your memory. There you can recommit yourself to what God previously accomplished in that place. Revisit in your mind the meetings and events where God spoke to you. The word "revival" means a "return to life." This can occur by returning to our former places of strength. In a revival we return to (a) New Testament Christianity where God poured Himself out on the Early Church, or (b) the place of our conversion where God first manifested His presence to us and we experienced the forgiveness of sins.

There are places where both God and demons want to manifest themselves. Elijah was from the northern kingdom of Israel. There he had his greatest victory on Mount Carmel. His homeland, however, was a land of idols. It was a place where Satan was manifesting himself through false gods. Elijah sought a new touch from the true God, so he returned to the place where God had originally revealed Himself to Moses.

Step 4: Fast to Hear the Word of the Lord

After Elijah arrived at Mount Sinai, "the Word of the Lord came to him" (v. 9). God had a message for Elijah, and he had to obey God to receive it. He had to travel to Sinai to get the message.

a. *Study to know what the Bible says, not what you think it says.* Many people who have destructive physical or emotional habits have convinced themselves there is no hope for themselves. Depressed people believe in the credibility of their memories. Because they remember something, they attribute omniscience to their insight. Because people are not perfect, neither are their memories perfect. People who are locked into negative cycles of thoughts and emotions need to look outside themselves to see what God says about the patterns. If God says a habit can be broken, it can be broken.

A depressed person needs to hear from God that:

The wrong desires that come into your life aren't anything new and different. Many others have faced exactly the same problems before you. And no temptation is irresistible. You can trust God to keep the temptation from becoming so strong that you can't stand up against it, for he has promised this and will do what he says. He will show you how to escape temptation's power so that you can bear up patiently against it (1 Cor. 10:13, *TLB*).

b. *Depressed people need to receive a positive external influence from outside their thinking.* To know only of your limitations is to believe in your limitations. The way to break that cycle of negative knowing and believing is to introduce new facts into your thinking. Carefully study the Word of God. Study portions about faith, hope, the power of God and victory. As you understand the promises of God to overcome a habit, you will gain strength to break that habit.

Step 5: Let the Word Reveal Your Weakness

When Adam sinned, God came asking him, "Where are you?" (Gen. 3:9). God knew where Adam was; He asked the question to cause Adam to reflect on where he was. When we read the Word of God, we begin to question "where we are" spiritually. We reexamine our presuppositions.

Only when we question our habitual thought patterns can the bondage of mental habits begin to be broken.

When Elijah arrived at Mount Sinai, the Word of the Lord came to him. "What are you doing here, Elijah?" God asked (1 Kings 19:9). Notice how God uses questions as a mirror to make people view themselves from outside their inner compulsiveness. During the Elijah Fast, use Scripture as this kind of mirror to show you your weaknesses—"where you are," emotionally and spiritually.

Step 6: Confess and Agree with God About Your Weakness

When the Word of the Lord came to Elijah on Mount Sinai, God began to penetrate his soul. Immediately, Elijah was embarrassed. In an attempt to justify himself, Elijah said, "I have been very zealous for the Lord God of hosts; for the children of Israel have forsaken Your covenant" (v. 10).

Although this sounded like a bold self-defense, this statement was actually Elijah's confession of failure. When we are filled with self-justification, we cannot confess our needs.

Elijah had covered his need with the claim to be defending God, not realizing that God can defend Himself. A wise Bible teacher once said that the Word of God is like a lion. No one has to defend a lion—just release the lion and he will defend himself. In the same way, we sometimes are zealous for God's honor, as we should be, but when we try to defend God, we use our own beautiful thoughts. Perhaps we simply need to tell people about God and allow God to defend Himself.

Step 7: Look for Quiet, Inner Meaning

Elijah was a broken leader, depressed and withdrawn from people. God did not perform a miracle or give Elijah outward power to correct his negative perceptions. God did not even solve Elijah's problem. Instead, He asked Elijah to look within himself for the answer.

> And behold the Lord passed by, and a great and strong wind rent the mountains, and brake in pieces the rocks before the Lord; but the Lord was not in the wind: and after the wind an earthquake; but the Lord was not in the earthquake: And after the earthquake a fire; but the Lord was not in the fire: and after the fire a still small voice. And it was so, when Elijah

heard it, he wrapped his face in his mantle, and went out (vv. 11-13, *KJV*).

Elijah found the answer in the Lord's still small voice, not in the powerful wind, the earthquake or the fire. The power was in the Word of God. Whether that voice was audible is not the issue. Elijah heard within his own ear the voice of the Lord speaking to him and telling him what he must do.

Some people go to the altar and ask, "God, take this habit from me." Sometimes this is an appeal to God for external power to overcome their habits. People want to put the ball in God's court, when all along God wants to give them the ball to empower them to be more responsible.

Habits are broken not by external forces, but from within. They must be broken the way they are formed, one act at a time—by submitting to discipline—by repeatedly choosing not to behave according to habit. Just as the habit of overeating was established one meal at a time, conquering that habit will require submitting to disciplined eating one meal at a time.

Remember that a habit is "frequent repetition." Disciplining yourself for one meal is not enough. There must also be frequent repetition of your discipline. Like the football player who builds up torso strength by employing daily workouts, so the Christian builds up strength to break a bad habit by using daily discipline to resist that habit. Our strength comes from within as we build up the inner person.

The Elijah Fast should not begin by asking God to do a supernatural miracle to take your habit from you. Of course He could—and may—do it in this way. Instead, begin by looking within the Word of God, and listening within your own "inner ear" to hear what God is saying to you. Perhaps He does not want to use His power to break your habit externally. Perhaps He wants you to build up your inner strength so you can break your habit. Be flexible in discovering God's will in the matter.

Step 8: Look for the Positive Through God's Eyes
Too often, we enter the Elijah Fast focusing on the "negative" emotional pattern, thereby trapping ourselves within the problem. Elijah's problem was his depression and pessimistic despondency. He continually reminded God, "I am the only one left." This proclamation was a manipulative way of bragging to God about his ability to be faithful. Elijah should have been seeking to view his problem from God's perspective.

God came to Elijah to give him a positive message, to get the prophet's eyes off his human weakness and onto God's strength. God told Elijah, "I have left me seven thousand in Israel, all the knees which have not bowed unto Baal" (18, *KJV*).

As long as we focus on our problems, we exercise faith in our problems. We are admitting that our problems are bigger than we are and even bigger than God. God wants us to focus on His power so we can have more faith in His power than in our problems.

Step 9: Plan Positive Actions
Habits are broken by taking positive actions rather than concentrating on negative traits. Notice that God does not tell Elijah to "quit being depressed" or to "stop grumbling."

The way to break a bad habit is to acquire a stronger positive habit. When a three-year-old boy wants to suck his thumb, a mother puts a toy in his hand. By substituting that which is more desirable, she can break the thumb-sucking habit.

God gave the depressed prophet some positive things to do. First He told him, "Go...anoint Hazael as king over Syria" (v. 15). Next, "You shall anoint Jehu the son of Nimshi as king over Israel" (v. 16). Even then God was not finished with Elijah. Next God told him to go commission Elisha, the prophet already selected to follow Elijah (v. 16).

Much of what we do in life is in response to the way we see ourselves. To break a bad habit, therefore, we must see ourselves successfully doing a new habit. It is good to develop the ability to see ourselves as we really are, but more importantly, to develop the ability to see ourselves as we want to be.

> You can't achieve
> What you can't conceive!

Step 10: See Potential Results
People break bad habits when they have goals that are stronger than the attractions of their bad habits. God had a plan for Elijah. By directing Elijah to go anoint Elisha to be his successor, God gave the pessimistic prophet a new vision of the prophetic potential in Israel. And when Elijah understood his importance in God's plan, he left his despondency behind.

HOW HABITS EVOLVE

"America is great because America is good!" concluded the French author Alexis de Tocqueville in his study of America's reasons for greatness. What he could not find in our nation's political and business institutions, he found in our churches. He coined the phrase "habits of the heart" to describe the moral character of the American people of that era.

Understanding how to develop moral character in our lives gives us the strength to break bad habits. In the words of a country farmer, "What's in the well comes up in the bucket." That is, our inner beliefs or convictions influence our expectations or visions. These in turn influence our attitudes and values, which influence our actions, which influence our habits, which shape our characters.

Faith is at the core of being a Christian. "Without faith it is impossible to please Him" (Heb. 11:6). One of the first descriptions of Christians in the Early Church was the expression "believers" (Acts 5:14). The kind of faith that impresses God and characterized those early Christians is faith that is evidenced in the way we live. "For as the body without the spirit is dead, so faith without works is dead" (Jas. 2:26). Our biblical faith must influence the way we live our lives. Our faith will build good habits, and break bad habits.

When people see the gospel making a difference in our lives, they will be attracted to us so they, too, can experience similar changes. Just as the bright petals of a flower draw a bee to the sweet nectar inside, so consistent Christian character will draw others to the Christ who indwells us and enables us to live the Christian life.

A correlation exists among what we believe (our creed or the content of our faith), the process by which we believe (the foundation of our faith), how we live (our actions and habits) and who we are (our character).

The apostle Peter (see 2 Pet. 1:4-8) summarizes the process of developing biblical character. Compare the steps of this verse, which I paraphrase here, to the above paradigm of character development:

> God has given us powerful, yet precious promises in Scripture that will break our old habits and change us into people of character. Give diligence to add to your (1) knowledge of Scripture, (2) faith by which you live, then (3) add the virtue of expectation. Next (4) add the attitude of self-disci-

pline, as a (5) consistent godly habit. If you have these (6) qualities of habit, you will not be ineffective and unproductive (author's paraphrase).

Look closer at each step in the process of developing character. This belief-system cycle is the basis for character development in our lives demonstrating how to make and break habits.

Changed Thinking Leads to Changed Beliefs

Character and habit development begin with thinking. Think differently about your habit and you will develop a deep belief about what to do. Scripture reveals that belief is not just a decision, nor is it a desire—it is a commitment. To say, "I believe God will help me break a habit" is saying "I know God can break my habit."

Belief, therefore, may be defined as the conviction that something is true. Scripture uses various words to describe aspects of belief that, when examined together, outline the usual steps to developing biblical faith.

First, the word "hope" describes the desires we may have. We may say, "I hope to break this negative emotional habit."

On the basis of hope, we make plans that reflect what we anticipate. We may say, "I plan to break this habit." As we are persuaded in our faith, we express our confidence. "I am confident I can break this habit."

The fullest expression of our confidence is the statement, "I know I can break this habit." When we come to that point in the growth of our faith, we have moved into the realm of biblical conviction.

FOUR STEPS TO BIBLICAL BELIEF
1. I hope.
2. I plan.
3. I am confident.
4. I know.

Faith is produced by the Scriptures, which are called "the word of faith" (Rom. 10:8). "So then faith cometh by hearing, and hearing by the word of God" (v. 17, *KJV*). This means that those who want to develop faith in God must begin by learning the basic facts of Scripture. Knowledge of Scripture must then become the basis upon which they live their Christian lives.

Changed Beliefs Lead to Changed Expectations

The second step in the process of character formation involves changing beliefs to effect a change in expectations. Your expectations or vision must come from God's Word. "Where there is no vision, the people perish: but he that keepeth the law, happy is he" (Prov. 29:18, *KJV*). Some people never break a bad emotional habit because their belief in God does not create new expectations from God.

There are at least six different responses people may have about vision. First, some never see what God wants them to see. They have mechanical problems. Others see it, but don't understand it. They have mental problems. Still others see it, but never pursue it. They have will problems. A fourth group see it, but never feel it. They have emotional problems. Then there are those who see it, and through obedience achieve it. Finally there are some who see and share it, demonstrating their capacities for leadership.

Biblical expectation will motivate you to overcome bad thought patterns and habits and to develop new biblically based behaviors. God's vision for your life can be grasped as you take these four steps: First, look *within* yourself to determine how God has enabled and gifted you. Second, look *back* to see how God has used past events to shape you and prepare you for something greater. Third, look *around* yourself to identify others you admire. (I often tell people, "Tell me who your hero is and I'll tell you where you'll be in 10 years.") Fourth, look *ahead* to determine what kind of life you want to live for God in the future.

Changed Expectations Lead to Changed Attitudes

A good attitude is not enough to break a habit, and you can't break a habit with a bad attitude. Where does a good attitude originate from? From changed expectations.

Your attitude is the predisposition of your life's focus. It may be defined as the habit of your attention. When you are a victim of a bad habit, you are on a downward cycle that results in "hardening of the attitudes." In contrast, creating positive emotional habits puts you on an upward cycle.

As you consistently apply attitudes, you develop habits that form your character. When you tire of always being late, you may decide to start being on time. As that attitude becomes more prominent in your thinking and is more consistently applied, you will begin to develop the habit of punctuality. This new habit helps shape your new character.

Usually four steps are involved in developing new attitudes. First, *identify the problem you wish to address.* In the illustration used previously, the problem was chronic lateness. Second, *identify the right thinking that will lead to changing an emotional habit.* Decide you want to be on time. The third step involves *relating to positive people.* You become like those with whom you associate. If you want to become punctual, you should begin associating with punctual people. Finally, *develop a plan that will encourage positive attitudes* and help develop a new habit. Begin by being on time for your next meeting, then the next one and so on. Being on time for one meeting at a time will eventually develop the habit of being on time, and you will become known as a punctual person.

Changed Attitudes Lead to Changed Actions
The dictionary defines an action as "anything done or performed." Actions may be wrong, ignorant, positive, lucky, planned or unplanned.

Your actions earn your reputation and communicate to others the kind of person you are. "Even a child is known by his deeds, whether what he does is pure and right" (Prov. 20:11). Jesus emphasized this principle by referring to the common practice of identifying a tree by the fruit it produces. "Every tree is known by its own fruit. For men do not gather figs from thorns, nor do they gather grapes from a bramble bush" (Luke 6:44). Our actions are the fruit by which others determine the kind of people we are.

Changed Actions Lead to Changed Habits
Actions are the things you do. When you do them repeatedly they become habits. An action or an accomplishment is the complete satisfactory outcome of an action. We often use the word "accomplishment" in a positive sense—for instance, when we say a person is "an accomplished musician." Actually, the word means "the final outcome regardless of its value, whether it is good or bad." The Scriptures use the word in the sense of completing something. The goal of the Scriptures is "that the man of God may be complete, thoroughly equipped [or "accomplished"] for every good work" (2 Tim. 3:17, paraphrase mine).

Changed Habits Lead to Character Formation
Your character is not indicative of one isolated event in your life. It is a result of the pattern of your activities. When you follow good habits, you

develop good character. Conversely, when you develop bad habits, you develop detrimental character.

Conclusion: Character Is a Process

Life is a process throughout which we develop character. First, we think about it. Then we know it. After that we dream it. Next we begin to focus on it. Then we act on it. Our action leads to accomplishing it. Ultimately, we become it.

PRINCIPLES TO REMEMBER

When you know what forms good habits, you know how to break bad habits. Study the material explaining character formation.

Focus on the biblical principles of strength developed by withdrawing to "a desert place," as Elijah did, during fasting and prayer. When you go to the quiet place to fast and pray, you gain inner strength from God. When you enter the Elijah Fast, separate yourself from external forces that reinforce your problem—television, newspapers and the usual influences of your life. You will gain strength in quietness before God. As mentioned in previous chapters, this is not just quiet meditation.

Bring your Bible and other study tools. Also, take material to read about breaking compulsive habits or bondages.

Fast and pray for God to give you a positive self-image mirroring biblical character. You want to be a good testimony for God. Character is constantly doing the right thing with the right attitude for the right purpose because you know what is right.

Fast and pray for the positive actions God would have you do. As you begin the Elijah Fast, make a list of those things. Some of these disciplines are spiritual, others involve the natural world. Remember, there is more than one solution to a problem; likewise, there is more than one way to break a habit. Perhaps you have tried in the past and failed. You did not try every means because there *is* a "way of escape" (1 Cor. 10:13).

Develop a list of prayer requests for times of fasting. As you continually pray through the requests, you will begin to see some of God's answers. Other requests may not realize an immediate answer. By keeping a written account of what God is doing, you can see objectively His working in your life. This insight gives you strength to break your habit. Watch your confidence grow as you seek His answers to your prayers.

Determine how long you should fast. An Elijah Fast is most effective when it is practiced an ongoing length of time in God's presence and/or practiced several times to break especially engrained mental habits. The more deeply rooted your habit, the more intense your fasting and prayer must be. The longer you've had the habit, the more times you will need to fast. Remember the words of Jesus: "This kind goeth not out but by prayer and fasting" (Matt. 17:21, *KJV*).

PREPARING FOR THE ELIJAH FAST

Aim: The Elijah Fast for breaking negative mental and emotional habits.

Affirmation: I believe in the power of God over the whole person, spirit, soul and body (see 1 Thess. 5:23). I believe that "He has given us not a spirit of fear, but of power and love and a sound mind" (2 Tim. 1:7, *KJV*).

Vow: God being my strength, and grace being my basis, I commit myself to the Elijah Fast for building godly character, to the glory of God.

Fast: What I will withhold _____

Beginning: Date and time I will start _____

End: Date and time I will stop_____

Purpose: I am fasting to break the mental/emotional habit of

_____

Bible Basis: 1 Kings 19

Bible Promise: "For He Himself has said, 'I will never leave you nor forsake you.' So we may boldly say: 'The Lord is my helper; I will not fear.'" (Heb. 13:5,6).

Resources Needed: _____

Prayer Partners: _____

Steps After Fast: _____

     Signed _____ Date _____

\|///

≡ 6 ≡

THE WIDOW'S FAST

A MEXICAN PASTOR IN CHIAPAS, MEXICO, RAN OUT OF BIBLES WHILE distributing them door to door. The people were hungry for the Word of God, so they immediately began to read their Bibles and learn God's message to them.

The pastor spent his salary and deprived himself of food to provide more Bibles. Three days later, some of the people realized that he was not buying food. Although this pastor did not enter a formal fast in the traditional sense, he followed the prescription for the Elijah Fast. Within his own admirable value system, it was a forced fast. As we shall see, those who joined the Widow's Fast shared a common situation with this pastor in which going without food seemed better than its alternative.

Zarephath was just another hot, dry village in Phoenicia (modern-day Lebanon). A widow traveled to the outskirts of town to collect dry sticks falling from dehydrated bushes. Zarephath had been suffering a drought. The bright, blue cloudless skies dashed any hopes for rain. Even if it did rain, it was probably too late for the widow and her son.

The village had not experienced the rainy season for the past two years. No one previously enjoyed the prolonged dampness that penetrated the bones during weeks of constant rain each spring; however, it would now be welcomed. The field grasses had turned brown, and trees prematurely shed their leaves. The local priest was summoned to do what was necessary to appease the village god so that the rains would once again bring life back to the earth. Several rituals had been performed, but still the gods of Phoenicia had withheld the life-giving showers from their village.

The entire Near East was suffering a drought. To judge the people of Israel (Phoenicia's neighbors), God had shut up heaven. Elijah the prophet "prayed earnestly that it would not rain; and it did not rain on the land for three years and six months" (Jas. 5:17).

Ahab, king of Israel, had married a girl from the region near the widow's home. She was Jezebel, known for her faithful worship of the gods of Phoenicia. "Ahab...did evil in the sight of the Lord, more than all who were before him" (1 Kings 16:30). "As though it had been a trivial thing for him to walk in the sins of Jeroboam the son of Nebat...he took as wife Jezebel...and he went and served Baal and worshiped him" (v. 31). Jezebel personally underwrote the living expenses of 450 prophets of Baal (see 18:19).

Very little is known about the Phoenician widow except that she was one of many widows in the land. She went about gathering sticks to cook her small evening meal. Life had been difficult but manageable when her husband was alive. There were good times and bad times. One of the best had been at the birth of their son. She recalled the proud look in her husband's eyes as she presented their boy to him.

Times went from bad to worse when her husband died unexpectedly. She had barely been able to make ends meet before the drought hit, and now it was almost impossible to find the basic necessities of life.

The sun was scorching hot; however, her chief problem was that she only had enough food for one last meager meal. She had reconciled her fate in her own mind. She would take the sticks she had gathered and make her last cooking fire. She might have enough flour and oil left to feed both her son and herself, but that was all. She would use their last resources to prepare one final meal. Then, like their predecessors, they would find a quiet place to wait for death from starvation to overtake them.

"Please bring me a little water in a cup, that I may drink," called a feeble male voice behind her (17: 10). The voice was so weak that she was compelled to help this stranger who had stumbled into her village. As she approached the well to draw water, she heard him call out one more time, "Please bring me a morsel of bread in your hand" (v. 11).

Years earlier, she would have been eager to help. That was just the way people were in her village. They took care of strangers who were in need of food and water. But now there was no food to eat. What she had was not enough to keep herself and her son alive. How could she give the little she had to a stranger?

She turned to explain to the stranger that there was no bread in her home. All she had was a little flour in the bin and a bit of oil in a jar. She was on her way home to prepare a final meal for her son and herself when the stranger asked for water. As she explained her situation to the stranger who had called to her, she knew she would have to do something. His appearance confirmed her awareness that he needed the food more than she did. She could not have known at the time that this stranger had been living in a *wadi*—a dry streambed—for the past few months, surviving off the carrion left by ravens.

"Don't be afraid," the stranger encouraged. "Go home and do as you have said. But first make a small cake of bread for me from what you have and bring it to me, and then make something for yourself and your son" (v.13, *NIV*). He assured her that his God would take care of her family if she followed his instructions.

The widow was special. God had prepared her for this moment and this task. God had told Elijah, "Go at once to Zarephath....I have commanded a widow in that place to supply you with food" (v. 9, *NIV*). By the time he arrived at Zarephath the prophet looked so unkempt and sounded so hungry and thirsty that it almost sounded funny to hear him deliver God's promise, "The jar of flour will not be used up and the jug of oil will not run dry until the day the Lord gives rain on the land" (v. 14, *NIV*). She might have laughed if her own hunger had been any less painful. Still, it was easy for her to decide. She would die with or without her meal, so why not share what she had with someone in need, someone who had not yet lost hope completely?

As she trudged home with the prophet Elijah, the widow had no idea that her houseguest would be a prophet who would later end this drought through a power encounter with the prophets of Baal. She only knew someone needed something that she had slighty more of than he had. Missing a meal to provide it was the very least she could do.

The Widow's Fast is named after this poor woman of Zarephath because she was willing to go without food to meet a humanitarian need in the life of another.

The Widow's Fast was not a long fast. Just as Elijah had promised, God intervened in her situation. She was able to continue feeding her son and new houseguest throughout the remainder of the famine. The prophet's promise was fulfilled and the flour and oil were not consumed. In expressing a willingness to deny herself to meet the needs of Elijah, the widow of Zarephath modeled a unique approach to the discipline of fasting.

THE WIDOW'S FAST IN THE BIBLE

The Scriptures reveal a strong emphasis about the concerns of God's people for the physical needs of those around them. It is not surprising that providing for people in need should become an important aspect of the discipline of fasting. Israel's need for reform had prompted God's question:

> Is this not the fast that I have chosen...to share your bread with the hungry, and that you bring to your house the poor who are cast out; when you see the naked, that you cover him, and not hide yourself from your own flesh? (Isa. 58:6,7).

The Widow's Fast enables us to see God meet the needs of others, especially humanitarian needs such as food and clothing. Eventually this fast was practiced far beyond the small village of Zarephath.

The New Testament introduces us to other widows who fasted. Anna is described as a prophetess who "never left the temple but worshipped night and day, fasting and praying" (Luke 2:37, *NIV*). From the little we know of Anna, she appears to have had a ministry of serving God by fasting. Did that ministry, like that of the widow of Zarephath, involve sharing her physical resources with others?

Jesus identified another dedicated widow while teaching in the Temple. As He saw a poor widow place her last two mites into the Temple treasury designated for the care of the poor, Jesus said,

> Truly I say to you that this poor widow has put in more than all; for all these out of their abundance have put in offerings for God, but she out of her poverty put in all the livelihood that she had (Luke 21:3,4).

She gave all she had. This widow was willing to sacrifice everything, probably including her next meal. The Widow's Fast describes this widow who gave up necessities to help others.

Widows were not the only ones mentioned in the New Testament who fasted in order to provide for the physical needs of others. The apostle Andrew found a young boy who was willing to give up his lunch consisting of five barley loaves and two small fishes so that 5,000 hungry people could be fed (see John 6:9). Someone else must have made a similar sacrifice when Jesus fed 4,000 people who had been fasting for three days (see Mark 8:1-9).

There is some indication that the spirit of the Widow's Fast was part of the spiritual discipline of the Early Church. Paul used the example of the Macedonian Christians to encourage the Corinthians to give sacrificially to meet a humanitarian need in Jerusalem. Concerning the Macedonian Christians, Paul wrote:

> In a great trial of affliction the abundance of their joy and their deep poverty abounded in the riches of their liberality. For I bear witness that according to their ability, yes, and beyond their ability, they were freely willing, imploring us with much urgency that we would receive the gift and the fellowship of the ministering to the saints (2 Cor. 8:2-4).

Although the discipline of fasting is not specifically mentioned here, the spirit of their giving is consistent with that of those who use the Widow's Fast to sacrificially give to meet the needs of others. Like the widow who gave her two mites, the Macedonian Christians gave out of their poverty to provide for others.

A LONG AND DISTINGUISHED TRADITION

(The citations in this section all come from Christian writers from the period immediately after the New Testament era.)

Fasting may or may not have been involved in these previous examples of giving to meet human needs; however, fasting to meet such needs quickly became part of church life in the postapostolic age. Fasting is mentioned often in the writings of the "Church fathers," and usually in the context of what we are calling the Widow's Fast. By the second century, fasting was practiced by Christians twice weekly—Wednesdays and Fridays. The discipline of fasting was considered better than prayer (see 2 Clement 16:4). The *Shepherd of Hermas* describes the practice of eating only bread and water during a fast, and designating the money otherwise spent on food for charitable pursuits.

The relationship between fasting and giving to charitable causes continued for some time in the Early Church. Saint Leo described fasting as a "praesidium"—a protection for the spirit against the control of the body. He advocated fasting to keep the body disciplined. Disciplining the body enabled the spirit to receive direction from God, such as a call to take the gospel to the unreached people of that day.

Leo insisted that the discipline of liberally giving to humanitarian causes always accompany fasting. According to the *Apology of Aristides*, when a Christian did not have enough money to help a poor fellow believer, the Christian would customarily fast for two or three days to raise the needed funds.

Throughout the Middle Ages, a modified form of the Widow's Fast was practiced by the early monks. Fasting in monasteries became part of an ascetic lifestyle before it later ended. Strong evidence suggests that the discipline of fasting was first practiced as part of an economy responsible for sending missionaries to the unreached world.

In the sixth century A.D., Saint Columba and other Irish monks were sent on evangelistic missions throughout Great Britain and northern Europe. These missions were possible because the limited resources of the monastery were given to missions rather than to provide an abundance of food and other luxuries. Similarly, the early Moravians and other pietist groups adopted a simple communal lifestyle that included the discipline of fasting. Their sacrificial living enabled them to release their limited resources to meet needs and to support outreach ministries.

The Widow's Fast was also a part of the personal discipline of many revivalists and revivalistic movements. The example of the Moravians has already been mentioned. John Wesley and other Methodist leaders in the Evangelical Revival adopted a simple lifestyle that included regular periods of fasting, and they encouraged others to do the same. Money that might have been spent on food for themselves funded a number of humanitarian projects, including the care of widows and orphans, the liberation of slaves and prison reform.

In chapter 1 we mentioned that hundreds of Christians skipped their lunches during the Layman's Prayer Revival in 1859. This enabled many to save money that would have been spent on meals to instead assist others directly suffering the effects of the bank collapse that occurred about the time the revival peaked. Although the purpose of the prayer meetings was not to fast, because people prayed through their lunch hours, fasting was the logical outcome.

Even today, many Christians in North America practice the discipline of fasting in the context of giving to humanitarian projects. Many churches and community groups have sponsored a "Thirty-Hour Famine" to raise funds for famine relief. Others have conducted church banquets featuring a menu of rice and beans reminding people of the world's underprivileged populations. They often donate money that would otherwise have funded a banquet, to feed the hungry. The Widow's Fast is also practiced by Christians in the emerging nations of the world.

A variation of the Widow's Fast is regularly practiced by Christians in the state of Mizoram, India. This is the poorest state in India, but Christians from that region have developed a unique strategy to raise money for foreign missions. When the women of Mizoram prepare the daily rice for their families, they remove one cup of uncooked rice from the total amount that would normally be prepared. This rice is set aside as a gift to missions. The women give this rice to their churches, who then resell it to their church members. Funds raised through recycling rice are used to send out missionaries to other provinces of India and neighboring countries.

The humanitarian emphasis of the Widow's Fast also appeals to those who do not identify themselves as Christians. Mahatma Gandhi believed people should live an "eternal, compulsory fast" to adequately meet the needs of others. Gandhi practiced fasting personally, and urged his followers to do the same. His simple lifestyle was apparently motivated by his concern for the needy. Surely Christians, who are to be characterized by their love for others, should be concerned for those who lack basic necessities (see John 13:34,35).

HOW TO OBSERVE THE WIDOW'S FAST

Before practicing the discipline of fasting in the context of the Widow's Fast, take time to prepare yourself adequately. Although it is possible to forfeit one or two meals to make a financial contribution to international relief projects, the experience of the Widow's Fast can be much more meaningful if you are prepared for it. Allow your fast to minister to you as you seek to minister to others.

Step 1: Become Others Oriented

Develop sensitivity to the problems of others by researching the needs of the underprivileged living in close proximity to you. One of the disadvantages of living in an "information age" is that we hear about so many hurting people that we easily become desensitized to their needs. We can overcome this natural tendency by proactively cultivating empathy and sensitivity for people who are enduring difficult circumstances.

Step 2: Recognize Your Own Blessings

Most Christians in this country are far better off than the poor of this world. Yet most of us find it easier to complain than to rejoice. Often we do not recognize how fortunate we are until we see others in greater need. A Bible student once complained he had only bread and jam to eat, until he learned of another student who had only crackers. The poorest in North America would be considered extremely wealthy in many parts of the world. Instead of complaining about not being able to purchase an expensive dessert with our restaurant meal, we should rejoice in God's provision of food for us. Many people in the world cannot count on a single meal consisting of a bowl of beans, rice or other cooked grain.

Step 3: Use Some of Your Grocery Money

The purpose of the Widow's Fast is to help release your giving to meet the needs of others by using resources that would normally be consumed for yourself. As a faithful steward of the resources entrusted to you by God, you can fast to economize your own food budget. The money you save will enable you to have more to share with the hungry. It is not possible to bring foreign famine victims to your dinner table each week, but it is possible for your family to fast through dinner so that a family in one of the famine regions can eat.

Step 4: Fast and Pray for Guidance

One person cannot meet the needs of every hurting person. Therefore, ask God for wisdom to determine the extent to which you should be involved in a specific humanitarian project. Rather than giving up in frustration because you are not able to feed all the hungry people in the world, ask God to burden you with a manageable portion of need.

Perhaps your family could provide food for a hungry family by fasting one day a week. Another family may designate the money saved through their Widow's Fast to purchase Christmas toys for poor children. Other families may contribute to a food bank, home for pregnant teenage girls or a local drug or alcohol rehabilitation center. Your fast will take on greater significance if you identify specific ways you can participate in the solution to the much larger problem.

Step 5: Pray for Those You Help
After you have identified the specific need of your Widow's Fast, set aside special times—perhaps mealtimes—to pray for the needy who will directly benefit from your Widow's Fast gift. When Jesus received the gift of five barley loaves and two small fishes from a young boy, He gave thanks before distributing it to the hungry.

Step 6: Identify with Others' Suffering
If you find it difficult to endure the afternoon without a candy bar, think of those who must survive the day or week on a small bowl of rice. Some families who fast together break their Widow's Fast with a simple meal of rice and beans, the staple diet of many people throughout the world, or a native dish of the people for whom they are fasting. Humanitarian agencies are often able to provide information to help prepare these dishes.

Step 7: Consider a Long-Term Investment
As you incorporate the Widow's Fast into your personal discipline of fasting, begin thinking of extending your involvement to the relief of human suffering. Consider making significant lifestyle changes that would enable you to continue contributing to others.

Many doctors encourage their fasting patients to develop healthier post-fast eating habits. Eliminating excessive sugars and salt from your diet could be translated into savings for the ongoing support of needy people. You may choose to fast a meal or day each week to extend your ministry to people in need.

PRACTICAL PRINCIPLES TO REMEMBER

The following are suggestions for extending the value of the Widow's Fast.

Learn to identify other specific human needs. The widow of Zarephath decided to abstain from eating for Elijah's benefit. Likewise, the boy who sacrificed his lunch saw it used specifically to feed the hungry multitude when he decided to fast. The Widow's Fast can sensitize you to people you may be able to help in other specific ways.

Learn the monetary value of the food you would consume in a typical day. This amount can be determined in one of two ways. You could lay out a daily typical menu estimating the cost of each meal, including between-meal snacks and morning coffee and doughnut purchases.

If your family is observing the Widow's Fast for a day, it may be easier to divide the family food budget by seven to estimate the savings realized by a typical day of fasting. If a family spends $140 a week on groceries and other food purchases, that family will save $20 in a one-day Widow's Fast. In this way you not only help feed the hungry, but you also get a better grasp of your own food budget.

Note the value of spending the money to meet the need before you begin fasting. The widow of Zarephath gave her food to Elijah before she fed herself and her son. The widow who gave two mites in the Temple and the boy who provided his lunch to feed 5,000 hungry people also gave before concluding their fasts. Giving first will help you identify the priority of your fast and eliminate the tendency to break your fast by spending your humanitarian gift on food for yourself.

Set specific goals. Set a goal of how much you would like to contribute to a specific humanitarian project. Then determine how long you should fast to save the amount you intend to give to this project. Most people will find it easier to fast one day a week for several weeks than to observe a longer fast. Some may choose to fast regularly, adopting a new project each month or two.

Learn to identify with those you serve. When you break your fast, do so with a meal that will remind you of the people for whom you are fasting. A bowl of cooked grain such as oatmeal, rice or grits is not unlike the daily meals of many people in the world. If you are fasting for people in a tropical climate, you may wish to break your fast with a banana or other serving of fruit.

Look for specific ways to reduce your personal cost of living to enable you to contribute more to meeting the needs of others. Many Christians in North America have so incorporated nonessentials into their personal lifestyles that they are now viewed as essentials. Our luxuries have become our necessities. A Widow's Fast can help us recognize nonessentials that may be eliminated to produce significant long-term savings. Many Christians have chosen to live simple lifestyles so they can give more to missions and meet the needs of others.

PREPARING FOR THE WIDOW'S FAST

Aim: The Widow's Fast, for diverting funds to meet the needs of others.

Vow: Lord, I vow to fast and pray according to the following outline on behalf of the specific people named. During the fast I commit myself to giving the funds that would normally provide my food to You through an agency or directly to the needy.

Specific Need: I will endeavor to meet the needs of _____

Specific Amount: I will contribute a total of $____to this cause, based on what I would have otherwise spent on my own meals.

Fast: What I will withhold _____

Activity: I will be praying at meal times specifically for _____ during the fast.

After Fasting: To identify with those for whom I am fasting, I will break my fast by _____

My Own Needs: The need in my own life I would like God to meet as I fast is_____

Beginning: Date and time I will start _____

End: Date and time I will stop_____

Bible Basis: 1 Kings 17.

Bible Promise: "The jar of flour will not be used up and the jug of oil will not run dry until the day the Lord gives rain on the land" (1 Kings 17:14, *NIV*).

Resources Needed: _____

Prayer Partners: _____

Steps After Fast: _____

Signed _____ Date _____

THE SAINT PAUL FAST

A MINISTERIAL STUDENT FASTED ABOUT ACCEPTING A POSITION AS associate pastor in a large, prominent church. Like Saint Paul on the Damascus road, the student needed God's guidance. During the fast, God removed the student's desire for that church position.

A month later the senior pastor resigned; consequently all staff members were also asked to resign. Prior to his Saint Paul Fast, the student was flattered by the prospect of ministering in that prominent church. But when he retreated into a quiet place and fasted for the will of God, the guidance he received proved to be providential.

FASTING FOR LIGHT ON THE ROAD

Because life will present all of us with major decisions, we can all benefit from the Saint Paul Fast at some time. Decisions can redirect our entire lives and destinies. A decision about whom to marry, for example, can make us or break us.

If we knew the future, it would be easier to make decisions. But we don't, so God promises that the fast He desires will cause His "light [to] break forth like the morning" (Isa. 58:8). This implies that if we focus on God's will instead of our own when we face major decisions, He will provide us with clearer perspective and the insight we need to make crucial decisions.

ORIGIN OF THE SAINT PAUL FAST

The apostle Paul (formerly Saul—persecutor of Christ and His followers) was confronted with a life-changing decision, a fast and a revelation of God's light on the Damascus road. After being struck down by the Lord, Saul was blind for three days, "and neither ate nor drank" (Acts 9:9). Having dedicated himself to persecuting Christians, he must have been stunned and "in the dark" about Christ and his future with Christ. It was only after Saul went without food and drink that he "saw the light." God sent the Christian Ananias to the house where Paul was staying. Ananias placed his hands on Saul the former persecutor, and he received the vision to become Paul the apostle.

HOW DOES GOD SPEAK TO US?

If we could talk to someone who knows the dangers, the rewards and the heartaches of the future, decisions would be easy. Jesus Christ is that someone.

Those who know Jesus Christ have an advantage in decision making. He knows the future because He is Alpha and Omega, the beginning and the end. Jesus is God; therefore, He is timeless and limitless. He stands on the other side of our decisions and knows what will happen to us. Thus, we ought to ask the Lord to help us make our decisions. God speaks to us through His Son Jesus Christ.

The Lord may not speak audibly to us as some heard Him in Scripture, but He will help us make our decisions. First, the Lord has given us principles for living in the Word of God. For example, we don't have to pray about whether to marry an unsaved person (see 2 Cor. 6:14), nor do we have to pray about whether to have sex outside of marriage (see Exod. 20:14).

Most of our decisions are not black and white. We often stand in the dimness of twilight, which is neither bright nor dark. Like driving at dusk, twilight makes it difficult to see people on the roadside. We miss important warning signs. There is always danger that we might lose our way or lose our lives. Life-changing decisions can make us feel as though we are driving through life in twilight.

In addition to the guidance He supplies through His Word, God has provided many other resources for decision making.

- He directs us by counsel with friends (see Prov. 11:14).
- He sovereignly guides (see Rom. 8:28).
- He directs us inwardly (see Acts 16:6; Rom. 8:14).
- He directs us by opportunities (see 1 Cor. 16:9).
- He directs us when we have a yielded spirit (see Rom. 12:1,2).
- He directs us through our spiritual gifts (see 1 Cor. 7:7).
- He directs us through our common sense (see Prov. 16:9).
- He guides us through prayer.
- Most importantly, God directs us through fasting.

The Saint Paul Fast involves focusing on our choices instead of our foods, and praying our decisions through to successful conclusions.

Decisions can be so threatening or obscure that we go through the previous checklist and still don't know what to do. What can we do to help us make the really big decisions?

We can fast.

When we fast, God gives us light that breaks into our thinking like the dawn of a new day. The light is His perfect will for our lives.

Although the Saint Paul Fast helps us to receive God's wisdom to make our decisions, its purpose is not to help make insignificant decisions for us. This fast is not for every minor decision in life, such as where to go for lunch or what minor purchases to make. The Saint Paul Fast offers help in weighty decisions such as choosing a mate, resigning a job and other life-changing choices.

John Maxwell makes some excellent observations about making decisions.

THE MAXWELL RULE FOR DECISION MAKING
1. The wrong decision at the wrong time is a disaster.
2. The wrong decision at the right time is a mistake.
3. The right decision at the wrong time is unacceptable.
4. The right decision at the right time is success.

Life is centered around decision making. We choose a college, then choose a major. When we graduate we choose a job and an apartment. We choose the car we'll drive, and we choose our friends. Mornings present us with the choices of what to wear, what to eat and what to include in our daily priority lists. We choose our attitudes. When we let little things annoy us, we even choose to be grumpy.

Most of life is a choice. Those who have reached the top have a history of making good choices. Like a heavyweight boxer who must win the important fights to become the world champion, those who succeed in life must make right choices in the important decisions that confront them.

Wrong Choices

Wrong choices can lead to disaster. Fasting will not automatically cause us to make better choices. Although it should help us focus on the elements of the decision God wants us to consider, we should also use our own initiatives to be aware of any factors in our lives that have contributed to wrong choices in our pasts.

Wrong emotional perceptions often lead to wrong choices. We choose according to how we perceive things. We think someone hates us when they don't; they just ignore us. The responses people have made to previous commitments can cause us to make choices for or against them. Tradition can cause us to make wrong choices: "We've never done it that way before." As every parent knows, peer pressure often leads to bad choices: "All the guys are going"—and that pressure can lead to poor parental choices. Pride can force wrong choices, causing us to make poor decisions simply to "save face."

As the president of a Bible college, I had to purchase a van for our traveling team one summer. Like all struggling Bible colleges, we had little money—not even enough to pay salaries. Four staff members wanted to buy an off-brand German van. Using it to make fund-raising tours would enable us to pay for it, they argued. I was not convinced we should do it, but was daily pressured into making the purchase. Finally, I called the four into my office. We all knelt around my desk and prayed for God to lead us to the right van. When we finished praying, I said, "Go ahead."

The van was purchased from a private party—not new from a dealership. It caught fire one block away from the place of purchase and was completely gutted. Fortunately, we had pre-arranged for insurance by telephone, so we were covered. But the parts did not arrive from Germany for six months, so we didn't use the van to raise money. Instead, we actually lost the use of the money. When the mechanic was finishing the repairs, he tightened a screw in the front windshield too tight, and cracked the windshield. Another three months' delay occurred before we obtained use of the van.

I made a bad decision, even after praying with four people. We were all convinced it was the right decision. We could easily have made the same bad decision had we been doing a Saint Paul Fast, because we simply did not have enough good information about that brand of vehicle.

> We make good decisions on good information.
> We make bad decisions on bad information.
> With no information, we make lucky decisions.

PREPARING FOR THE SAINT PAUL FAST

Before you begin the Saint Paul Fast about an important decision, you need to have a decision-making strategy. The following strategy will be used throughout the fast, and will become the basis of the decision making process. The five steps of this strategy were not developed especially for this book, but are generally accepted steps that should be followed in any decision-making process. I don't believe God "drops" an answer out of the blue on us. He is a rational being who guides us through our own minds—first to understand Him and second to apply the principles of His Word to our lives. Fasting can avail us to the application of good decision-making principles.

FIVE STEPS TO DECISION MAKING

1. Honestly face any problem that clouds your decision. Begin your fast by admitting you have a problem. Sometimes this involves confession of sin. "We have sinned" (Dan. 9:5), Daniel confessed, as he faced decisions in captivity. It is useless to fast just to avoid your responsibility to confront a problem. For example, a man may know he has to make a decision about a job, so he says to his friends, "Let's pray about it." This is another way of admitting that he doesn't know what to do. And while they pray, they don't follow any strategy in decision making.

The Saint Paul Fast is a means of admitting you must do something about the problem. You have decided to withhold food to help yourself find a solution. One great benefit of this fast is knowing that you are doing something about your problem.

2. Define your problem. Be hard on yourself as you approach the Saint Paul Fast. Buckle down to work. Don't just meditate about symptoms, but write out your problem. Seeing your problem in black and white may result in a different idea about the solution. Also, a well-defined problem is a half-solved problem. When you have clearly defined your problem, you can marshal all your energies toward the solution. During your fast, write and rewrite the problem three or four times. Each time you process the information about the problem, you get a different viewpoint. Rewrite the problem again. Eventually you will clearly understand the problem, and your mind will focus on an answer.

3. Gather information. This involves reports, charts, articles—anything and everything pertaining to your problem. You may need to summon your diary, or other written documents that will give you a "handle" on the problem.

As you gather information, ask, "Why?" Force yourself to look at causes. Why are things as they are?

4. Make a list of all possible solutions. Gathering information will force you to think through all potential solutions to your problem. Brainstorm! Write down every way the problem might be solved. List the obvious as well as the foolish solutions. Write everything that comes to your mind. A weak answer may trigger the best answer. Don't try to answer your problem until you've exhausted the list of potential solutions. If you grab too soon at one solution, you may circumvent a better solution. It is important to write out as many solutions as possible to your problem. This way you will find your mind working overtime on each of the solutions.

5. Choose the best decision. The act of decision making is not sitting around praying for an answer to drop out of the blue. Nor is it suddenly trying to come up with a better answer. It is choosing the best solution among many. The best solution is uncovered by sifting through all the available facts, and even then, it might not be a perfect solution. Only God and His Word are perfect. So after you have looked at all the data and examined all the solutions, choose the one best for you.

Someone has said, "Make a decision...make it work." The first step in making a decision work is to make a *commitment* to the decision. Because you know the facts, you must exercise your will; your emotions will follow your will. The whole personality becomes steeled toward the decision—intellect, will and emotions.

A man who wanted to lose weight was looking at various diets. He realized that the amount of sugar in his coffee put him way over his calorie count each day. He loved three teaspoons of sugar per cup of coffee in the five cups he drank daily.

Someone suggested that if he would drink black coffee without sugar for seven days, he would never add sugar again. He accepted the challenge. For six days he drank black, sugarless coffee, but he didn't like it. On the last day his wife suggested, "Add a little cream to take away the bitter taste." He did. Ten years later he drinks his coffee without sugar, just a little cream. When someone mistakenly gave him coffee with sugar, he couldn't drink it. What kind of decision radically transformed his coffee habit? He knew with his intellect what he wanted (i.e., to cut calorie intake). His emotions of enjoyment were important. He marshaled his will. The total personality made a decision—a permanent decision.

PRESCRIPTION FOR THE SAINT PAUL FAST

The Saint Paul fast began at a time when Paul needed to correct his horribly wrong idea about Christianity. The New Testament introduces Paul as the young man who held the coats of those who stoned Stephen (the first recorded Christian martyr) to death. Later, Paul testified that he persecuted Christians to the death (see Acts 22:4). Paul had a misconception about God. He saw Him as a narrow, Jewish God. Paul did not understand God's love for the world. He went door to door arresting Christians and throwing them into prison. On what charge? They were followers of the Way—Jesus Christ who said, "I am the Way" (John 14:6). Paul was traveling down the wrong highway, doing the wrong thing, with the wrong attitude.

What could turn him around? Jesus Christ, who radically changed his life as he traveled down the highway—better known as the Damascus road. How did that change take place? For three days after meeting Christ, Paul fasted without eating or drinking. In those three days he reassessed and rethought his views of both God and Jesus Christ. During that time God spoke to him, gave him revelations and laid the embryonic foundation for the entire theology of the New Testament.

The Saint Paul Fast is for gaining insight and wisdom. Paul gained life-changing insight and wisdom from this fast, and it became the basis for Paul's changing the direction of Christianity. The Saint Paul Fast became the most important fast in the Christian Church. The following 10 principles drawn from Paul's original fast can direct your own.

Step 1: Make Time to Listen for Jesus' Voice
As he was traveling down the highway to Damascus, Paul heard the voice of Jesus and fell to the earth (see Acts 9:4). Paul was directed into a house off Straight Street in the city of Damascus. There he had time to meditate upon what he had heard. We, too, when we hear the voice of Jesus speaking to us, must know we are listening to the One who can help. God is too loving to deceive us and too kind to hurt us. Begin your Saint Paul Fast by listening for the Lord to speak to you. "Be still, and know that I am God" (Ps. 46:10).

Some will pray for one day, not eating food for 24 hours. (See glossary for the typical fast.) Some will eliminate liquids. Others will pray one day a week for three or four weeks. Some will fast for three days as did Paul. During whatever time frame is chosen, they listen for God and concentrate on the decisions before them.

Step 2: Ask and Answer Questions About Yourself
The greatest thing about the Saint Paul Fast is that we can look into the mirror of self-examination to see ourselves. At the beginning of the fast, we still see ourselves as we think we are. Time invested in the presence of God will cause us to see ourselves as we really are.

When Paul was on his knees on the Damascus road, God asked, "Saul, Saul, why are you persecuting me?" (Acts 9:4). Paul honestly thought he was serving God when he was persecuting Christians. Sometimes we think we are on God's side when we're really not. We think we are making a decision that is right—a decision that is in the will of God—but it's not. When God comes looking for His people, He often asks a question to make them ask themselves "where they are"—just as He came asking, "Adam,...where art thou?" (Gen. 3:9, *KJV*).

Obviously, God knew where Adam was. Adam was hiding naked in the bushes. God asked the question not to locate him, but to make Adam realize what he was doing.

God came asking Cain why he was downcast (see Gen. 4:6). Obviously, God knew why Cain was angry, but He wanted Cain to face his feelings. A question is often God's way of teaching us what we need to do.

When you fast, let God ask questions. You can do this by first studying what Scripture says about the issues pertaining to your decision. Second, in quietness allow God to speak to your conscience. After God had asked Paul a question, the confused Jew in turn asked God a question, "Who are you, Lord?" (Acts 9:5). Paul didn't recognize the transfigured Son of God who had stopped him from entering Damascus with vengeance in his heart. Paul asked an appropriate question. Until we know who God is, we cannot know what to do. God will not show us an answer until we want to know Him. He will not show us an answer until He shows us Himself.

Step 3: Recognize the Objective Truth

As we approach a decision we may be confused, discouraged or, at least, "shut up" to our own thinking. The Saint Paul Fast will change our introspection. The answer may be silently awaiting our discovery. The answer is not within—it's without. Although Paul was stunned and confused, he recognized that the answer was in the Lord ("Who are you, Lord?" Acts 9:5), not in himself.

Sometimes God speaks with loud authority. At other times He speaks with a still, small voice. We have to listen to hear Him. God's silence can feel threatening; however, in those quiet moments, we tell God by our fasts that we are searching for Him and for His answer.

Truth stands without us like a sentinel on guard. But too often we ignore the truth. Yet, like gravity, truth stands whether or not we agree with it. When we fast, we signal our willingness to accept God's truth instead of our own subjective musings.

Often we try to justify ourselves and our decisions. We try to make things go our own way. We don't look at all the facts, and we don't understand the facts we do look at because we are blinded by our presuppositions. We think we are never wrong. Two paramount problems in decision making are (1) our omniscient memories (we think we are always right because we remember being right before); and (2) our omniscient insights (we think we must be right because we thought of the answers).

The more we consider the facts, read the Bible and look into the heart of God, the more we realize that our answers may not be what we originally thought. We can lie to ourselves about truth, but truth remains truth. Truth, like a hot stove, always burns us when we touch it.

What is the best way to start a fast? Start as Saint Paul did. The Bible says he fell to the ground, "trembling and astonished" (Acts 9:6). When he asked, "Lord, what do You want me to do?" he was confessing even in his confusion that Jesus is Lord. When Paul recognized Jesus, his life was turned around. Paul began his fast by simply calling on the One who could help him.

Step 4: Stop All Self-Effort and Yield to God

There is a time for initiative and self-effort. There is a time to get up from our knees and work because the night is coming. The Bible tells us, "Whatever you do, do it heartily" (Col. 3:23). We are supposed to work hard. But there are times to stop working and to be quiet before God.

When you enter into the Saint Paul Fast, stop all self-effort. Fasting is not a time to work; it is a time to wait. Fasting is not a time to sweat; it is a time to sacrifice. Fasting is not a time to labor; it is a time to plunge deep into the heart of God in yieldedness to Him.

Step 5: Pay Attention to the Physical

The outer affects the inner. Sometimes it's important to go away to a completely different location for a fast. Sometimes it is important to enter into your closet or go into your private room where no one will bother you. Sometimes it's important to kneel, at other times to bow humbly before God, at still other times to stand before God with hands lifted, reaching out to God as Solomon did at the Temple dedication (see 1 Kings 8:2). It may be appropriate to lie flat on the ground before God, as did the apostle Paul in his encounter with Christ on the Damascus road. The outward stance should reflect the inward stance of the heart.

Step 6: Pay Attention to the Spiritual

a. *Submit your spirit.* When Paul said "Lord," it was a great admission by an antagonistic Jew that Jesus was his master. When Paul called Jesus "Lord," he was admitting that his past actions were wrong. He yielded his prejudices. He submitted.

Begin your fast by admitting to the times you were wrong. You might even list them—not to show to others, but to see yourself as you really are. Then, submit any future self-efforts to God. Why? Because you know you were wrong in the past. Use the Saint Paul Fast to search your inner person for answers and wisdom.

When Paul began his fast, he added, "Lord, what do you want me to do?" (Acts 9:6). In essence, Paul began a three-day search for truth by asking the Lord to help him.

b. *Search with your whole heart.* God has promised, "You will seek Me and find Me, when you search for Me with all your heart" (Jer. 29:13). At times we think we are honestly searching for God, but the longer we stay in His presence the more we realize that the self has crawled onto the throne of our hearts. The longer we stay in the presence of God, the more we discover devious motives in our hearts. We might be making decisions for money, glory or even sinful reasons that rebel against God. During the Saint Paul Fast, we search for answers and find them when we search with our whole hearts.

c. *Allow the Lord to search you.* What does it mean to allow God to search us? He said, "I, the Lord, search the heart" (17:10). God already knows our hearts, but when we ask Him to search us, we symbolically hand Him the flashlight and willingly allow Him not only to see into our hearts; but also ask Him to show us what is there. He already knows what is in our minds. God knows us better than we know ourselves. But with the flashlight in hand, He allows us to see what is there.

d. *Allow the Holy Spirit to teach you.* When you enter into the Saint Paul Fast, you are asking the Holy Spirit to be your teacher. Just as an earthly teacher will inform and enlighten you, so when the Holy Spirit becomes your teacher, God shows you what to do. "The Helper, the Holy Spirit...will teach you all things, and bring to your remembrance all things that I said to you" (John 14:26).

One of fasting's great rewards is connecting with the Holy Spirit. This doesn't mean the Holy Spirit will teach us every detail about what we should do. For instance, we can't fast instead of studying for the chemistry exam. We don't fast in place of hard work, claiming that He will teach us all things. That is not the purpose of fasting, nor is it God's way. We are to study, memorize, apply ourselves, pray and perhaps fast— then we take the chemistry exam.

Again, notice what Jesus promised. He said the Holy Spirit "shall teach you all things...whatsoever I have said unto you" (14:26, *KJV*). The Spirit will help you recall what Jesus said. You will gain insight into the Word of God and come to know the person of God. When you begin the Saint Paul Fast, pray, "Open my eyes, that I may see wondrous things from Your law" (Ps. 119:18).

e. Study diligently. While we wait upon the Holy Spirit to teach us, the Scriptures also tell us "Be diligent to present yourself approved to God...rightly dividing the word of truth" (2 Tim. 2:15). We are to give diligence to learn the Word of God. When we study best, God speaks to us the most. When we study best, we get the most from meditation. When we study best, we become most like Christ. So during the Saint Paul Fast, bring your Bible, dictionary, concordance and Bible encyclopedia. Study His Word to find out His will.

f. Pray. What do we pray as we search for answers during the Saint Paul Fast? We can do no better than to pray, "Search me, O God, and know my heart; try me and know my anxieties...and lead me in the way everlasting" (Ps. 139:23,24).

Step 7: Obey What You Learn

Paul had been knocked to the ground on the Damascus road by the revelation of Christ. But he had to do more than meet Christ. "The Lord said to him, 'Arise and go into the city'" (Acts 9:6). This was a very clear command. What did Paul do? He arose, and allowed his companions to lead him to Damascus (v. 8). Saul got up from the ground and began following the only thing he knew the Lord wanted of him: to go to Damascus. Later in life, Paul spoke about the incident in these words: "I was not disobedient to the heavenly vision" (26:19).

Just as there are twin propellers that keep the power boat cruising straight on the lake, so there are twin forces that keep the Christian life on an even keel. These "propellers" are *knowing* and *doing*. Some people veer off course by only studying to know. Others rush in to do, not having biblical knowledge. Biblical faith involves the balance of both knowing and doing. We are told, "Trust in the Lord with all your heart, and lean not on your own understanding; in all your ways acknowledge Him, and He shall direct your paths" (Prov. 3:5,6).

As you continue the Saint Paul Fast, use pencil and paper to make a list of everthing you will do after this fast. What will be the outcome of your decision? How will you inform others of your decision? How will you stay accountable? For what will you pray?

Step 8: Be Willing to Be Patient

When Saul met Jesus Christ, God did not give him a complete road map of his future. He was only given his next assignment. He was told to go into the city. There he would get his next orders. "Arise and go into the city, and you will be told what you must do" (Acts 9:6).

In your first Saint Paul Fast, you may get only preliminary direction. You may have to fast a second or third time. Remember, Paul went three days without eating or drinking before Ananias came with further direction (v. 9).

How does God speak to us? Sometimes the answer will come gradually, like the dawn of a new day. Long before the sun peeks over the horizon, there is some light through the windows. Slowly, more light creeps into the room. Then suddenly, the sun bursts over the horizon. But even then, it is not as full daylight as it will be at noon.

In the same way, God may give us some light in our first Saint Paul Fasts. We see a few things vaguely, such as the shapes in the backyard that begin to appear before the sun appears over the horizon. We may have to plan to fast again to get the full sight of noon. Some may have to fast several times to get the answers they seek.

This doesn't mean there will not be times when God breaks into your world with full insight the first time you fast. Remember, Paul was a blind and prejudiced Jew on his way to arrest Christians in Damascus. Suddenly he was blinded by a great light—Jesus Christ. He could only respond, "Lord."

Likewise, you may get a sudden insight from fasting. You may have been praying and fasting for several hours when suddenly God shows you what you must do. The Greek philosopher Archimedes was commissioned to determine the total amount of space in a gold sculpture. The task was difficult without melting down the statue. Archimedes put the problem aside to take a warm bath. He then noticed that the water rose when he submerged himself into the tub. Suddenly he realized he could measure the amount of water his body displaced to determine the space of his body. When he realized he could do the same thing with the statue, he jumped from the tub yelling, "Eureka!" (Greek for "I have found [it].") From that story, we still use "Eureka!" when we get sudden insight.

Step 9: Be Open to Insights from Others

You will probably embark on the Saint Paul Fast alone, as did Paul. Even in your solitude, however, realize that God may give an answer through someone else. Although God spoke in a limited way to Paul, He gave additional insights through Ananias (see Acts 9:10,11). Similarly, God may use others to give you direction. While you are fasting, God may be giving the answer to someone else. Even though you end the Saint Paul Fast without the answer, that doesn't mean there is no answer. It simply means you do not have the answer at that time. God may have given someone else the answer, and you may have to wait for that person to come into your life.

God had prepared Ananias to pray for Saul's spiritual and physical condition. "Ananias...entered the house; and laying his hands on him he said, 'Brother Saul, the Lord Jesus...has sent me that you may receive your sight and be filled with the Holy Spirit'" (v. 17). We might have thought that because the great apostle Paul had just met Jesus Christ he could have prayed for himself. But no! God used Ananias to pray for Paul to receive his sight and to be filled with the Holy Spirit.

You may discover during the Saint Paul Fast that you cannot heal yourself; you cannot find the answer yourself; you do not even know what is wrong. God may bring a more mature person into your life to give you instruction after your fast. So what was the purpose of fasting? You have prepared your heart to receive the message from someone else. So when you leave the Saint Paul Fast, don't be surprised if God answers your prayers through the life of someone else.

Step 10: Prepare to Be Misunderstood

Paul was journeying from Jerusalem to Damascus accompanied by several men. Some were probably his servants, and others his companions who would search the houses for Christians, arresting them. Notice that God did not speak to the men who were with Paul. "The men who journeyed with him stood speechless, hearing a voice but seeing no one" (v. 7). Only Paul saw Jesus Christ.

- The others did not see Jesus.
- The others did not fast.
- The others did not receive an answer from Ananias.

When God leads you to the Saint Paul Fast, He may not lead other members of your family or even those who are involved in your decision to fast with you. Usually the Saint Paul Fast is a lonely fast. You stand alone before God; your communion is solely with Him. Do not be surprised if others do not understand.

PRACTICAL PRINCIPLES TO REMEMBER

Practical suggestions abound to help the Saint Paul Fast become effective. The following are just a few to remember as you begin on your journey:

The more weighty your decision, the more often and the longer you should follow the Saint Paul Fast. As we have noted, when fasting was first introduced, it was probably because people who went through deep distress and life-changing pressure just did not want to eat or drink anything. They were so consumed with their problems that food was the last thing on their minds. Whether Paul was taken up with the distress of his immediate emergency (i.e., blindness) or whether he truly fasted for God's blessing, the text is not clear. But it is true that the more severely your problem shakes your equilibrium, the more intense should be your fasting.

Plan Bible reading that is not directly related to your decision. As you read from various portions of Scripture, your mind will relax in God's presence. Then perhaps the answer will "pop" into your mind. In the quietness of peace, God may speak to you about a topic you are not presently studying.

During the Saint Paul Fast, you should purpose to read the entire New Testament in one day. If that is too much, surely you should purpose to read chosen books of the Bible.

Know and apply principles of decision making. Write out the five steps of decision making previously mentioned. As you fast, review your data in addition to these steps and follow them systematically. Following this formula, like a pilot who goes through a checklist before the plane takes off, guarantees that nothing is left out of the procedure. In the same way, as you go through the strategy of decision making, the steps become your "checklist" for solving crucial issues.

Write and rewrite the decision you need to make during the Saint Paul Fast. Don't be satisfied with one writing of the problem facing you. Each time you study the data, clarify your thinking. Each time you go through the strategy of decision making, rewrite the problem or the decision you must make.

Write out facts that influence your decision and review them with prayer. Reading through all of the facts in a folder will help, but rewriting them on a sheet of paper will give you greater insight. As you rewrite the facts, you objectify the situation. Sometimes it helps to draw a line down the middle of a sheet of paper listing the reasons for "yes" on one side and the reasons for "no" on the other side. This "scales" approach transfers the problem from your mind to the paper in front of you to study objectively.

Write out all possible solutions before attempting to make a decision. The best decision is usually one of several possible decisions. Add to the list even those decisions you first rejected. Look at all possible decisions before you make the final decision.

Wait for inner confidence in your darkest hour. It may not be in a dream or a vision, but in your darkest hour when God will give you inner confidence about what you must do. He may give it to you through a phone call, letter or an open door of opportunity. The servant of the Lord must wait as did Eleazar, Abraham's servant, who said, "Being on the way, the Lord led me" (Gen. 24:27). If you commit to being "on the way," genuinely seeking God's will, God will give you inner confidence that the world can never give. You can be "led by the Spirit of God" (Rom. 8:14).

PREPARING FOR THE SAINT PAUL FAST

Aim: My Saint Paul Fast is for wisdom and decision making.

Vow: I will delight myself in the Lord so that my desire becomes what He wants in this decision (see Ps. 37:4). I will seek first the kingdom of God and His righteousness in my life so I can follow His principles in analyzing and making a decision (see Matt. 6:33). I will seek the Lord for His answer to the problem. I am fasting because I want to make the best decision and be in the center of His will (see Rom. 12:1,2).

Bible Basis: "And [Saul] was three days without sight, and neither ate nor drank" (Acts 9:9).

Bible Promise: "Your light shall break forth like the morning" (Isa. 58:8).

Fast: What I will withhold_____

Begin: Date and time I will start _____

End: Date and time I will stop _____

Resources
Needed:

God being my strength, and grace being my basis, I
commit myself to the Saint Paul Fast for God's glory.

Signed _____ Date _____

≋ 8 ≋

THE DANIEL FAST

IN APRIL, 1985, DEAN OF STUDENTS VERNON BREWER OF LIBERTY University was diagnosed with cancer. The doctors gave him a short time to live. Vernon Brewer was a well-liked dean because he was fair in handling discipline problems. His life magnified the Lord Jesus Christ. Word about his cancer grieved the entire student body.

All 5,000 students were asked to join in prayer and fasting for Dean Brewer's healing. The students were given several days to prepare themselves for the fast and to learn what fasting would do. Then the students began a 24-hour prayer vigil in the school chapel. The chapel only seated 200 people, so the students were asked to alternate 1-hour segments throughout the night and day. The chapel was always overflowing; therefore, the chapel windows were opened, allowing students sitting on the grass outside to join in the time of prayer with those inside.

The number of those praying during the darkest hours of the night was greater than during the day when classes were in session. The food services of the university shut down, except for a small serving line for about 50 diabetic students who had to eat and could not physically join in the fast. Even then, those whose conditions required them to eat prayed just as intently as those who were fasting.

After fasting and praying, three medical procedures were performed to save Dean Brewer's life. First, a five-pound cancerous mass was surgically removed from his chest. Next, he received both radiation and chemotherapy. As I write this story 10 years later, Vernon Brewer is alive, and as healthy as he was before we fasted and prayed. He directs World Help, a missionary and humanitarian organization. Every time I see Vernon Brewer, I know God heals in answer to prayer and fasting.

FASTING, HEALTH AND HEALING

God has promised, "Is not this the fast that I have chosen...[that] your healing shall spring forth speedily" (Isa. 58:6,8). When we begin fasting and praying for physical health and healing, we must realize that it is God who heals. His name Jehovah Rapha means, "I am the *Lord* who heals you" (Exod. 15:26, emphasis mine).

We enter the Daniel Fast for two physical reasons: (1) as therapy when we are sick and need healing, or (2) as prevention to keep us from becoming sick or getting a disease.

Preventive Healing
In the setting of Exodus 15, the Lord was promising preventive healing. He promised His divine protection to keep his people from becoming sick, rather than just "prescriptive" healing—removing an illness from them. "If you obey me by doing right and by following my laws and teachings, I won't punish you with the diseases I sent on the Egyptians" (Exod. 15:26, *CEV*).

Preventive medicine is like the mother who gives her children vitamins and bundles them in warm clothing before sending them off to school in the snow. Curative medicine is like putting the children to bed, providing medicine and rest.

An example of God's preventive healing power is the Old Testament law prohibiting eating blood and animal fat (see Lev. 3:17). Recent medical research seems to show that bacteria and disease reside primarily in blood and fat. God wanted his people to enjoy good health.

We also know that despite the way rich food and desserts pander to our tastes, they aren't the best for our health. The Daniel Fast withholds extra rich foods such as "finger food," "party food" and desserts. Those who enter the Daniel Fast eat only necessities to (1) cleanse the digestive system, (2) rest the body and (3) renew the system.

Curative Healing

God has promised that prescriptive healing can come by faith and prayer: "The prayer of faith will save the sick, and the Lord will raise him up" (Jas. 5:15). Faith and prayer must be joined. Faith is an instrument of healing when it is joined to the tool of prayer. Even when you have faith and pray, it is still God who heals, or maintains health. The Daniel Fast rests on a three-platformed foundation: (1) faith, (2) prayer and (3) fasting.

Kevin Romine, a student at Liberty Baptist Theological Seminary, sat through my course "Spiritual Factors of Church Growth" during the summer of 1994. One of the assignments is to fast for a project, and/or faith event. Kevin had injured his back delivering packages while working to put himself through seminary. He was not only disabled, but he was also in intense pain. Often he had to stand in my classroom because of back pain.

In February of 1995, Kevin pitched a tent in his backyard in the county where he lived. For three days he fasted, taking neither food nor drink. He prayed for deliverance from pain, and for healing. He said, "Withholding food and drink was not the difficult part—it got extremely cold in that tent!" At the end of the 3-day fast, he continued with a 21-day fast, taking only liquid and juices.

"The pain is completely gone!" he told me three months later. "However, I haven't tried to pick up any heavy boxes, thinking I might reinjure my back." This student is looking forward to full-time Christian service in evangelism.

God Can Heal Through Fasting

God has placed within every physical body the ability to heal itself. Technically, doctors, surgical procedures and medicine do not heal people. In the study of pathology, we see that disease and germs cause illness in the human body. When the doctor, surgery or medicine removes the cause of the disease, then the body will heal itself.

God has given each of us a wonderful physical body that He calls "the temple of the Holy Spirit" (1 Cor. 6:19). Every normal person is born with internal mechanisms whereby the body reproduces itself and heals itself. When a person eats a proper diet, at the proper time, in the proper way, that person will have a healthy body if disease or other physical barriers to health are not present.

A correct diet will make you healthy because you are what you eat. The Bible is neither a health book nor a diet book; however, it gives principles that can help you enjoy good health. Eat unhealthy food and you will be sick or sickly. Eat the correct food and you will normally enjoy good health.

This book is not about diets and correct nutrition, although fasting is one discipline that will improve your health. Fasting's physical benefits include eliminating impurities, and resting the physical system so that its functions may begin balancing themselves.

The Daniel Fast may be preventive (joined with the John the Baptist Fast), keeping us from disease. Or it can be curative, moving God to intervene as the Great Physician if we already have a disease. God's promise, "I am the *Lord* [Jehovah Rapha] who heals you" (Exod. 15:26, emphasis mine) includes both preventative and curative action. As you pray for good health, the Daniel Fast allows God to restore or maintain your body's health.

BACKGROUND OF THE DANIEL FAST

The Hebrew, Daniel, had been taken into captivity by the Babylonian army as a young man, and transported to the city of Babylon. He and his three friends from Judea were being trained as diplomats/bureaucrats to serve in the Babylonian government. It was probably King Nebuchadnezzar's plan to have them carry out his administrative policies over the Jewish remnant.

The plan included giving the four Hebrews the finest delicacies and wine from the king's own provisions (see Dan. 1:5). But for reasons we will discuss later, such food was not acceptable to the Hebrews. So Daniel proposed to the king's servants that they be allowed to "fast" from the king's sumptuous fare, and to eat only vegetables and drink only water (v. 12). If, after 10 days, they were not in better health than their Babylonian counterparts, Daniel promised that they could be dealt with as the Babylonian guards wished. (The fact that they were allowed to demonstrate the effectiveness of their vegetarian diet indicated how important Daniel and his three friends were to the Babylonian government.)

At the end of the 10-day test period, Daniel and his friends were healthier in body and mind than the men who were served food from the royal palace (vv. 19,20). As a result of his faithfulness, Daniel lived a long and useful life. Captured by Nebuchadnezzar as a teenager, he lived until the reign of King Cyrus of Persia, 73 years later. He was over 90 years old when he died.

THE DANIEL FAST PRESCRIPTION

The following are some steps for fasting for preventive or curative health, drawn from the biblical account of Daniel.

Step 1: Be Specific

Daniel was not vague in his objection to the Babylonian diet. He defined the problem immediately, and had a clear solution to suggest to the king's servants. Although it was an act that had social and political implications and may well have cost him his life, Daniel was specific about his plan.

With so much at stake, why did Daniel reject the delicacies offered by the king? Three possibilities have been suggested: (1) The king's food was against Jewish dietary laws; (2) Daniel and his three friends had vows against partaking of the alcohol (wine) that was included; and (3) the king's food had been offered to foreign idols/demons.

The exact reason Daniel refused to eat the king's meat is not clear. Two principles, however, are evident: (1) Daniel felt it was a religious test of his faith (he "would not defile himself" [v. 8]); (2) Daniel had a desire for a strong physical body in which to serve the Lord.

Step 2: Fast as a Spiritual Commitment

The Daniel Fast consists of more than just a diet adjustment or the withholding of food. Those who have a weight problem or other physical problems will not be successful with solely a physical solution. The Daniel Fast involves a spiritual commitment to God. "Daniel purposed in his heart that he would not defile himself" (Dan. 1:8). Although he bargained with his overseer, the whole process began with a spiritual commitment to God. The Daniel Fast requires a spiritual equation, not just a physical solution.

Step 3: Reflect Inner Desire by Outer Discipline

Many people have an inner desire for better health, but they can't discipline themselves to avoid junk food, finger food, or other "party food." If you want a strong physical body, you must make a wholehearted commitment to discipline your body. You must say no to improper food and yes to healthy food. Out of Daniel's deep spiritual commitment he said to his overseer, "Please test your servants for ten days, and let them give us vegetables to eat and water to drink" (Dan. 1:12).

The physical health you seek from God may be more than an answer to prayer. Your physical health may be linked to any of the following factors.

a. Your food choices. When you enter the Daniel Fast, you not only modify your diet, but you also begin praying for God's wisdom to make appropriate choices of food in your diet, adding some and deleting others. After you have prayed for wisdom, begin learning about proper diet by reading books, listening to audio tapes and talking to knowledgeable people.

b. The level of your spiritual commitment as reflected in constant prayer during the fast. It is not enough to do without food; you must pray during your Daniel Fast that God would give you the strength of your commitment to stay on the fast.

In case of illness, you must also pray for God to touch your physical body with healing; that the disease will be flushed out of your body; and that by eating the proper food you will be able to build up your body.

c. Your time commitment. Be sure to fulfill your fast to the conclusion of your commitment. If you make a 10-day commitment to God, be sure that you do not stop on the ninth day. As an illustration, suppose you have a sinus infection, and that the doctor prescribes penicillin. You begin taking your medicine, and in a few days you start to feel better. It's tempting to quit taking your medicine at that point; but the doctor said to continue taking penicillin after you feel well because the entire prescription is needed to completely kill the infection. You don't quit taking medicine when you feel better, but when the infection is eliminated.

The same can be said of a physical diet. Suppose you've made a 10-day commitment to the Daniel Fast, and after 7 or 8 days of a vegetable diet you begin to feel better. You think, *Just one hamburger won't hurt.* But there is a deeper issue here: You made a spiritual commitment to God for 10 days; therefore don't violate your fast. In all things, "We are God's fellow workers" (1 Cor. 3:9). As you do your part by sticking to your fast commitment, God will do His part in giving strength and health to your body and soul.

d. Your testimony commitment. Your Daniel Fast is a statement of faith to God that you want Him to heal your body. It is also a statement of faith to yourself and to other people. A Daniel Fast is a faith statement for a specific purpose. Jesus said, "If you have faith...you will say to this mountain [your physical problem], 'Move from here to there'" (Matt. 17:20). Maintaining your fast is a testimony to yourself and to others that you believe God can move mountains.

Faith is foundational to the Daniel Fast. Do not minimize the role of faith in healing your body. There is a strong tie between mental and physical health. Those who have strong self-esteem and who feel good about themselves help their bodies make better use of food, leading to better physical health. The Bible recognizes this tie between mental and physical health in such statements as, "A merry heart makes a cheerful countenance" (Prov. 15:13). James tells us that "the prayer of faith will save the sick" (Jas. 5:15). And God tells us to visit the sick to encourage their faith and spiritual growth. Therefore, make a dual commitment in your Daniel Fast for physical strength to keep the fast to the end of your commitment, and for faith and emotional strength for your spirit.

Step 4: Pray to Perceive Sin's Role in Poor Health
When my children were growing up, my wife would ask, "Why are they sick?" when they got a cold or some other illness. I answered in jest, but with long-range theological implications, "Sin—sin makes them sick." She would laugh and say, "No I don't mean that." Of course she didn't. She wanted to know the immediate cause so she could apply an immediate remedy. But theologically, sickness comes into the world because of Adam and Eve's sin against God. If our first parents had not sinned, neither they nor we would have the physical problems of sickness, pain and death.

The issue of sin and healing is addressed by James in his Epistle. Although there is not always a direct cause-effect relationship between sin and sickness, there probably is a correlation. You are not likely suffering immediate sickness because you sinned, but the opposite will probably be true: continued godly living will usually produce continual physical health. Of course this is one basic reason for the Daniel Fast. Notice what James says:

> Is anyone among you suffering? Let him pray. Is anyone cheerful? Let him sing psalms. Is anyone among you sick? Let

him call for the elders of the church, and let them pray over him, anointing him with oil in the name of the Lord. And the prayer of faith will save the sick, and the Lord will raise him up. And if he has committed sins, he will be forgiven. Confess your trespasses to one another, and pray for one another, that you may be healed (5:13-16).

Notice the implications revealed in this passage:
• Sin is sometimes related to the cause of sickness.
• Lack of health/healing may be the result of spiritual rebellion, i.e., adultery, lying, blasphemy, unforgiveness, bitterness or similar sins.
• Lack of health/healing may be the consequence of the sin of wrong intake, such as alcohol, drugs, cigarettes or other destructive substances. It could be a poor diet, consisting of fatty, poisonous or unhealthy foods.
• Repentance is linked to health in James's prescription that believers should call for the elders to deal with their sins so that they can be forgiven and healed from the cause of their sicknesses.
• A church's elders have a role in healing both spiritual and physical health. They not only have faith to pray, but they also deal with public sins in the church. Sickness rooted in sin can be evidenced by public spiritual rebellion such as adultery, lying, blasphemy or other sins that might bring about both poor health and damage to the entire Body's reputation.
• Sick people must desire to be well. Hence, their total personalities—knowing, feeling and will—become involved in their healings. They are exercising faith by calling for the elders, and asking for healing.
• The "anointing of oil" has at least three interpretations: (1) it could be medicinal for healing; (2) it could be symbolic of the Holy Spirit (not real oil), signifying the filling of the sick person by the Holy Spirit, which qualifies that person for healing; (3) it could be real oil (like real water in baptism), which is only the outer symbol of God's Holy Spirit that heals within.
• Prayer alone may not heal a person; in the passage from James we see that faith is also a factor.
• Not all sicknesses are included in James's statement. In verse 15, the word "sick" is derived from the Greek word *kamno*, which suggests "to be weary, weak, incapacitated or have a general sickness." James could have used the word *astheneo* (as he did in verse 14), which implies "dis-

eased, impotent or a pathology." Or he could have used the word *sune-cho*, translated "diseased by illness, tormented." This verse does not refer to severe pathologies such as blindness, palsy or a disease that has attacked a limb/organ.

• Attitude is important for healing. James said, "Is any among you suffering? Let him pray. Is anyone cheerful? Let him sing psalms" (v. 13). Apparently James links sickness to mental orientation. Those who have positive attitudes toward their lives, toward their bodies and toward God have strong foundations for getting well.

Step 5: Fast as a Statement of Faith to Others

Most people define faith in the words of Scripture, "Now faith is the substance of things hoped for, the evidence of things not seen" (Heb. 11:1). Faith may also be defined as "affirming what God said in His Word." Daniel was making a statement of faith when he asked for only vegetables to eat and water to drink, then dared to ask the overseer to compare the appearance of the four sons of Israel with the young men who ate the royal food (see Dan. 1:13). Daniel's statement of faith, therefore, was not just a private act. Faith is acting on God's Word. When you modify your diet for a biblical goal to accomplish the will of God, you are acting on faith, and expressing your willingness for it to be a public act.

Jesus recognized that some fasts should be private: "When you fast, do not be like the hypocrites, with a sad countenance...that they may appear to men to be fasting" (Matt. 6:16). There are times when you do not tell anyone you are fasting. Occasionally I have been invited to a meal with others while I was fasting. They were situations I didn't plan and couldn't cancel. For example, recently the pastoral staff at my church was called at 11:30 A.M. for a luncheon that day. I didn't make a big deal of my fast, but said nothing. When the waitress asked for my order, I simply said, "I just want coffee." Because I didn't call attention to my fast, no one else treated it with significance. My fast continued privately to God.

There are times when fasting makes a statement of faith to other Christians and to the world. "The official told Daniel, 'I am afraid of my lord the king,...Why should he see you looking worse?'" (Dan. 1:10, *NIV*). When you modify your diet over a long period of time, others will notice. It is important that you have the right attitude during the Daniel Fast and that you don't become hyperspiritual or reclusive.

There are several ways to appropriately involve others in the Daniel Fast:

a. More than one can agree to fast together, providing support and unity.
b. You can announce to others the purpose of the fast.
c. In the case of sin, you can relate it to those it involves.
d. You can involve church leaders, as directed in James 5:14.

Through the years, I have not immediately agreed to fast when people have asked me to fast with them. I first talk with them to determine their level of commitment. I'm afraid that some people want me to join in their fast because they trust in my "ability" to get things from God rather than in their own ability. I want to put the ball in their court. After they fast I want to ask them what has happened. How did they pray? What did God do? When I sense their commitment to healing, then I may join in the fast.

Step 6: Learn the Effects of the Foods You Eat

During the Daniel Fast, you should study proper nutrition and diet. Daniel understood what he had to eat to be healthy. "So the guard took away their portion of delicacies and wine...and gave them vegetables" (1:16).

Proper diet will generally cause a person to live longer. People who have healthy bodies are usually able to fight off bacteria or germs and overcome the threat of disease. Yet some very healthy people will be infected with germs or diseases in spite of their good diets. Learn what to expect from good nutrition from qualified nutritional experts.

Step 7: Yield All Results to God

When Daniel fasted, he submitted himself to the consequences of his convictions. "As you see fit, so deal with your servants" (1:13). The following is a little quiz:

a. Did Daniel say, "I won't eat it, so you will have to punish/kill me"?
b. Did Daniel say, "If my diet doesn't make me better, I'll eat the king's food"?

   c. Did Daniel say, "My diet will make me better; then you'll decide to leave us on it"?

Actually, none of the above. Daniel's conviction was based on his faith and trust in God. So he submitted himself to God and trusted Him for the consequences.

Step 8: Deal with the Possibility of the Fast's Failure

You may enter the Daniel Fast—either for yourself or for someone else's healing—and the person doesn't get better. Despite prayer, the illness seems to increase. What should be your reaction?

First, don't terminate your fast, or cut it short. A fever frequently gets worse before it is broken, and health returns. Keep your commitment to God.

Second, realize that some diseases are so advanced that healing is not possible.

Third, recall that all healing is subject to the will of God. He may have in mind a purpose in this illness that you cannot see. Remember that God controls all of our lives; no one dies prematurely. When God does heal, it is temporary, because "it is appointed for men to die" (Heb. 9:27). God controls the hands of the clock that determines the death of all people. Some healthy people die by accident, yet other diseased people live on for years.

The Daniel Fast may fail for several reasons:

   a. The disease has endangered other vital physical organs/ functions and the body can't function without them.

   b. You are too late to fast and pray for healing. Perhaps you should have fasted earlier, but you didn't obey God. As a result, your disobedience allowed the disease to progress to the place where it is terminal, just as the doctor tells a patient, "You should have seen me before your cancer advanced to this stage...it's too late." We must always be readily available and obedient to enter the Daniel Fast when God directs us.

   c. Your fasting and prayer were not wholehearted. God is not moved by shallow repentance or prayers that do not come from the bottom of your heart. Repentance is also necessary. When we pray with sin in our hearts, God cannot answer (see Isa. 59:1). Unknown sin in our lives proves that we have not spent time in the presence of God so He can show us our sin. As a result, our prayers do not get through.

PRACTICAL PRINCIPLES TO REMEMBER

The Daniel Fast will lead to spiritual insight. The results of fasting were ongoing in the lives of Daniel and his three friends. "To these four young men God gave knowledge and understanding" (Dan. 1:17, *NIV*). The knowledge God gave them was apparently the reward of their fast. Withholding food does not make us smart. God gives wisdom and knowledge to those who have the self-discipline to withhold food and to spend their time praying, reading His Word and seeking His will.

After Daniel and his three friends completed their fast, "The king talked with them, and he found none equal to [those who fasted]" (v. 19, *NIV*). These men who had self-determination, "In all matters of wisdom and understanding about which the king examined them, he found them ten times better than all" (v. 20).

The Daniel Fast is longer than one day. Your poor health/sickness developed over a long period of time, therefore, it will likely take a long time for your diet modification to produce a renewed state of health.

The Daniel Fast is a partial fast. Although other fasts involve no food or drink for one to three days, the Daniel Fast usually does not eliminate all food and water.

The Daniel Fast includes healthy food. Inasmuch as "the body heals itself," you must eat basic foods during the Daniel Fast to strengthen the body so it can heal itself.

The Daniel Fast requires abstinence from "party food." There may be times to enjoy party food, but the Daniel Fast is a return to basic nutritional necessities.

PREPARATION FOR THE DANIEL FAST

Aim: The Daniel Fast is for health and healing. Specifically, I am fasting to_____

Vow: I believe God has given me my physical, mental and emotional nature in which to glorify Him. Therefore

---

I renew my pledge to honor Him in every area of my life (see 1 Cor. 10:31). I believe sickness is a result of our first parents' sin, and I renew my faith in the daily cleansing from sin available through Christ's blood (see 1 John 1:7). I believe in Jehovah Rapha, that following His principles will give me health and that He can heal sickness. Therefore, I commit myself to God's healing/health and will fast and pray for it.

Bible Basis: "Is this not the fast I have chosen...your healing shall spring forth speedily" (Isa. 58:6,8).

Bible Promise: "The prayer of faith will save the sick, and the Lord will raise him up" (Jas. 5:15).

Fast: What I will withhold _____

Beginning: Date and time I will start _____

End: Date and time I will stop_____

Resources Needed: _____

God being my strength, and grace being my basis, I commit myself to the Daniel Fast for God's glory.

Signed _____ Date _____

≡ 9 ≡

THE JOHN
THE BAPTIST FAST

A WOMAN WHO ATTENDED A CHRISTIAN CHURCH SPREAD LIES ABOUT ITS
pastoral ministry and church integrity. The church's board did not capit-
ulate to her demands, but fasted once a week for the testimony of the
church and the pastor. When the woman threatened to sue the church
over alleged damages, and the threatened suit was publicized in the local
newspaper, the board thought its worst fears were realized and that God
hadn't honored their fast.

Then the board received letters from two other churches saying that
the woman had "pulled the same stunt" in their churches. Unfortunately,
they had given in to her demands and paid her off. The newspapers printed the letters, and the lawyer who had threatened to sue the church
changed his mind and refused to represent the woman. He suggested the
church had a legal complaint against her, but that he couldn't get
involved. The church board did not sue her, but fasted and prayed for the
woman's spiritual health.

EXTENDING OUR TESTIMONIES

Christians are commanded to be testimonies to others: "You are the light
of the world" (Matt. 5:14). The John the Baptist Fast is a tool for believers

to use to extend their lights. As in the case of the godly church board just mentioned, this fast is an important way to extend a faithful testimony even in a bad situation.

Christians have a double obligation: (1) to live godly lives and (2) to actively extend their influence to others for the glory of God. "Let your light so shine before men, that they may see your good works and glorify your Father in heaven" (v. 16).

Sometimes, however, unbelievers are not attracted to our godly lives. Because we don't participate in their sins, they criticize us. Worse, our godly lives convict them of their own sinfulness, so they attack us. When we try to positively influence them, we are persecuted for "righteousness sake."

Peter describes both the problem and the solution: "Having a good conscience, that when they defame you as evildoers, those who revile your good conduct in Christ may be ashamed" (1 Pet. 3:16).

A CASE IN POINT

A public school teacher attempted to live for Christ in his classroom and among the school's staff. He was, however, criticized by the personnel director as being "too straight" because he wouldn't compromise or go to "happy hour" with the staff. The teacher was extremely conscientious, investing extra time with students and going the extra mile in preparation. Finally, at a staff meeting where there was a policy disagreement, the personnel director told the Christian teacher, "I'm gonna get you fired...I won't rest till you're gone."

On Friday of that week the Christian teacher fasted and prayed for the personnel director. He didn't pray for vengeance on his "enemy"; instead, he prayed in accordance with Jesus' words, "Bless those who curse you, and pray for those who spitefully use you" (Luke 6:28). He prayed for the personnel director's salvation and success in employment and family relationships. The Christian fasted to bless his enemy, not to merely "heap coals of fire on his head" (see Rom. 12:20).

On that very Friday, the day the Christian teacher was fasting in prayer, the personnel director was caught violating district policy. Security escorted him from the building, and the locks were changed on the doors. Eventually the Christian who fasted was named "Teacher of the Year."

EXTENDING OUR "RIGHTEOUSNESS"

The John the Baptist Fast is for those who want to be good influences, or for those who have not had good testimonies, but want to be influential for God. Isaiah promised, "Is not this the fast that I have chosen...[that] your righteousness shall go before you" (Isa. 58:6,8).

This means that the believer's "righteousness" or testimony will extend beyond physical limitations. The John the Baptist Fast enables us to ask God to reach those who know about us so our "righteousness" may have greater influence.

Extending What We Do Not Have

An explanation about our "righteousness" is in order. In one sense we cannot refer to our own righteousness because the Bible says, "There is none righteous" (Rom. 3:10). Before we are saved, we are sinners, "For all have sinned and fall short of the glory of God" (3:23). This does not mean we all commit every possible sin, or the same sins, nor does it mean no one does good works. It means that although our works may be "good" in the eyes of others, they are not good enough to get us to heaven (see Eph. 2:8,9). This is because "By the deeds of the law no flesh will be justified in His sight" (Rom. 3:20).

No one can jump to an island located 10 miles out in the ocean. A small child may be able to jump 1 foot, an Olympic champion may jump 25 feet; but both fall short of the 10-mile jump. Similarly, there are people who are "good" in the eyes of their friends. They contribute to charities, they coach soccer teams or they give their time as candy stripers at the local hospitals. These people make positive contributions to society. They are not robbers, rapists or criminals. Society therefore may think these people are "good" in contrast to those who contribute nothing. But compared to God's standards, "there is none righteous, no, not one" (Rom. 3:10).

We Are Given God's Righteousness

When we come to Jesus Christ we receive a double blessing. First, our sins are forgiven; second, the righteousness of Jesus Christ is given to us. "The blood of Jesus Christ His Son cleanses us from all sin" (1 John 1:7). We no longer have any sin on God's record book. Instead, the righteousness of Jesus Christ is entered into our records, "that we might become the righteousness of God in Him" (2 Cor. 5:21).

This means that everything Christ did that was right is entered on our records. We now have "righteousness" not in ourselves, but God's "right" actions are added to our accounts. We are saved to obey Jesus Christ and to do good works. These works are described as the fine linen of the bride of Christ, which is "the righteous acts of the saints" (Rev. 19:8).

Fasting to Reverse Criticism

Use the John the Baptist Fast to reverse criticism when people don't understand the good things you do. Let me illustrate. Suppose you don't go with your buddies to the bar for a drink after work. They criticize you and make statements that hurt your job advancement. Or you lose an account or miss a sale because you no longer laugh at the prospect's filthy story, or use foul language as he does. Or when you and coworkers are sent to an out-of-town seminar, you refuse to go to an X-rated film and you're not considered "one of the group."

The John the Baptist Fast can reverse the attitudes of people blinded to the constructive contribution of your clean living and make you more influential.

FACTS TO FACE ABOUT FASTING

Like the other fasts described in this book, the John the Baptist Fast must be entered with a realistic attitude.

Fasting Is Sacrifice

During fasting you pay a price by giving up life's necessities, as well as its delicacies (i.e., good food). The heart of fasting is sacrifice.

Fasting is associated in Scripture with "afflicting the soul" (see Isa. 58:5). We have previously observed that the practice of fasting grew out of deep despondency or despair. It was the result of an emotional upheaval. In despair and grief, a person cried to God for an answer. After time, people reversed the cause and effect. The original cause (deep grief) drove people to the effect (not eating). Later, when people needed answers from God, they returned to the effect (not eating) so they could afflict their souls to the place where they would pray with all of their hearts (cause).

Fasting Doesn't Always "Work"
Some people fast without apparent or immediate results. God anticipated the questions that would arise because of this: "'Why have we fasted,' they say, 'and You have not seen? Why have we afflicted our souls, and You take no notice?'" (Isa. 58:3). In Isaiah's day, people were not grieved over sin and injustice when they fasted, so their fasting was ineffective. David's response to unanswered prayer was to humble himself (see Ps. 35:13). David said that when he prayed without results, he had to humble himself through fasting to make his prayers effective.

ESTABLISHING A GREAT TESTIMONY

Every Christian should want to establish an effective testimony to friends and relatives. As we saw in 1 Peter 3:16, we are commended for having good testimonies. We want to have a godly influence upon others.

No one had a more effective testimony than John the Baptist. This is not the opinion of people, but the observation of the Lord Jesus Christ.

The greatest influence. Jesus said, "Among those born of women there has not risen one greater than John the Baptist" (Matt. 11:11). No sin is recorded about John the Baptist; apparently he continually did the will of God. He witnessed to his generation that Jesus was the Christ (see John 1:7). We, too, can become great witnesses by following John the Baptist's example of fasting "often" (see Matt. 9:14) and observing a special diet (drinking "neither wine nor strong drink," Luke 1:15).

His Nazirite diet. Before John the Baptist was born, his father, Zacharias, was told that his son would follow the Nazirite vow. "For he will be great in the sight of the Lord, and shall drink neither wine nor strong drink" (Luke 1:15). This was one of the requirements of the Nazirite vow, which is named after a Hebrew word meaning "vowed" or "dedicated." Another qualification was that a person could not cut his hair. So John's vow would make him different from the average person on the street. When people saw his long hair, they would identify him as a Nazirite—a dedicated or consecrated man. He would be perceived to be influential before both God and man. *John the Baptist was Spirit filled.* Not only did John have an outward testimony of long hair, but he also had an inner power that touched people. His father, Zacharias, was promised before John's birth that "he will also be filled with the Holy Spirit, even from his mother's womb" (Luke 1:15).

Those who enter the John the Baptist Fast will not automatically be filled with the Spirit by refraining from eating. The "filling of the Spirit" means the Holy Spirit controls you. To be filled with the Spirit you must follow God's prescription, "Do not be drunk with wine...but be filled with the Spirit" (Eph. 5:18).

HOW TO BE FILLED WITH THE SPIRIT
- Empty sin from your life.
- Yield yourself to God.
- Ask the Spirit to enter your life.
- Have faith that He will come.
- Obey God's word.
- Walk continually by the Spirit.
- Let the Spirit continually empower you.

The evangelistic effects of John's testimony. Zacharias was told that his son would be different from other children, and that he would be filled with the Spirit. This would result in John's evangelistic success and powerful influence upon his generation:

> He will turn many of the children of Israel to the Lord their God. He will also go before Him in the spirit and power of Elijah, "to turn the hearts of the fathers to the children," and the disobedient to the wisdom of the just, to make ready a people prepared for the Lord (Luke 1:16,17).

Establishing your influence. Although John the Baptist's testimony was the greatest seen at that time, his influence was not for selfish or ego-building purposes. We must not enter the John the Baptist Fast for self-centered reasons. We want to influence others, but we must realize our sinfulness, failure and shortcomings. When we come to recognize our "nothingness" in God's sight, then He can use us.

Realizing that we are "the least in the Kingdom" establishes our foundation for being a greater influence than was John the Baptist: "He who is least in the kingdom of heaven is greater than he" (Matt. 11:11).

Jesus said, "Blessed are those who hunger and thirst for righteousness, for they shall be filled" (Matt. 5:6). He was not referring to physical fasting, but to spiritual hunger and thirst. Denying ourselves food and drink for a time, however, can sharpen our spiritual appetites, and move us closer to realizing Jesus' promise: "For they shall be filled."

PRESCRIPTION FOR THE JOHN THE BAPTIST FAST

Step 1: Attach Your Diet/Fast to Your Desire for Influence
Begin the John the Baptist Fast knowing the kind of influence you want to be. Remember, there are not only positive and negative influences, but also degrees of influence. On a scale of 1-10, Phil may be a 7, Kara may be only a 2. Much of the difference among various influences depends on desire.

It was predicted about John the Baptist, "he will be great in the sight of the Lord, and shall drink neither wine nor strong drink" (Luke 1:15). Although the angel told John's father, Zacharias, that John was to accept a Nazirite vow, that decision had to be desired and confirmed by John. There is power in that kind of decision—one that controls your life. You must make a decision to serve God, then you must daily make that decision work.

There is also power in a separated life. Some want to imitate their friends in dress, music and entertainment to avoid being viewed as weird or "spiritually fanatic." The world is drifting into a lifestyle of pleasure, ease, lust-fulfillment, homosexuality and rebellion against God. Christians must dare to be different from the world to be influential for God. Just as the flower children and hippies of the 1960s established a counterculture to communicate their values and lifestyles, so Christians today will have to establish a godly counterculture.

Step 2: Write Out the Testimony You Want
When you begin the John the Baptist Fast, write down specifically what you want to accomplish. Decide (a) the areas in which you want to influence others; (b) the people you want to influence; (c) the events you want to influence; (d) the place where you want to establish your testimony.

John the Baptist had a unique mission in life. "There was a man sent from God, whose name was John. This man came for a witness, to bear witness of the Light" (John 1:6,7). The purpose of John's testimony was to be a light for Jesus Christ. What is your purpose in life? God has a unique purpose for you to accomplish. Why were you sent into the world?

Step 3: Determine to Be a "Person of the Vow"

John the Baptist was dedicated as a Nazirite from birth. The word "Nazirite" comes from *nadar*, "to vow"; hence, a Nazirite was "a person of the vow." He was one who decided to serve God and to reflect his decision in the food he ate, the clothes he wore and the length of his hair.

A Nazirite vow could be either temporary (usually 30 days) or permanent. The vow was usually initiated by stress or trouble. In John the Baptist's case, the nation of Israel was enslaved to Rome, blinded by its legalism and spiritually in trouble. Because of its distress and trouble, God called John to a lifelong Nazirite vow to influence an entire nation.

Nazirites were not celibates, nor did they live monastically (i.e., apart from people). They lived among people, but lived by different standards:

> If any of you want to dedicate yourself to me by vowing to become a Nazirite, you must no longer drink any wine or beer or use any kind of vinegar. Don't drink grape juice or eat grapes or raisins—not even the seeds or skins. Even the hair of a Nazirite is sacred to me, and as long as you are a Nazirite, you must never cut your hair...you must never go close to a dead body, not even that of your father, mother, brother or sister. That would make you unclean. Your hair is the sign that you are dedicated to me, so remain holy (Num. 6:2-8, CEV).

Likewise, when you undertake a John the Baptist Fast, you establish a distinct diet while living among people. You "vow a vow" to God, and you demonstrate your vow by being different. You eat differently and you live differently because you expect a different influence from your life than people of the world expect from their lives.

Step 4: Submit Your Total Lifestyle to Christ

To become an influence for God, bring your total life into conformity with Jesus Christ. The success of the John the Baptist Fast begins with repentance—a heartfelt turning from sin. Remember Israel's problem, "Why have we afflicted our souls, and You take no notice?" (Isa. 58:3). The answer was that the result of fasting is determined by more than an outward physical abstinence from food. There must be a heart response to God, and a total life commitment to being a testimony for Jesus Christ.

Clothes. The way we dress must bring honor to Jesus Christ. "John himself was clothed in camel's hair" (Matt. 3:4). Some people believe this was camel *skin*, but the peasants wore cloth woven with camel hair, and this may be what John wore.

We don't have to wear peasant clothes to be effective today. During the John the Baptist Fast we will dress like other people, unless their dress is immoral or sends a wrong message. We must want the way we dress to bear a Christlike testimony. We should wear modest clothes to protect ourselves from sending the wrong signal about our bodies or our desires.

Christians should not call undue attention to themselves by the clothing they wear. They should avoid distasteful fads. When my children were growing up, questions arose about wearing what the world wore, such as skirt lengths and the kinds of jewelry that could be worn. Very early I taught my children a principle that was repeated often within our home.

> Be not the first by which the new is tried;
> be not the last by which the old is laid aside.

Our clothing should not be so outdated that we bring attention to ourselves by looking odd. Nor should we wear the latest fads before they are accepted by society.

There are two factors to consider about clothing. (1) Do not offend your own personal conscience. "If you don't do what you know is right, you have sinned" (Jas. 4:17, *CEV*). (2) Do not offend the "corporate conscience" (i.e., the conscience of the Christian community or the local church). You must live by what they expect of you if you intend to extend your Christian testimony.

Food. The Nazirite vow prohibited drinking strong drink and the fruit of the vine. The Bible indicates what John ate: "His food was locusts and wild honey" (Matt. 3:4). Some teachers have claimed that the word "locust" is a corruption of the original term "lotus plant," meaning that John the Baptist was a vegetarian; but there is no basis to support that view in Scripture. The locust was simply an insect that was "clean" food in the Jewish dietary law, and was specifically approved for eating (see Lev. 11:22).

On one of the islands off South Korea, a village of elderly people boast that some of their women live to be 200 years old by eating locusts and honey. They grind up the locusts, mix them with honey and sell the mixture in jars to the tourists. The validity of their claim has not been verified; but many elderly people do live there, and what they sell represents what John the Baptist ate.

Those who follow the John the Baptist Fast may prohibit themselves from certain foods, usually for the rest of their lives. They also maintain lifelong separated lifestyles.

No strong drink. Those who participate in the John the Baptist Fast will separate themselves from strong drink. The John the Baptist Fast requires making a strong statement of separation from alcohol of any kind. This says nothing about the harmful effects of alcohol on your body, but it says everything about your testimony—especially your witness to small children, your spouse, the Christian community and the world.

Home. John did not live in a house as did ordinary people. The Bible identifies "the wilderness" as the place where the Word of God came to John (see Luke 3:2). We are not told whether he lived in a cave, a man-made shelter or outdoors. Scripture simply indicates that John did not live in town among people. Some Nazirites lived among people, but John the Baptist separated himself from people. You can live a normal life and go to work during the John the Baptist Fast; however when you pray, you must seek a quiet place to spend time alone with God, as did John the Baptist.

Step 5: Decide Whether Your Fast Is an Event or a Process
Some fasts are for crisis events (the Disciples Fast) and some fasts are lengthy (the Daniel Fast), but the John the Baptist fast can be both because our testimonies have ongoing influence.

Fast-event. Although John the Baptist maintained his strict diet throughout his entire lifetime, there were times when he entered a fast-event. He and his followers fasted "often" (see Matt. 9:14). This meant that on certain occasions they fasted for a specific purpose. Similarly, you should enter the John the Baptist Fast on certain occasions for your testimony/influence.

Diet/Process. The John the Baptist Fast may require a lifelong diet adjustment as an ongoing process, resulting in a stronger testimony to yourself, God, other Christians and the world. Just as a Nazirite could alter his testimony either for 30 days or for a lifetime, so you may need to alter your diet as a long-term process.

Step 6: Adjust the Fast's Duration to the Problem
The act of separating yourself for spiritual purposes may be a lifelong practice, depending on the nature of the testimony for which you fast. Alcoholics who go to Alcoholics Anonymous make lifelong commitments never to drink again. They recognize that within their bodies lurks an alcoholic who if given one drink will drink continually. Therefore they take lifelong pledges never to drink again.

Each of us is susceptible to the menacing cancer of addiction. When we take pain drugs, we subject ourselves to the potential of becoming drug addicts. If we ignorantly and naively take drugs, we can become slaves to them. The point is that the John the Baptist Fast should alert us to the ongoing risk of lapsing into habits that damage our influence.

BEFORE ENTERING THE
JOHN THE BAPTIST FAST:
- Write out your dietary changes.
- Determine the duration of your fast.
- Write out the purpose (the more exact your aim, the better you can attack an unanswered prayer).
- Make a vow and sign it. (See the form at the end of this chapter.)

Step 7: Short-Term Fasting for Your Testimony
When an issue concerning your Christian influence distresses you, you should fast immediately and specifically for that issue. Sometimes the issue is not clear and you are confused about the problem, such as when a friend suddenly seems distant or estranged. That is all the more reason you should enter the John the Baptist Fast. You begin (1) praying for

insight to understand the problem, (2) praying for a strategy to solve the problem, (3) praying for strength to deal with the issue and (4) praying for God to providentially work behind the scenes to restore your influence.

Be aware of the four basic desires of the ego or personality. Although these desires may seem natural and prescriptive, they may also grow out of a selfish heart that puts ego on the throne. These desires drive us to the John the Baptist Fast.

- *Protect me.* We feel threatened by losing life's basic necessities.
- *Exalt me.* We feel embarrassed or feel that others minimize us.
- *Accept me.* We are alienated or frozen out of the group.
- *Respect me.* We feel threatened because of criticism or direct attacks.

When we feel a threat to our emotional equilibrium or self-esteem, we should enter the John the Baptist Fast to strengthen our testimonies and our influence upon others.

Step 8: Know the Nature of a Christ-Centered Testimony
If you are not aware of how to be a good Christian witness, read Christian books and listen to instructive tapes to help you learn during your fast. Keep the following factors in mind:

Recognize your limitations. Concerning Jesus, John the Baptist admitted, "I would not have known him, except...[God] told me" (John 1:33, *NIV*). His disciples told John, "All are coming to him" (3:26). You want your testimony to be effective, but beyond your influence remember the most important principle, "He must increase, but I must decrease" (v. 30). This means that you are not fasting to protect your ego, but to exalt Jesus Christ.

Recognize your unworthiness. John would not let other people exalt him, not even his disciples. He told the religious authorities from Jerusalem, "I am not worthy" (1:27).

Evaluate your desires. During the John the Baptist Fast, we should seek out any hidden selfish desires. John the Baptist said that in merely bearing witness to Christ, "This joy of mine is fulfilled" (3:29). This happens when Jesus Christ is exalted.

PRACTICAL PRINCIPLES TO REMEMBER

Determine time limits for the short- and long-range fast/diet. When you get ready to fast, make these a matter of prayer and write out the duration before you begin the diet/fast.

Determine diet modifications before you begin. Write down what you will or will not eat before you begin the fast. In making this determination, ask yourself:

- Is this healthy for me?
- Will this harm me?
- Would this be a testimony if others knew what I was doing?
- Is this mere legalism? (Trying to please God through a work of the flesh.)
- Why am I withdrawing from this food/liquid?

Determine testimony-objectives before you begin. It is good to write out the purpose of your fast/diet before beginning. We have been told, "You do not have because you do not ask" (Jas. 4:2). Frequently when we write out our petitions, we suddenly see ego staring back at us from the paper. The process of writing out our objective clarifies our petition and its motive.

Determine the sincerity of your vow-decision before you begin. We test our sincerity in light of God's standards—the Word of God in Jesus Christ. John the Baptist's sincerity could not be questioned, for he spoke of Jesus as the one "Who, coming after me, is preferred before me, whose sandal strap I am not worthy to loose" (John 1:27). Also, he was willing to pay for his testimony with his life, which was cut short by King Herod (see 14:1-12). (Although some might think this shows that the John the Baptist Fast wasn't successful, John's death merely extended his testimony!)

The point is that we must not enter the John the Baptist Fast for selfish or self-protective reasons. We must make sure that we desire to extend our influence for good only to ensure that in all things Jesus Christ will be honored.

Remember, we have the right and obligation to eat. Paul asked rhetorically, "Do we have no right to eat and drink?" (1 Cor. 9:4). Then he said, "Therefore, whether you eat or drink, or whatever you do, do all to the glory of God" (10:31).

PREPARING FOR THE JOHN THE BAPTIST FAST

Aim: To expand and increase my testimony to Jesus Christ through the John the Baptist Fast for testimony and influence.

Vow: I will be free of alcohol, cigarettes, drugs and any influence that destroys my testimony because I want Christ to be magnified in my body (see Phil. 1:20,21). I will be sexually pure for my life-partner, because I want my body to be the temple of the Holy Spirit (see 1 Cor. 6:19). I will keep my body under subjection so my life will communicate Christ to others (see 1 Cor. 9:27).

Sacrifice: What I will abstain from for life _____

Fast: What I will withhold _____

Begin: Date and time I will start _____

End: Date and time I will stop _____

Bible Basis: "Let your light so shine before men, that they may see your good works and glorify your Father in heaven" (Matt. 5:16).

Resources Needed: _____

God being my strength, and grace being my basis, I commit myself to the John the Baptist Fast for God's glory.

Signed _____ Date _____

⇒ 10 ⇐

THE ESTHER FAST

MY FRIEND JERRY FALWELL RECEIVED SEVERAL DEATH THREATS FROM those who opposed his leadership of the Moral Majority.

I was with Jerry in the summer of 1982 when he visited Australia. More than 1,000 Moral Majority opponents rushed the National Legislative Building in Canberra, the capital. The evening news described their actions as a "national disgrace." The Parliament had never been threatened.

The following Sunday afternoon, a mob showed up at the Sydney Civic Center to protest Falwell's presence. Only a few uniformed patrolmen were present to keep the mob behind police barricades. As I watched, a thousand people plunged through the barricades and broke down the front door. I wondered if we would be killed.

Since that experience, I have raised the preventive wall of the Esther Fast as I pray for the safety of Jerry Falwell and other men of God. Outsiders may presume that those for whom I fast get "lucky breaks"; but we who have wrestled with the evil one know what happens. We know that the Esther Fast is effective.

THROUGH MANY DANGERS

The Christian life presents many dangers. We are susceptible to physical attacks, as in the case of Jerry Falwell's Australian opponents, and to spiritual threats from Satan and his demons.

Taking a stand for Christ can be costly. Rivals may attempt to get you fired, or lie about your effectiveness. They may steal from you or take credit for your efforts. High school students have been known to physically attack Christian students. In Muslim countries, Christians have been martyred for their faith. The Esther Fast can release God's protection upon His children.

Although spiritual attacks are more subtle, devious and vicious, in some cases they also pose physical threats. Whether physical or spiritual, these threats have only one source. Paul tells us, "We do not wrestle against flesh and blood, but against principalities, against powers, against the rulers of the darkness of this age, against spiritual hosts of wickedness in the heavenly places" (Eph. 6:12).

Most Americans, including many Christians, do not believe in evil forces or demonic spirits. They believe demons exist only in fairy tales and discount their significance in the Bible.

Perhaps this is because America has been living under the umbrella of God's protection. Unlike the darkness of heathen society, America has experienced few instances of active, public demonism. Demonic attacks are much more common on the mission field than in America. Also, the use of demonic medicine men and witches has not been openly practiced in America. Although America has been far from Christ-centered in many of its activities, at least our Congress opens with "Christian" prayer and our president is sworn into office with a Bible. The Ten Commandments have been taught in public schools and Christian churches have been the dominant influence in our nation. This Christian umbrella has shielded America from the hot glare of satanism and demonic destruction that have tormented other societies.

As America is becoming more secular and pluralistic, we are seeing more evidence of demonic attacks in our nation. Therefore, Christian leaders must understand the potential of demonic influence on their ministries, and they must know how to seek protection from the evil one.

God has promised, "Is not this the fast that I have chosen...the glory of the Lord shall be your rear guard" (Isa. 58:6,8). As we shall see, the Esther Fast is designed to be this kind of rearguard protection from danger and demonic influence.

WHAT THE ESTHER FAST IS NOT

We understand the purpose of the Esther Fast better when we understand what it is not.

It Is Not an Exorcism
First, the purpose of the Esther Fast is not to exorcise demons from a person. Exorcism is a totally different process, and only those who are fully equipped and trained for the process should enter into that exercise.

Second, the Esther Fast does not break the bondage/addiction a person has because of demonic influence. Such situations call for the Disciple's Fast (see chapter 2).

Third, the Esther Fast is not designed to heal a person who suffers a pathology because of demonic influence and/or possession. Although at times the presence of a demon in a person *may* cause psychological or physical problems, usually such problems have no trace of demonic influence. In either case, the Esther Fast is not designed to target this problem.

The Esther Fast *may* be used as a protective weapon against the demonic. The previously mentioned problems are unusual, and the vast majority of Christians are not troubled by them. Many Christians, however, are tempted to sin, or they are enticed to heresy (doctrine of devils) or immorality. All of these temptations can stem from demonic sources. Also, Christians can be harmed physically, mentally or emotionally by satanic attack; therefore they need protection. And protection is one purpose of the Esther Fast.

Satanic attacks have hurt the work of God and Christians in several ways. When my friend accepted the pastorate of a small Mississippi church, the attendance was fewer than 75. He sought God's power, which resulted in an anointing that lined the altar with converts and caused the attendance to grow to 800.

One day as this pastor was on a church visit, a drunk driver crossed the highway, striking the pastor's automobile head-on. He died instantly. As demoralizing as his death was to the church, the aftermath was even more disastrous. The next two or three pastors were not able to preach with the same power, or lead with the same wisdom and effectiveness. The church declined and decayed until it reached its present attendance of 150.

I have often wondered whether my friend's death was the result of mere circumstance or God's will to take him for some reason I don't understand. Could his death have been satanically inspired? Not having enough information to make a conclusion, I personally believe the last answer is probably accurate.

Occasionally I have felt that God has delivered me from the evil one. For example, I conducted a Sunday School seminar, at a Holiday Inn in Hollywood, California, for a small crowd of between 50 and 60 church leaders. At the end of the seminar, I asked if I could conclude by dedicating the leaders and their churches to God. I asked all present to either kneel by their chairs, stand before God or sit with bowed heads, using the chairs in front of them as altars.

I knelt in the front row and dedicated all of the delegates and their churches to God. I ended my prayer as I usually do, asking for God's protection for our travel home. Using the words of the Lord's Prayer, I prayed, "And God as we travel, deliver us from the evil one who would snuff out our lives." Upon saying amen, I arose and moved back to the podium.

Immediately after leaving my place of prayer, a heavy window frame fell out of the wall onto the spot I had just left. Several who were present cried out with fear. People leaving the room almost unanimously agreed that God had just answered my prayer, and that my moving from underneath the heavy window frame was God's protection of me. I agree.

In 1977 I spent New Year's Eve in Haiti. I was told that New Year's Eve was the Devil's Night, and that demonic activity would occur that evening. I slept on the laundry-room cot in the home of a missionary, Bob Turnbull, president of Haiti Baptist Mission. I'd gone to bed about 10:00 P.M., not caring about any of the New Year's Eve activities.

About 11:50 P.M., I awakened with a cold shudder. Immediately I began praying and calling out loud for "the power of the blood of Jesus Christ." I knew that demons and Satan could not stay in the presence of Jesus Christ and the power of His blood. As midnight approached, I could hear the whistles and sirens ushering in the New Year. I sensed a cold, demonic oppression, and continued to pray in the name of Jesus Christ and the power of His blood until His sweet peace flowed into my heart. I went back to sleep and slept securely.

It Is Not for Daily Protection
The Esther Fast is a tool for obtaining protection in events of epic pro-

portions, not for protection from the temptations and dangers we face daily. I teach my students that the final petition of the Lord's Prayer— "And do not lead us into temptation, but deliver us from the evil one" (Matt. 6:13)—should be used as a daily umbrella of protection. But the Esther Fast is reserved for those crisis situations that are much larger than our need for daily protection.

The protection that God gives through the Esther Fast is similar to the protection God gave Israel as it fled Egypt for the Sinai wilderness. "The Lord went before them by day in a pillar of cloud...and by night in a pillar of fire" (Exod. 13:21). When Egyptian armies attacked Israel from the rear, "the pillar of the cloud went from before them and stood behind them" (14:19). The Esther Fast is an appeal for God to become the "rear guard" for ourselves or others, protecting us when we are most vulnerable.

It is important to know during the Esther Fast that God is on our side, but it is more important to know that we are on God's side. We must know whose side we're on before we can win. The Esther Fast is a statement that we are on God's side and we expect His protection in our lives and ministries.

Paul warns us not to be ignorant of Satan's devices (see 2 Cor. 2:11). The evil one is "out to get us." He is a "roaring lion, seeking whom he may devour" (1 Pet. 5:8). Paul told the Christians in Corinth, "The people you forgive for sinning against your church, I forgive, because Satan gets to you if you have an unforgiving spirit. I forgive them because I live in Christ. I am not ignorant of Satan's devices to get to me" (2 Cor. 2:10,11, author's paraphrase).

THE PROBLEM FACING ESTHER

Esther was a Hebrew maiden living in the land of Persia, where the Israelites had been carried away as captives in the sixth century B.C. At that time the land was ruled by Nebuchadnezzar, king of Babylonia. Esther was a beautiful girl who was raised by her cousin Mordecai after her parents died.

When Queen Vashti of Persia displeased King Ahasuerus (or Xerxes), Esther was among several young women taken to the king's palace as possible replacements for the queen. Sure enough, God's sovereignty became evident when Esther was chosen over all the other maidens and elevated as queen of the Persian Empire. Esther did not reveal her identity as an Israelite; and some scholars believe that the name Esther means "hidden," reflecting her hidden identity.

Haman, the prime minister of Persia, hated the Jews because Esther's cousin Mordecai would not bow down to him (see Esther 3:1-6). Haman used his position to pass a law calling for a holocaust against the Jews, planning to slaughter all Hebrews living in Persia. When the proposed slaughter was announced, Mordecai told Queen Esther, and she determined to appeal to the king to save her people.

Esther, however, faced a problem. According to Persian protocol, if she went in to see the king uninvited she could lose her life. But she summoned her courage, and called on Mordecai to stand with her in her ordeal by gathering the Jews in a three-day fast (see Esther 4:15,16). As you recall, God was with her—the king extended his staff toward her in a gesture of acceptance. Later, again in God's sovereignty, Haman's plot against Mordecai and the Jews was turned against him. He was hanged on the gallows that had been built for Mordecai, and the holocaust was averted.

In ways very similar to the story of Esther, people/Satan hate Christians today because they will not bow down nor compromise to ungodly principles. The Esther Fast provides a means of protection.

PRESCRIPTION FOR THE ESTHER FAST

Step 1: Recognize the Source of Danger

Sometimes you will know that a particular trial, temptation or problem is from Satan. The nature of the attack against you is obvious. So when you begin the Esther Fast you know you are fasting for divine protection from Satan.

If you get a "cold" feeling of satanic oppression or internally sense "demonic attack," flee to God for protection and begin the Esther Fast immediately. Some of the other fasts mentioned in this book might not be initiated for two or three days, or even two or three weeks; however, the Esther Fast is an immediate response to danger.

The Esther Fast can also be used as a tool to prevent danger. You may enter the fast not because of an immediate threat, but to keep any danger from threatening you.

Esther knew exactly what she was up against. Mordecai provided Esther through her servant with a copy of the decree that would have destroyed the Jews (see Esther 4:8). Until Esther knew of the decree, she could do nothing about it. She looked out of her window and saw Mordecai in sackcloth and ashes, praying for God's help. Esther sent clothes to Mordecai, but he refused them.

This is an example of two believers, one who knows of the imminent danger and the other who is unaware of it. This may be your situation. Someone else may know about the foreboding danger in your life, but you don't. When they inform you of the threat, you should immediately enter into the Esther Fast. On the other hand, you may be the one who knows about the threat, and you have friends like Esther who are not aware of the problem. You have to communicate the threat to them just as Mordecai communicated with Esther.

Step 2: Realize the Nature of Your Battle

As previously stated, not every battle you face will be the result of demonic attack. But you should realize that you do have an enemy behind all your problems: "Be sober, be vigilant; because your adversary the devil walks about like a roaring lion, seeking whom he may devour" (1 Pet. 5:8). The Christian life is not easy; it is a struggle against darkness and heresy. When you know the nature of the battle and who your enemy is, you can take adequate steps to protect yourself.

When the Israelites entered the Promised Land, they defeated the nations that inhabited Canaan—the Philistines, the Canaanites, and many other nations. But after they defeated their enemies, Israel allowed their enemies to settle among them. What their enemies could not do in battle they did in peace. Although they could not defeat Israel, they enslaved the nation through the "Canaanization" of God's people. Notice four steps that brought Israel into bondage as surely as if they had suffered a military defeat:

THE CANAANIZATION OF GOD'S PEOPLE
- They tolerated the Canaanites.
- They intermarried with them.
- They worshiped Canaanite gods.
- They adopted the Canaanite lifestyle.

Your relationship to Satan is the same as Israel's was to its enemies. Satan has been defeated in the cross of Jesus Christ. His defeat was predicted by Jesus: "Now the ruler of this world will be cast out" (John 12:31) and "the ruler of this world is judged" (16:11). Satan, like the Canaanites, has been defeated; but he acts no more like a defeated foe than did they. He may even come to you as a Christian to try to defeat you—especially if you made the choices the Israelites did to tolerate satanic influence, intermarry with satanic attractions, worship the idols of the world and adopt its lifestyle.

When you sense danger and direct temptation from demonic forces, you should enter into the Esther Fast. You should also enter this fast when your temptation is not an immediate threat but an ongoing attraction.

Step 3: Recognize Whose Authority Protects You
When Haman threatened to destroy all the Jews, Mordecai told Esther that she should "go in to the king to make supplication to him and plead before him for her people" (Esther 4:8). Given the special permission that had to be granted to see the king, this took courage and faith in a power beyond Esther herself. Just as she took a stand by faith in God's power, so your fast will require such a stand. Relying on God's authority involves three steps:

• *Remove.* You should remove yourself from any circumstance or environment where you will be tempted. The Bible says, "Flee these things" (1 Tim. 6:11).

• *Resist.* Not only should you vacate the place of evil influence, but you should also "Resist the devil and he will flee from you" (Jas. 4:7). Paul also tells us, "Fight the good fight of faith" (1 Tim. 6:12).

• *Rebuke.* You cannot rebuke the devil in your own power, but you can allow God to rebuke him. Notice the caution given to us in Scripture: "Michael the archangel, in contending with the devil...dared not bring against him a reviling accusation, but said, 'The Lord rebuke you!'" (Jude 9). You can rebuke the evil one in the name and power of Jesus Christ because His name is a strong name.

Step 4: Fast and Pray for Protection
When faced with a life-threatening situation, Esther proclaimed a fast (see Esther 4:16). Only then did she go in to the king in an attempt to save her people. Although this fast was for a specific time and place in life, the Esther Fast can also be coupled with intense prayer for protection from

future attacks. Because of this, I teach that a Christian should pray every day the seventh petition of the Lord's Prayer, "Deliver us from the evil one" (Matt. 6:13).

Step 5: Know the Limitations of Prayer and Fasting

Don't expect the Esther Fast to produce omnipotent powers, because fasting and prayer is not a "fix all" solution. Esther realized her fast might not work. Notice that she sent word to Mordecai that she would "go to the king, which is against the law; and if I perish, I perish" (Esther 4:16). She was going to fast for three days, but was still not certain if she would live. Esther was going to be faithful to God and do what she had promised no matter what the cost. She determined to go to the king. Note what fasting did not do for Esther and Mordecai:

> ### WHAT FASTING DID NOT DO
> - It did not change the decree.
> - It did not make the king call the queen.
> - It did not solve the crisis.

God did not conspicuously reveal Himself in the circumstances Esther faced. Instead, He worked through the circumstances to accomplish His glory and purpose. God does not violate the free will of people, nor the nature of His laws. Because His laws are an extension of His nature, God cannot go against Himself. The Persian king had to make a new law that was more powerful than the old law (see 8:7,8). The king did not violate his law; likewise God does not violate His laws. When you enter the Esther Fast, you must realize that some things will not be changed. At times evil may have already been set in motion, and you cannot undo history. For example, you cannot take back evil, cursing or blasphemy that has been spoken. Our words are like the feathers of a pillow—once they have been thrown into the wind, we will never get all the feathers back into the pillow.

Step 6: Gain Power from Corporate Fasting

Some fasts are designed to be private—for example, the Disciple's Fast. Other fasts are more effective when others join you. Esther told Mordecai to "Go, gather all the Jews...and fast for me; neither eat nor drink for three days, night or day. My maids and I will fast likewise" (4:16).

Because this was a national problem, Esther called for all God's people to fast in response. When the problem is personal, the fast should be personal. When the problem is national, the fast should be national. The principle to follow is that the circle of those involved in the fast must be large enough to include the circle of those who are affected by the problem.

Step 7: Fast to Overcome Spiritual Blindness

As you enter the Esther Fast, ask God to help you discern the nature and purpose of the spiritual attack upon you or of any other threat. When you understand Satan's purpose, you can fast to counter him. Otherwise, "As the serpent deceived Eve by his craftiness, so your minds may be corrupted from the simplicity that is in Christ" (2 Cor. 11:3).

One of the reasons there has been so little demonic activity in America is that the light of the gospel, shedding understanding and spiritual discernment, has largely repelled it. Usually, Satan's wiles have not been exerted overtly or openly, but covertly. Perhaps one of the greatest demonic activities is in liberal seminaries where apostasy is taught. Paul called heresy the doctrine of devils, predicting that "in latter times some will depart from the faith, giving heed to deceiving spirits and doctrines of demons" (1 Tim. 4:1). Such are those "having a form of godliness but denying its power. And from such people turn away!" (2 Tim. 3:5).

One of the purposes of the Esther Fast is to increase such discernment. One of the spiritual gifts is the "spirit of discernment"; however, we also gain discernment from experience, from talking to experienced Christians and from studying the Word. Understand that Satan will try to wipe out any discerning spirit you have. The most obvious form of satanic attack is not overt demonism. Satan's first strategy is to blind your mind from understanding spiritual things.

• *When Satan blinds you, demons don't need to attack you.* For the past 200 years in this country, the demonic has not manifested itself in outward manifestations as much as it has in blinding even believers to the truth. "The god of this age has blinded" many, "lest the light of the gospel of the glory of Christ...should shine on them" (2 Cor. 4:4). Satan blinds the unsaved from seeing the gospel so they won't become saved. He blinds believers from knowing and doing God's will for their lives.

Even ministers can become spiritually blind, denying the fundamentals of the faith. Paul warned against "False apostles, deceitful workers, transforming themselves into apostles of Christ. And no wonder! For

Satan himself transforms himself into an angel of light. Therefore, it is no great thing if his ministers also transform themselves into ministers of righteousness" (11:13-15).

• *When you overcome blindness, beware of attacks in other realms.* When you successfully study the Word and understand the will of God, you begin to grow in Christ. If Satan can't blind you, he will then attack you in other realms. Sometimes if he can't hold you back from knowing God's will, he will make a fanatic out of you and you will run past the will of God. There is no better place than the center of God's will.

• *Fast for a strategy of victory.* Even with the king's permission, the Jews had to protect themselves. Esther appealed to the king for protection, but the king could not change his decree. The law of the Medes and Persians mandated that it could never be changed. All the king could do was to have another law written that was more powerful. This new law allowed Jews to defend themselves. God's strategy was to counter one law by another law, "that the Jews would be ready on that day to avenge themselves on their enemies" (Esther 8:13). As a result, the Jews smote all their enemies.

At times, the Esther Fast releases defense for you against the unseen world. God will send His angels to protect you. At other times, the fast will reveal strategies you must take for your own protection. You may discover anew the importance of getting enough sleep and eating properly so you will have physical strength. Remember, when you are physically weak you lose your initiative to fight and your inhibitions are low. Other strategies may involve study, programs and other initiatives.

Step 8: Fast with Common Sense, Not Recklessness
Notice that the immediate success of Esther's fast didn't end the problem. It gained her access to the king, but she and the other Jews then had to defend themselves. Too often we pray and enter into a fast, then sit in our rocking chairs waiting for God to solve our problems. The Esther Fast gives us power to attack our problems, so we leave the fast ready to become active in service. Note the things Esther had to do after she had fasted:

• *Be in the right place.* Esther "stood in the inner court of the king's palace" (Esther 5:1). After you have fasted in private, then you will have to follow the Lord's leading, perhaps into a public place.

• *Wear the right clothing.* Esther didn't just pray for God to change the heart of the king. She put on the right apparel that would be attractive to him. She understood that while you are on your knees, you must pray as though everything depends on God; but when you arise, you must work as though everything depends on yourself. "Esther put on her royal robes" (v. 1).

Today we too must "put on the whole armor of God, that you may be able to stand against the wiles of the devil" (Eph. 6:11). The clothing for standing against Satan is like the armor of a soldier. Because we are in a warfare, we must possess a siege mentality. If we are not ready to fight, we will be defeated. Dressing properly for the fight is the best preparation for winning. The following list shows the prescribed attire:

THE CHRISTIAN'S ARMOR
For the hips—Truth
For the chest—Righteousness
For the feet—Preparation of the Gospel
For defense—The Shield of Faith
For the head—The Helmet of Salvation
For a sword—The Word of God

A look at this battle dress tells us that defeating Satan takes the *total* resources of the *total* person against an enemy who will bring his *total* evil plans against us. There is not one inclusive method Christians can use to defeat the devil, such as quoting the Bible. Although quoting the Bible is imperative, it is not the only weapon needed in spiritual warfare. We must take truth with us not only in the spoken word, but we must also be clothed with truth as an attitude. We must not only have faith, but we must also know that God wants to help us and will defend us as certainly as we know that Satan is our enemy. Defeating Satan takes total preparation of our bodies, our inward lives and our relationships to God.

• *Use good judgment and wisdom.* When Esther stood before the king and he held out his scepter to her, she did not rush into his presence and blurt out a request. Nor did she fall at the king's feet and beg for protection. Every request to a king must be rightly framed. It must be preceded by proper preparation to build anticipation. So Esther prepared with wisdom and logic. She invited Haman and the king to a banquet she prepared (see Esther 5:5).

Before the banquet, circumstances occurred that turned the heart of the king toward Esther. He could not sleep that evening, so he had the royal diary brought in. The diary revealed the story of how Mordecai had discovered a plot against the king's life—in essence saving the king. The next morning, the king asked Haman how he could honor a person who had done a great service for him. Haman, thinking the king wanted to honor him, thought of the most elaborate honor of all—that the person be allowed to ride throughout the city on the king's horse wearing a royal robe. Then the king told Haman to honor Mordecai in just that way. Haman wound up leading his enemy on a horse throughout the kingdom.

Finally, at Esther's banquet, she named Haman as the man who had issued the decree that she and her people should be annihilated. The king was aghast, and as though to control his wrath he stormed from the room. Meanwhile, Haman fell across the couch where Esther sat, begging for mercy. Just then the king returned and mistakenly thought Haman was trying to assault the queen. Immediately he issued orders to hang Haman on the very gallows he had prepared for Mordecai (see Esther 7).

In the original Esther Fast, God had prepared the heart of the king to do the righteous thing in protecting the Jews. But by fasting, Esther had also gained the good judgment to devise a plan that resulted in the death of the wicked Haman.

Step 9: Pray for Spiritual Protection

God has angels who are spirits to help and protect us. "Are they [angels] not all ministering spirits sent forth to minister for those who will inherit salvation?" (Heb. 1:14). God has not called us to pray *to* angelic spirits for protection; however, we can pray *to God* for protection and God will send His ministering angels. "The angel of the Lord encamps all around those who fear Him, and delivers them" (Ps. 34:7). "For He shall give His angels charge over you, to keep you in all your ways" (91:11).

When Daniel was cast into the hungry lions' den to be eaten alive, the king came and asked, "Has your God, whom you serve continually, been able to deliver you from the lions?" (Dan. 6:20). Daniel answered him, "My God sent His angel and shut the lions' mouths, so that they have not hurt me" (v. 22).

PRACTICAL PRINCIPLES TO REMEMBER

The greater the spiritual attack, the more often or the longer you should fast. The more severe the attack from Satan, the more intense should be your prayer and fasting. This means you will have to fast longer—perhaps a three-day fast—or you may have to fast one day on three different occasions. When faced with a severe problem, Jesus said, "This kind does not go out except by prayer and fasting" (Matt. 17:21).

The greater the spiritual attack on you, the more people you must get to fast and pray for you. Just as the prayer of one person is effective, the prayer of more than one intensifies the results. Jesus said, "If two of you agree on earth concerning anything that they ask, it will be done for them by My Father in heaven" (18:19).

When you tell someone what you want God to do, your request becomes a statement of faith, and when you pray aloud, your prayers become a statement of faith. When you expect an answer, the anticipation is a statement of faith. These expressions of faith have the power to increase faith in others who agree together in your behalf.

The greater the spiritual attack, the more preparation you must make for your fast. Correlate the time and place of your fast and the study tools you will use with the intensity of the attack. Look at the preparation outline at the end of this chapter to make sure you bring all the needed materials to your Esther Fast.

The Esther Fast is also for the spiritual protection of your pastor or other church leaders. Satan knows that if he can destroy the credibility of church leadership, those following will lose their way. Therefore, there are intense attacks by Satan on leadership. The Esther Fast is not only for each Christian who feels a satanic attack or the need for protection in other situations, but it also has special application for spiritual leaders as protection from attacks upon them.

One of the best books for Christian leadership is *Prayer Shield* by C. Peter Wagner (Ventura, Calif.: Regal Books). Peter Wagner is my close friend, and I told him jokingly that this was not the best title for the book. He should have called it, "How a Pastor Can Get People to Be His Intercessors to Protect Him from the Evil One and Make His Ministry More Effective." This book provides an outstanding study during the Esther Fast, especially for spiritual leaders and pastors.

PREPARING FOR THE ESTHER FAST

Aim: The Esther Fast, for protection from the evil one.

Vow: Because I believe God loves me, and can protect me, and that only God controls the day of my death, I pledge to enlist His protection against all opposing forces. I also believe there is an evil one who would attack me and harm me (see 1 Pet. 5:8). Therefore, I vow to fast for God's protection for me and others, that I might serve Him and bring glory to Him (see Eph. 6:12).

Fast: What I will withhold_____

Beginning: Date and time I will start _____

End: Date and time I will stop_____

Decision: Specifically, I am fasting to_____

Bible Basis: "Is not this the fast that I have chosen...the glory of the Lord shall be your rear guard" (Isa. 58:6,8).

Resources Needed: _____

God being my strength, and grace being my basis, I commit myself to the above fast for God's glory.

Signed_____ Date_____

\\\\\

APPENDIX

⋑ I ⋐

FASTING: GIVING OUR BODIES A BREAK

BY REX RUSSELL, M.D.*

IF I PUT UP THE SWING SET AND DISCOVER THAT TOO MANY PIECES ARE left over, and that it's not balanced right, I might want to look at the directions!

My investigation into fasting as a means of healing of diseases began in just that way. When I observed the lives of several people who are near and dear to me, it was clear that they were out of balance.

Sue, a bright, cute nine-year-old, had severe dyslexia. Her loving and interested family had the means to take her to the best medical facilities in the country for evaluation. She was being tutored by a teacher who was an expert in learning problems.

At one point, Sue became ill with the flu and couldn't eat for several days. When the teacher returned, he found to his surprise that Sue could

---

*From *What the Bible Says About Healthy Living* by Rex Russell, M.D. (Ventura, Calif.:
     Regal Books, 1996). Used by permission.

read! He remarked to the parents, "I don't know what you are doing but please don't quit. She is reading above her expected reading level."

Does this mean that rest, fever and fasting will correct dyslexia?

When Sue resumed her normal diet, her reading problems returned. Later, when she experimented and ate only unfamiliar foods, her reading skills improved. Further testing revealed that she was sensitive to sugar, corn, white flour, margarine, honey and several other frequently eaten foods. As you might suspect, the foods she liked best were the most offending.

Another observation I made was in my immediate family. We had a son who was hyperactive. Several kinds of therapy were unsatisfactory. Another plan included a three-day fast prior to treatment. Having never considered fasting before, we were a little scared and apprehensive. Rather than a water fast, we let our son eat only foods he had never eaten before—plums, kiwis, fish, cashews, etc.

We were absolutely astounded by the third day to see him being very calm. We thought he was lethargic, but he was probably just acting normal. Many of his favorite foods stimulated him to extremes of activity and lack of concentration. Of course it was hard—almost impossible—to keep him eating certain foods instead of junk foods, so our troubles weren't completely over. Knowing that some help might be available somewhere, however, was hopeful. We decided to investigate further into what happens when the body is deprived of certain foods. *What is fasting, anyway?* we wondered.

WHAT IS A FAST?

According to Grolier's Encyclopedia, fasting is:

> The practice of abstaining from food, either completely or partially, for a specified period. It is an ancient practice found in most religions of the world. Traditionally, fasting has been a widely used form of asceticism, and a penitential practice observed for the purpose of purifying the person or atoning for sins and wrong-doing.
>
> Most religions designate certain days or seasons as times of fasting for their adherents, such as Lent, Yom Kippur and Ramadan. Certain events in the lives of individual persons

have been considered appropriate times for fasting, such as the day or night before a major personal commitment. The vigil of knighthood is a historical instance of this practice.

Prayer is supposed to accompany fasting. In this respect, fasting should be distinguished from abstinence.

HISTORY AND BACKGROUND

Hippocrates, the father of medicine, used fasting to combat disease 2,400 years ago. The ancient Ayurvedic healers of the Hindu religion prescribed fasting weekly for a healthy digestive system. Most nationalities, religions and languages have a tradition of fasting handed down from their ancestors.

Most secular historians speculate that fasting evolved from people living without food during troubled times. Eventually they learned to go without food *because* they were troubled. I think there is a better explanation.

The Chinese have fasted since their beginnings, which some scholars think was four generations after Noah's family. The earliest writings in the Chinese language are found on bones and pottery, dated 2000 B.C. These writings include stories of a seven-day Creation, the Fall of humans from their favored place in a garden, a great flood and many other accounts also recorded in Genesis. Similar flood stories are found in more than 200 ancient languages, including several native American accounts.

The fact that fasting is found in many languages would indicate that this practice occurred before the Tower of Babel. This story is history—the ruins of the tower can be seen in present-day Iraq. The people of Babel were the descendants of Noah. The practice of fasting may have been handed down through Noah's offspring. Did Noah, in turn, receive the tradition from the very week of Creation itself, when God "rested" on the seventh day? The Sabbath rest may have been designed for the digestive system as well as for a religious observance.

FOUR KINDS OF FASTING

1. The *normal fast* is going without food for a definite period. The duration can be one day, as in Judges 20:26, *NIV:*

Then the Israelites, all the people, went up to Bethel, and there they sat weeping before the Lord. They fasted that day until evening and presented burnt offerings and fellowship offerings to the Lord.

Biblical fasts were also held for 3 days, 1 week, 1 month and as long as 40 days. Extreme care should be taken with longer fasts, and medical advice from one's physician is necessary.

2. The *absolute fast* is going without food or water, and should be short. Moses' 40-day fast would kill anyone without supernatural intervention. Be sure to test the spirit that tries to talk you into a 40-day fast without water, because normally it is a physical impossibility.

3. The *partial fast* includes omitting one meal a day, or omitting certain foods for a certain period. Eating only fresh vegetables for several days is a good partial fast. John Wesley ate only bread (whole grain) and water for many days. Elijah fasted (partially) twice. John the Baptist and Daniel with his three friends are other examples of partial fasts. People who have hypoglycemia or other diseases could use this kind of fast.

4. A *rotational fast* involves avoiding certain foods periodically. For example, food families such as grains are eaten only every fourth day. Three days of fasting without grains of any kind may be followed by one day in which grains are eaten. The various food families are rotated so that some food is available each day.

BENEFITS OF FASTING

From the very beginning, before the Fall of man, our bodies were probably designed to take periodic rests from food. The seventh day was designed for rest; and the digestive system needs rest just as much as the rest of the body.

Healing and Rest

One of the main benefits of a night's sleep includes rest for our digestive system. It is no accident that in English the first meal of the day is named break-fast. A 12- to 14-hour fast can also be beneficial for the system. One school of thought once taught that there are many health benefits gained by skipping the traditional breakfast and waiting until noon or later to eat. (Many like to do this now, but receive criticism from Mom, medicine and man. Are you too afraid of them to miss a meal?)

We know that foods (nutrients) are necessary for health. Because of this line of thought, it was once very hard for me to recommend fasting. My logic was that if eating is healthy, not eating was harmful. I now realize that this logic was faulty. You fast, whether you call it that or not, when you don't eat from 9:00 P.M. until 6:00 A.M. Extending this fast for a reasonable time won't harm you either.

Your body was designed to respond to sickness in a certain way. Fever, fasting and rest are part of the design. Do you remember the last time you were sick? Did you want to eat? Did you want to party? No! You had a temperature, could not keep any food down, and only wanted to crawl into your bed and be left alone.

Why do we work so hard to lower our temperatures? Fever causes us to ache, and to want to lie down. We fight going to bed because we are motivated by several excuses. "Strong people don't quit!" and "They can't work without me!" (Of course fever as high as 106 degrees can cause death or brain damage, and should be treated quickly. Body temperature should be kept under 104 degrees.) Rest, fever and fasting seem to be part of the design to shorten viral infections.

Have you heard that you can "sweat off a cold"? It sounds bizarre, but if the work causes your body to warm up, it might help. Researchers have also discovered that many harmful viruses do not multiply at temperatures much over 100 degrees. Fever is also reported to increase the mobility of the white blood cells, which destroy bacteria and viruses. Researchers are now heating the blood of AIDS patients to reduce viral counts, hoping to gain remissions.

The body is designed to heal itself at the cellular level. The biochemical mechanisms of the cell are billions of times more complex than the precise mechanisms that cause the universe to function. These processes utilize proteins, carbohydrates and fats to gain calories and nutrients for untold other reactions. Each reaction also produces waste products. The cells have ways to clear this waste, but apparently they can become overloaded. Fasting helps unclog the system, and also eliminates poison from it. The cell uses periods of rest to process and eliminate waste or other toxins. Modern research, ancient healers and more importantly the Word of the body's Designer, God, indicate that one benefit of fasting is healing.

In Isaiah 58, God took Israel to task for abusing the fast. He said that if they really fasted according to His will, "Then your light will break forth like the dawn, and your healing will quickly appear" (v. 8, *NIV*).

Many years ago, Dr. Isaac Jennings learned to prescribe rest, fasting and fresh pure water as a treatment for fever—instead of the blood-letting, heat and water-deprivation that were conventional medicine's practices at the time.[1]

Dr. Jennings developed a reputation for reversing many chronic illnesses. He prescribed various colored pills, powders and water, while withholding food for various periods of time (partial fasting). His success was so phenomenal that Yale University conferred an honorary degree upon him.

When Dr. Jennings revealed that his pills and powders were small, stained fragments of bread, his acclaim dwindled. He had discovered the placebo effect. But had he also rediscovered the far-encompassing benefits of fasting?

Fasting and Cancer Research

Research by Dr. George Thampy, a biochemist at the University of Indiana, on 60 healthy subjects who participated in a three-week fast revealed interesting results: (1) significant lowering of cholesterol; (2) lowering of blood pressure; (3) relief from arthritis; (4) loss of body mass and weight (as much as 40 pounds during the three-week fast).[2]

Those subjects who broke the fast and maintained a Genesis 1:29 (vegetarian) diet did not regain much weight even one month after breaking the fast. Those subjects who abruptly switched to a normal diet regained significant weight (as much as 15 pounds) during the first week of refeeding.

Currently Thampy is "chasing" a certain factor that is known to kill tumor cells. This factor is absent in tumor patients, and may be elevated in fasting subjects.

Fasting has also been shown to be an effective treatment for rheumatoid arthritis, and can reduce joint pains, swelling and morning stiffness in just a few days. In one experiment, 27 rheumatoid arthritis patients stayed on a Genesis 1:29 diet—basically a vegetarian diet—and showed remarkable improvement. Another group of patients in the same test did not stick to the partial fast, and suffered relapses.[3]

Fasting and Mental Health

Some mental benefits of fasting include a calming affect, the ability to focus on priorities and a generalized improvement in mental functioning.

Don't expect mental miracles on your first fast. Addiction and withdrawal symptoms (irritability, anger, etc.) could override any first-time benefits. However, examples of fasting's positive effect on the mind are even more striking.

A Kansas couple I talked with, both of whom were physicians, had an autistic son. They discovered fasting when the boy was 12 years old. After a three-day fast, the son began to respond to them for the first time in his life. Through testing it was learned that he had an enzyme deficiency that made him sensitive to certain foods. After a general fast of a few days, a rotational fast was used to keep from overwhelming the son's enzyme system. At age 18 the boy was reading and showing great improvement, according to his parents.

The symptoms of many other mental illnesses such as hyperactivity, dyslexia, incorrigible delinquency, schizophrenia and depression apparently have cleared temporarily during short fasts. These syndromes are usually blamed on early childhood/parental relationships. What if they are more closely related to diet?

The psychoanalysts who followed Sigmund Freud's theory for years did so with almost cultlike devotion. He is still revered as the father of psychiatry. Freud's guilt-producing theory on the subconscious id, ego and super-ego was primarily accepted because academia was using a new definition for science that excluded the supernatural. A cocaine user himself, Freud formulated his theory and gained his fame by treating patients with cocaine. They reported wonderful results! He produced a bizarre theory! ("There is a way that seems right to a man, but in the end it leads to death" [Prov. 14:12, *NIV*].)

Actually, in the strictest definition, Freud's methods became a religion. But since his day, most of these psychological diseases have been shown to have organic causes. Some of the symptoms of these mental illnesses have reportedly disappeared after kidney dialysis, which filters toxic products from the blood. These products rebuild rapidly, and within a few hours the symptoms may return.

Could the toxins come from incompletely metabolized foods, or accumulation of waste products? Can chemicals or drugs cause bizarre symptoms? Sure!

The mind is a precious thing. Fasting can give the body time to clear itself of toxic products. Eating things designed for food in their purest form could be great for the mind, just as it has been shown to maintain our joints, our weight and our immune system.

Dr. Yuri Nikolayave, a psychiatrist at the University of Moscow, treated schizophrenics with water fasts for 25 to 30 days. This was followed by eating foods in their purest forms for 30 days. Seventy percent of his patients remained free from symptoms for the duration of the six-year study.[4] In patients who have these advanced illnesses, profound biochemical changes do occur during the fast.

Allan Cott, an M.D. at New York University, has used this fasting treatment on 28 schizophrenic patients. He reported a 60 percent recovery rate from this dreaded disease.[5]

For many similar cases, read *Brain Allergies* by neuropsychiatrist William Philpott. He treated food reactions by withdrawal of the offending foods for three months. Then he rotated meals by food families every four days. Dr. Philpott uses this treatment for all kinds of physical and psychological problems, including arthritis, with surprising success.[6]

The rotation diet is complex and difficult, even for highly motivated patients. It appears to me that a yoke of bondage to foods and chemicals is more easily broken by frequent periods of abstinence (fasting). A three-month withdrawal of the offending food is the equivalent of a fast from that food.

Pediatricians, cardiologists, internists and many other specialists use this form of unconventional treatment for many ailments with interesting results. Supervision is a necessity.

FOOD ADDICTIONS

It is possible to make an item of food your god by becoming addicted to it. Anything that becomes an addiction displaces God from His rightful throne in our lives. "Jeshurun (Israel) grew fat and kicked; filled with food, he became heavy and sleek. He abandoned the God who made him" (Deut. 32:15).

In his classic devotional work, *My Utmost for His Highest*, Oswald Chambers wrote: "Make it a habit to have no habits." He emphasized that Christ is your Lord, which means "boss." If you are Christ's slave, then even good habits may keep you from serving Him. Eating is a necessary habit that some have elevated to the realm of worship. Don't let any chemical, food or drink become your god.

On the same principle, don't become addicted to *fasting* either. Don't be deceived into believing you should not eat healthfully. You need many nutrients at frequent intervals. Occasional fasting is the exception to the rule of eating.

Our society is addicted to alcohol, sports, food, drugs, education, wealth, power, work, relationships, nicotine, gambling, shopping, etc. According to some researchers, more than 10 million people in the United States alone are negatively affected by the use of some toxic substance.[7] According to *The Kellogg Report:*

> As peculiarly contemporary illnesses, they are caused by affluent overloads of once rare substances, from nicotine to sugar to cocaine, that now flood our society.[8]

Many things to which we are addicted are good in themselves. Food, sex, money, work, etc., are all wonderful blessings if used under the guidelines for their design. In my experience, these guidelines are best found in Scripture. Diet, however, is usually affected negatively by addictions. We have only to note the harmful effects of alcohol, eating disorders, drugs and smoking. Because these addictions cause us to eat improperly, the solution involves proper food and proper intake, as well as proper emotions. Both eating and emotions are affected positively by proper fasting.

Other addictions that affect us negatively include sugar, fat and caffeine. These substances not only cause us to neglect essential nutrients, but they also make the body lose its ability to digest, absorb and utilize the nutrients it needs. If addictions were broken or prevented by fasting, nutrients designed for our cells could be digested, absorbed and utilized. When fasting is combined with eating the things created for food, "then your healing will appear."

Prevention of health problems is much easier than recovery. In general, fasting will prevent addiction to foods.

Humans have imperfect enzyme systems (remember that the Fall of man placed limitations on the body: "Cursed are you" [Gen. 3:14, *NIV*]). Each person's "fallen" enzyme system is unique. This is why one person may be sensitive to milk and the next person can consume large amounts without any problems. One person could spend a lifetime trying to evaluate how each particular food affects his or her body.

Regular intervals of fasting appear to be a better way of protecting ourselves from a deficient or an imperfect enzyme system. Fasting prevents low levels of enzymes from being overwhelmed by gluttony or overconsumption. Perhaps fasting is a way to counter this aspect of the Fall—a way designed from the beginning when our Creator created a day for rest.

It is said that the brain wants the very substance that is doing it the most harm. In truth, we cannot even trust our own brain to want what is best for us. That is another reason we need food standards like those found in Scripture. The brain tells us it wants more sugar, fat and other luxuries found in what is popularly called "fast food." The brain likes this food, but if too much is consumed, the body begins to rebel with sickness and/or poor health, and if the cycle is constantly repeated, gluttony and addiction begin to form. Proverbs 23 warns:

> When you sit to dine with a ruler, note well what is before you, and put a knife to your throat if you are given to gluttony. Do not crave his delicacies, for that food is deceptive (vv. 1-3, *NIV*).

Dr. Joseph Beasley compares the behavior of addicted persons to a burning building:

> Every cell of [the body] is gradually being consumed and destroyed by the effects of their addiction or compulsion. Without a recovered body, neither the mind nor the spirit can reach its full potential.[9]

Dr. Richard Weindruch of the University of California in Los Angeles reported that mice that fasted frequently lived longer and with significantly less disease than mice that were allowed to eat anytime they wanted.[10]

An addiction to foods such as sugar, salt, fat or caffeine will not be cleared by a 24-hour period of abstinence. Often food addictions require from three weeks' to three months' abstinence from the offending food to clear the system. Frequent short periods of abstinence may help eventually to clear bondage to food.

What to Expect, How to Start

Three days before you start your fast, eat only things God created for food, and in the purest, most natural form possible—before basic nutrients have been processed out. Drinking pure water during a fast is wise.

On the first day of a fast, I recommend drinking only water and juice, with no sweeteners. This helps counteract hypoglycemic symptoms many people experience during their first fast. The number of symptoms and their severity may depend on the food addictions you have accumulated. Most symptoms will be mild, consisting of a headache, weakness or irritability. Other symptoms may include bad breath, frequent urination, sleeplessness or a sensation of coolness.

If you feel sick, eat. You do not get extra "macho" points by making yourself suffer. Then try to fast again in a few days, trying to extend the duration of your fast a little longer.

Try stretching the hours by eating lunch, then skipping supper. You will be sleeping during the toughest time of the fast. Then you can "break fast" with praise for the food God has designed for you. Before long you will be able to go for 24 hours with water or juice only. You will feel great throughout most of your fast! Fasting like this once or even twice a week may be a great benefit for you. Later you can extend the fast to three days every month or two. Study books about fasting. Let God direct you for longer fasts. You will not be the first to complete a long fast.

For partial fasts, you may want Day 1 to consist of juices, raw fruits and vegetables, and soups.

On Day 2, you could add whole-grain breads, nuts and cooked vegetables and legumes.

Take note of any symptoms that develop as you gradually replace your fast with food. If you develop symptoms after adding one or another food, try avoiding it for several months.

After fasting, make meats only an occasional or celebrative food.

Most people who rely heavily on fasting for health purposes recommend an occasional weekend fast or even a weeklong fast. I can assure you that if you're healthy, this kind of fasting won't be harmful to you. Many examples in human history show people completing fasts of up to 40 days without harming themselves. As well, many have recovered from a variety of maladies during times of fasting.

Supplementing your fast with freshly squeezed juices and broths may be helpful. Even a partial fast with vegetables may reduce symptoms. Seek medical or nutritional advice for your specific problems.

Fasting is not a competitive sport. You do not have to set any records. Your body does not get healthier if you out-fast your friend or opponent. Don't sulk if your spouse "out-fasts" you. God does not give you more pleasure or a special crown for suffering more than anyone else. There is no scorecard!

Protesters in Ireland who have refused food showed no ill effects until genuine hunger developed. When real hunger develops, the body is beginning to deteriorate and food is needed. Some Irish protesters who were very healthy after 50 days of partial fasting died within 2 weeks after the onset of real hunger.

Avoid all chemicals possible during a fast. Distilled or pure water and freshly squeezed juice are preferred. Remember also Jesus' counsel:

> When you fast, do not look somber as the hypocrites do, for they disfigure their faces to show men they are fasting. I tell you the truth, they have received their reward in full. But when you fast, put oil on your head and wash your face (Matt. 6:16,17, *NIV*).

Jesus assumed we would pray, give alms, fast and forgive. His teachings assumed that all believers practiced these disciplines. For Him to give instruction in these practices to the believers was like discussing breathing, sleeping or eating, which were all assumed to be a part of a normal person's life.

The rewards of observing a fast include spiritual, mental and physical benefits. I believe that fasting is a very valuable way to experience the divine design for total health.

Although the Bible and valid research indicate fasting is beneficial, it will still be hard to fast because of peer pressure and counsel from our families and medical advisors. Even weight loss programs teach us to eat every meal. If we need three meals a day, does that mean every day? Are three meals a day needed? Who said? Is that really healthy? (We often forget that three square meals can make us round!) Which is the healthier—fasting or never missing a meal?

Why do so many of us find fasting difficult?

THE ROOT OF OUR PROBLEM

Our major problem in fasting is the same as in other practices we know are good and wholesome, but we have difficulty doing. It is both a *time* problem and a *spiritual* problem. We are too busy—not only to fast, but to study God's Word, to engage in good works, to reflect on God's will for us, our community, church, family, nation, etc. We are too busy to use the tools for the redeemed that would allow us to flourish.

Think about this, however: fasting could give us at least three extra hours a day. Consider all the time we spend in food preparation, in eating—and in post-meal bloated drowsiness! Even more time is often spent in deciding where, what, when, why and how we are going to eat.

Is there any evidence in history that godly people were so preoccupied with eating? On the contrary, many heroes and heroines of the faith spent time fasting—people such as Moses, David, Nehemiah, Esther, Daniel, Elijah, Hannah, Jesus, Paul, John and his disciples, and Anna.

Furthermore, many leaders God has used throughout history have practiced fasting, including Luther, Calvin, Wesley and Knox. Reading about their lives and work makes it evident that fasting was vital both to their relationship with their Creator and to their leadership and influence.

Recently Dr. Bill Bright of Campus Crusade for Christ asked 300 Christian leaders to join him in Orlando, Florida, to fast and pray. Surprisingly, 600 people from various organizations came and fasted with him for three days! Books such as Dr. Bright's *The Coming Revival* (Nashville: New Life Publications, 1995) and Arthur Wallis's *God's Chosen Fast* (Fort Washington, Pa.: Christian Literature, 1993) document the movement of the Holy Spirit on people of our time when they practice the discipline of fasting.

Perhaps fasting will bring revival to our land. I would like to be a part of it—wouldn't you?

Notes

1. Albert Anderson, M.D., "Creation Health—Forgotten Medical Science" (self-published booklet), p. 2.

2. George Thampy, Ph.D., "The Effect of Fasting" (Abstract 2252), in a report from a conference about "Food Intake and Body Weight Regulations" received from the author [Dr. Russell] at the Fort Wayne Center for Medical Education, Indiana University, Fort Wayne, IN 46805-1499.

3. J. Kjeldsen-Kragh, M.D., "Controlled Trial of Fasting and One-year Vegetarian Diet in Rheumatic Arthritis," *Lancet* 338:8772, October 12, 1991, pp. 899-902.

4. Yuri Nikolayave and Allan Cott, "Continued Fasting Treatment of Schizophrenics in the U.S.S.R.," *Schizophrenia* 1:1969, p. 44.

5. Allan Cott, M.D., "Treating Schizophrenic Children," *Schizophrenia* 1:1967, p. 3.

6. William Philpott, M.D. *Brain Allergies* (New Canaan, Conn.: Keats Publishing Co., 1980), p. 28.

7. Karolyn Gazella, "Addictions: Breaking Free Is Possible," *Health Counselor*, 7:1, 1995, pp. 27-31.

8. Joseph Beasley, M.D. and J. M. A. Swift, *The Kellogg Report* (Bard College Center, N.Y.: Institute of Health Policy and Practice, 1989), p. 371.

9. Joseph Beasley, M.D., *Food for Recovery* (New York: Crown Trade Paperbooks, 1994), p. 5.

10. Richard Weindruch, M.D., "Dietary Restriction in Mice," *Science* 315:4538, pp. 1415-18.

FASTING
GLOSSARY

Abuses of Fasting

The discipline of fasting was abused in at least five ways in Scripture. (1) Some separated the formal practice from internal devotion to God and repentance from sin, which it was supposed to represent (see Isa. 58:5; Joel 2:13). (2) Fasting was sometimes practiced to cover other sinful motives and/or practices (see 1 Kings 21:9-13; Isa. 58:41). (3) Others fasted for economic rather than spiritual or ministry reasons (see Isa. 58:7). (4) Some Pharisees fasted for appearances rather than as a genuine act of worship to God (see Matt. 6:16). (5) Fasting, probably for ascetic reasons, was demanded by some false teachers in the Early Church (see 1 Tim. 4:3).

Breaking the Fast

You will want to break your fast biblically. If you have fasted biblically, meaning you have mourned and repented of your sins, then you will want to break the fast in the same spirit as you carried out your fast. I don't think you can go from a spirit of earnest prayer to levity and banqueting.

Some do not keep their fasting vows—the time of the fast or abstaining from the food/liquid that symbolized their vows. I believe this breaks the effectiveness of their vows, and that they must start again from the beginning. I do not believe they can take up where they have left off (i.e., if they make a three-day vow, and eat something after two days, they can't return and fast for one day).

The Yom Kippur fast of the Jews was from sundown to sundown. Because the stomach is empty after fasting, some have shocked the body at sundown or at another end of the fast by filling themselves with food, thinking they need to make up for food not eaten. The human body doesn't need that shock. Also, don't break the fast with rich food. Soup or a light sandwich are appropriate. One man told me after an extended fast that a bowl of bullion broth was "heavenly," and the best thing he ever put in his mouth.

The term "breakfast" comes from the biblical phrase "breaking the fast." The term occurs in the original language of John 21:12,15. "So when they had eaten breakfast [broken the fast], Jesus said to Simon Peter" (v. 15).

After Jesus arose from the dead, He told the woman at the tomb that he would meet the disciples at Galilee (see Matt. 28:10). Out of frustration, the disciples returned to their old occupation of fishing. Perhaps they had forgotten that Christ had called them to leave their nets and follow Him (see Mark 1:16). When Christ appeared to them, they were discouraged, backslidden and perhaps out of the will of God. He told them to cast their nets on the other side of the boat where they would catch fish. When they got to the shore, they found fish, bread and a fire. Jesus invited them to "Come, break your fast" (John 21:12, author's paraphrase). They ended their fast with Jesus Christ.

They were no longer spiritually blinded, but knew who Jesus was. "None of the disciples dared ask Him, 'Who are You?'—knowing that it was the Lord" (John 21:12). After this experience Jesus could commission the apostle Peter: "Feed My lambs" (v. 15).

When you break the fast, you should be in fellowship with Jesus Christ. You fasted and sought the presence of God in your life; now exit the fast with Him.

Break your fast with a "holy meal." This doesn't mean the Lord's Table, nor does it mean you have religious "things" to eat or religious "things" on the table (e.g., candles, etc.). When you break your fast, be sure to give thanks to God for the food you eat, and ask Him to give you physical strength through the food. You should eat your food with the same attitude as you had when you abstained from it. "Whether you eat or drink, or whatever you do, do all to the glory of God" (1 Cor. 10:31).

Breaking Your Fast and Christian Service

Jesus and the disciples ate breakfast on the shores of Galilee. When they finished, Jesus turned to Simon Peter and asked him three times, "Do you love Me more than these?" (John 21:15). The word "these" refers to the nets, boats and Peter's occupation as a fisherman. Jesus was asking Peter if his love for Him was greater than his love for making a living and getting food to eat. That is also the question of fasting.

In two questions in this conversation, the Lord used the "deep" word for love—*agapao*. In this question Jesus was asking Peter, "Do you love Me with all of your heart?" Peter was honest. Knowing he could not say that he loved the Lord that much, he used the shallow word—*phileo*—in response. In effect, he said, "I have affection for you, Lord."

The third time the Lord asked Peter the question, "Do you love Me?" He used the shallow word for love also, as though to ask, "Peter, do you *really* have affection for me?" Then Peter could only answer, "Yes." Because of Peter's honesty, the Lord was able to give him a command for Christian service: "Feed my sheep" (v. 17).

At the end of this night's fast, Peter was ready for Christian service. He was no longer a boasting servant. He had learned his limitations through defeat. Because of his repentance, the Lord commanded him to feed His sheep. The apostle who had denied His Lord three times was graciously reintroduced into Christian service.

After you have fasted, you must get up off your knees and go to work for Jesus Christ. It is one thing to withhold yourself from food; it is another thing to give yourself in dedicated service. Fasting should lead to soul winning, Sunday School teaching, sacrificial giving of your money or some other form of service to the Lord.

The proof of your fasting is measured by the energy of your service after you break your fast. Jesus said, "You shall be witnesses to Me" (Acts 1:8). As a result of fasting, we should be better witnesses so we can become better soul winners.

Breaking Your Fast with Celebration

The Jews understood both fasting and feasting, or celebration. Each year Israel observed the Day of Atonement. The trumpet sounded throughout the land on the tenth day of the seventh month. On this occasion, the high priest went into the holy of holies and made "atonement for himself, for his household, and for all the assembly of Israel" (Lev. 16:17). The emphasis on the Day of Atonement was upon the sins of the nation. As the high priest did his work of priestly intercession and atonement, the people joined in fasting (see 23:27-29).

"For any person who is not afflicted in soul on that same day shall be cut off from his people" (v. 29). This verse means that those who did not fast, confess their sins and repent of their evil would not enter into the forgiveness that was otherwise available on the Day of Atonement.

The Day of Atonement, as a solemn occasion, was properly symbolized by a fast, but it was always ended by a great celebration unto the Lord (see v. 32).

Breaking Your Fast with Praise
Hannah was a godly wife. She wanted to serve the Lord, but most of all she wanted a son. Each year she went to the house of God and prayed for a son. On one occasion she fasted and "did not eat" (1 Sam. 1:7). Hannah fasted and prayed for her request.

The high priest Eli saw her praying in the Temple. The Bible says, "Eli watched her mouth" (1 Sam. 1:12). Because of her intensity in prayer, Eli thought she was drunk and he rebuked her. She replied, "I am a woman of sorrowful spirit. I have drunk neither wine nor intoxicating drink, but have poured out my soul before the Lord" (v. 15). Obviously, Hannah cried to God and was of a solemn spirit because she wanted God to answer her prayers. She was under the burden of fasting.

After she had fasted and prayed, "[she] bore a son" (1 Sam. 1:20). Immediately after her son's birth, Hannah went to the house of God. Hannah's beautiful song of praise is recorded in 1 Samuel 2:1-10. She cried out, "My heart rejoices in the Lord" (v. 1), and "The Lord makes poor and makes rich; He brings low and lifts up" (v. 7). Hannah ended her fast with praise.

Broken Fast
(See Violated Fast.)

Corporate Fast
A fast conducted by a group of persons in concert with one another.

Group fasts may be a spontaneous response to a movement of the Spirit of God within the group, or an organized event within a church or group of churches often designed to encourage divine intervention in a matter of joint concern, such as national or international policy. For examples of corporate fasts in Scripture, see appendix 5.

Danger as a Motive for Fasting

Several biblical examples reveal people practicing the discipline of fasting when faced with actual or potential dangers. These include (1) Jehoshaphat, when threatened by the people of Moab and others (see 2 Chron. 20:3); (2) Jehoiachim, who proclaimed a fast as a sign of penitence to avoid God's punishment (see Jer. 36:9); (3) Ezra, as he prepared to travel to Jerusalem (see Ezra 8:21); (4) the Jews in Shushan, when threatened by Haman's plot (see Esther 4:3); and (5) Joel, when faced with a locust plague (see Joel 1:14; 2:15).

Daniel Fast (See Chapter 8)

Problem. When faced with a physical problem of health/healing, you limit your diet to basic necessities that strengthen the body to heal itself of sickness or to maintain good health.

Key Verse. "Please test your servants for ten days, and let them give us vegetables to eat and water to drink" (Dan. 1:12).

Prescription. (1) Begin your fast by defining the problem, then pray for a specific answer to the problem. (2) Fast as a spiritual commitment to God for His answer. (3) Your fast-commitment is an outer test that reflects an inner desire. (4) Fast and pray to understand the role of sin that keeps you from health/healing. (5) Your fast is a statement of faith to others. (6) The Daniel Fast is not done privately. (7) Know the potential of the food you eat during the Daniel Fast. (8) Yield all physical results to God.

Practical aspects. (1) The Daniel Fast will lead to spiritual insight. (2) It is longer than one day. (3). It is a partial fast, not a complete fast. (4) The Daniel Fast involves eating healthy food. (5). The Daniel Fast involves abstinence from "party" food.

Day of Atonement

The only prescribed fast in Scripture. This annual fast was established by divine revelation (see Lev. 16:29), whereas other fasts in the Jewish calendar (e.g., Purim) find their origins in historic tradition. On the Day of Atonement, rabbinic law required people to abstain from eating, drinking, bathing, anointing themselves, wearing sandals and conjugal intercourse. The Day of Atonement is described as "the Fast" in the New Testament, and may have been observed by the early Christians (see Acts 27:9).

Disciple's Fast (See Chapter 2)
Problem. A besetting sin, one that holds a person in bondage. Usually the person had repeatedly but unsuccessfully tried to break free of that sin.

Key Verse. "However, this kind does not go out except by prayer and fasting" (Matt. 17:21).

Prescription. (1) Renounce any control over your mind that is not from Christ, affirming your desire to be free. (2) Acknowledge that an external power is responsible for the bondage (see Matt. 17:18). (3) Forgive anyone you have blamed for the problem. (4) Submit your desire to God's desire for you. (5) Take responsibility for the way you may have contributed to your own bondage. (6) Disown all evil influences that tempt you to remain bound.

Discipline Fast
Fasting in response to a spiritual conviction from God that a fast should be undertaken even if there is no apparent goal.

Disputed Texts About Fasting
Four references to fasting included in the Textus Receptus are absent in the earliest manuscripts. These include Matthew 17:21; Mark 9:29; Acts 10:30 and 1 Corinthians 7:5. Those who believe the references to fasting are later additions usually claim they were added to support the increased emphasis on asceticism during the Middle Ages.

Elijah Fast
Problem. This fast is for those who want to break an emotional or mental thought pattern that may or may not be sin. A habit is a behavior pattern acquired by frequent repetition reflected in regular or increased performance.

Key Verse. "So he arose, and ate and drank; and he went in the strength of that food forty days and forty nights as far as Horeb, the mountain of God" (1 Kings 19:8).

Prescription. (1) Prepare physically for the Elijah Fast. (2) Recognize and face your limitations. (3) Revisit the place where God revealed Himself and gave spiritual victories. (4) Fast to hear and understand the Word of God. (5) Let the Word of God examine you to reveal your weakness. (6) Confess/agree with God about your weakness. (7) Look to God's Word for quiet inner meaning about your problem, not to external power for breaking the habit. (8) Lay out a set of positive actions. (9) See the positive through God's eyes. Don't focus on breaking bad habits, but on establishing good habits. (10) Envision the potential results in your life when you obey God.

Practical aspects. While Elijah fasted for 40 days he had supernatural assistance, and such a lengthy fast is not recommended in this dispensation. The lengthy time Elijah fasted suggests: (1) You may need to fast several times to break a habit. (2) The more intense a habit, the more intense your prayer. (3) The longer you've had the habit, the more fasting time you may need to break it.

Esther Fast

Problem. Use the Esther Fast when facing a threat from the evil one, or fast for ongoing security so you will be protected from satanic forces.

Key Verse. "Go, gather all the Jews...and fast for me; neither eat nor drink for three days, night or day. My maids and I will fast likewise" (Esther 4:16).

Prescription. (1) Recognize the source of danger and destruction (2) Realize you are under demonic siege. (3) Recognize whose authority protects you. (4) Fast and pray for protection. (5) Know the limitations of prayer and fasting. (6) Get power in corporate fasting and prayer. (7) Fast to overcome spiritual blindness. (8) Fasting must be done with common sense, not reckless abandonment of principles. (9) You need spiritual protection against evil spirits.

Practical aspects. (1) The greater the spiritual attack, the more often or the longer you must fast. (2) The greater your spiritual attack, the more people you must recruit to fast and pray for you. (3) The greater the spiritual attack on you, the more protection preparation you must make for the fast. (4) While you pray daily for protection from the evil one, you do not fast daily. (5) Fast and pray for spiritual protection of your spiritual leaders/pastor.

Ethics in Fasting

Only you and God can know whether you are sticking to your vow to fast, or whether you "sneak" a bit of candy or take a sip of water. Your integrity determines how you fast. Fasting is not just getting answers to prayer; it is also about how you do it. The same values you hold in your life will guide you in your fast decisions. Fasting is not only the right thing to do to get results, but also an exercise in your character growth and development.

Ask yourself some hard questions after you fast:

1. Did I do what I said I was going to do?
2. Did I do it the way I said I was going to do it?
3. Did I accomplish the purpose I wanted to accomplish?

Ezra Fast

Problem. Facing a problem in your physical life or a barrier to your Christian testimony. Ezra called all the Jews traveling through a dangerous wilderness to fast for protection from the journey.

Key Verse. "So we fasted and entreated our God for this, and He answered our prayer" (Ezra 8:23).

Prescription. (1) Recruit those involved to fast with you (see Ezra 8:21). (2) Share the problem (v. 21). (3) Fast seriously to God (v. 21). (4) Fast before attempting a solution (v. 15). (5) Fast on site with insight (v. 21). (6) Fast for step-by-step guidance (v. 21). (7) Take practical steps along with your fast to solve the problem (v. 24).

Fast (Required) (See Day of Atonement)

The only required fast was on the Day of Atonement when a lamb was offered for the sins of the nation of Israel. Note the procedure followed by the High Priest. "You must offer the bull as a sacrifice to ask forgiveness for your own sins and for the sins of your family" (Lev. 16:11, *CEV*). "You must next sacrifice the goat for the sins of the people" (v. 15, *CEV*). The "scapegoat" was next brought in. "You [the High Priest] will lay your hands on its head, while confessing every sin the people have committed" (v. 21, *CEV*).

The people became involved by fasting. "On the tenth day of the seventh month of each year, you must go without eating to show your sorrow for your sins" (v. 29, *CEV*). They fasted for self-examination and to demonstrate remorse. "On the tenth day of the seventh month there shall be a Day of Atonement. It shall be a holy convocation to you; you shall afflict your souls, and offer an offering made by fire to the Lord" (23:27).

Paul and his companions may have observed the Day of Atonement fast on his journey to Rome (see Acts 27:9).

Jesus supported fasting when He taught people how to fast: "When you fast" (Matt. 6:17). He did not command fasting. Fasting is described as a discipline to help believers in their prayer ministries: "Fast...to your Father who is in the secret place; and your Father who sees in secret will reward you openly" (Matt. 6:17,18).

When John the Baptist's disciples asked, "Why do we and the Pharisees fast often, but Your disciples do not fast?" (Matt. 9:14), Jesus said they have Me (deity) and don't need to fast. He added that "the days will come when the bridegroom will be taken away from them, and then they will fast" (v. 15).

Fasting is not required, nor is it a "church ordinance" that should or must be followed. It is a discipline that strengthens believers and a tool that provides answers to prayer, when correctly implemented.

Fast (Root Meaning)
The noun "fast, a fasting" is *tsom* in Hebrew, and *nesteia* in Greek. It means voluntary abstinence from food. The Hebrew word is a compound of the negative *ne* attached to the verb *esthio*, "to eat," hence "not to eat." The Greek adjective *asitos* is also a compound of the alpha-negative *a* attached to the noun *sitos* "corn" or "food."

First Mention of Fasting in Scripture
The first mention of the discipline of fasting in Scripture is the 40-day fast of Moses when he met with God on Mount Sinai and received directions about the building of the Tabernacle and the tablets of stone inscribed with the Ten Commandments (see Exod. 34:28; Deut. 9:9). This was followed by a second 40-day fast, during which time the tablets of stone were replaced (see Deut. 9:18).

History of Fasting
Old Testament historical development. The verb "fasting" comes from the Hebrew term *tsum*, which refers to the practice of self-denial. Most scholars believe the practice of fasting began with the loss of appetite during times of great distress and duress. At such times, abstinence from food was necessary. Hannah was greatly distressed about her barrenness and "wept and did not eat" (1 Sam. 1:7). Also, when King Ahab failed in his

attempt to purchase Naboth's vineyard, he "would eat no food" (1 Kings 21:4). Therefore, fasting began as a natural expression of grief.

After a time it became customary to reflect or prove one's grief to others by abstaining from food and/or showing sorrow. David used fasting to demonstrate his grief at Abner's death (see 2 Sam. 3:25). Many references in Scripture describe fasting as "afflicting" one's soul or body. Fasting came to be practiced externally as a means of demonstrating and later encouraging an internal feeling of remorse for sin.

Because fasting was a perfectly natural expression of human grief, it became a religious custom to placate the anger of God. People began fasting to turn away God's anger from destroying them. Eventually, fasting became a basis for making one's petition effective to God. David defended his fast before his child died, but promptly ended his fast when the child died. He indicated that while the child was alive, he hoped his prayer might be answered. But after the child's death, he knew his prayer and fasting would not produce the desired result (see 1 Kings 21:27).

When fasting became a national mode of seeking divine favor and protection, it was to circumvent God's wrath against a nation or His removal of blessing from a nation. It was only natural, therefore, that a group of people should associate themselves in confession, fasting, sorrow for sin and intercession to God.

Fasting in the New Testament. In the New Testament, fasting (Greek *nesteia*) was a widely practiced discipline, especially among the Pharisees and the disciples of John the Baptist. Jesus began His public ministry with an extended fast of 40 days. When the apostles were criticized by both the Pharisees and the disciples of John the Baptist for not fasting, Jesus defended their actions by implying they would fast later, but not during His ministry among them.

Jesus gave His disciples no specific guidelines concerning the frequency of fasting. He taught that their fasting should differ from that of the Pharisees. They should fast to God rather than to impress others with their supposed spirituality. Later, fasting was practiced in the Early Church, especially when ordaining elders and/or designating people for special ministry projects (see Acts 13:2). Fasting was apparently practiced by Paul and other Christian leaders fairly regularly.

Fasting in Early Church history. Epiphanius, the Bishop of Salamis born in A.D. 315, asked, "Who does not know that the fast of the fourth and sixth days of the week are observed by the Christians throughout the world?" Early in the history of the Church, Christians began fasting twice weekly, choosing Wednesdays and Fridays to prevent confusion with the Pharisees, who fasted Tuesdays and Thursdays.

The practice of fasting for several days before Easter to prepare oneself spiritually for the celebration of Christ's resurrection was also commonly practiced. Later, this fast took the form of a series of 1-day fasts each week for several weeks prior to Easter. Remnants of these Early Church fasts are seen in the Catholic traditions of substituting fish in meals on Fridays and the observation of Lent during the 40-day period prior to Easter. It was also customary for Christians in the postapostolic period of church history to fast in preparation for their baptisms.

Fasting in revival movements. The discipline of fasting has long been associated with reform and revivalistic movements in Christianity. The founders of the monastic movement practiced fasting as a regular discipline in their spiritual lives. Although later monasticism grew to practice fasting and other forms of asceticism in a vain attempt to achieve salvation, it is probable that the earliest monks fasted in their desire for revival and reform in the Church.

Each of the reformers also practiced fasting, as did the leaders of the Evangelical Revival. Jonathan Edwards fasted for 22 hours prior to preaching his famous sermon, "Sinners in the Hands of an Angry God." During the Laymen's Prayer Revival of 1859, Christians fasted during their lunch hours to attend prayer meetings in churches near their places of employment.

In the worldwide awakening in 1905, prayer was often accompanied by fasting as people sought the Lord for spiritual blessing. Billy Graham reports fasting and praying during his voyage to England to conduct his first British crusades. The response in his meetings at that time has been described by some observers as "revival in our time." Many revival movements have advocated a return to the early Christian practice of fasting two days each week.

Fasting for divine intervention. Periodically, political leaders have declared a national day of prayer and fasting for divine intervention in crisis situations. In 1588, Drake's victory over the Spanish Armada was widely recognized as an act of divine intervention by English contemporaries. The Pilgrims fasted the day before disembarking from the Mayflower in 1620 as they prepared to establish a mission colony to reach the native people of North America.

It was common for political leaders in many New England villages to call for a fast when they faced a crisis. Friday, February 6, 1756, was designated a day of solemn fasting and prayer in England as it faced the threat of being conquered by Napoleon. Abraham Lincoln also called for a national day of prayer and fasting during the Civil War. On both occasions, military victories by England and the Northern States respectively were viewed as divine interventions by contemporaries.

Such days of prayer and fasting have been proclaimed by political leaders as recently as World War II. In the midst of the Battle of Britain, George VI designated Sunday, September 8, 1940, as a day of prayer and fasting. In a radio broadcast made days after this day of prayer, British Prime Minister Winston Churchill compared Britain's state with the earlier threats of the Spanish Armada and Napoleon to the island nation. In his memoirs, Churchill identified September 15 (the Sunday following the day of prayer) as "the crux of the Battle of Britain." After the war, it was learned that Hitler decided to postpone his planned invasion of Britain two days later (September 17). Similar calls for a day of prayer also accompanied the D-day invasion of Europe by the allies (June 6, 1944).

Individual Fast
A fast engaged in by a solitary person without the knowledge of others. Because of Jesus' teaching about fasting in the Sermon on the Mount, many Christian fasters feel most comfortable with this approach to fasting. For examples of individual fasts in Scripture, see appendix 5.

Isolation Fast
Fasting done in isolation, allowing the person fasting to concentrate more clearly and totally on God and spiritual matters. This is usually a fast toward a specific goal.

John the Baptist Fast
Problem. The John the Baptist Fast is for those faced with distress or trouble concerning their testimonies or influence. "And your righteousness shall go before you" (Isa. 58:8).

Key Verse. "For he will be great in the sight of the Lord, and shall drink neither wine nor strong drink" (Luke 1:15). "He...ate grasshoppers and wild honey" (Matt. 3:4, *CEV*).

Prescription. (1) Attach your special diet/fast to your desire for influence. (2) Write out the area in which you want a better testimony. (3) The John the Baptist Fast makes you a "person of the vow." (4) Recognize that you become influential by doing more than fasting. (5) The John the Baptist Fast is an event and a process. (6) Long-term vows (because of long-term problems) are reflected in long-term fasts/diets. (7) Short-term fasts are for immediate results. (8) Know the steps to a Christ-centered testimony before you fast.

Practical aspects. (1) Determine time limits for the short-term or long-term fast/diet. (2) Determine your diet's limits before you begin (3) Determine your testimony's objective before you begin. (4) Determine the sincerity of your vow-decision before you begin.

John Wesley Fast
The founder of Methodism often fasted for several days, eating only bread and drinking only water.

Lipid Fast
In 1996 the American Heart Association released diet guidelines for health and called it fasting. The Lipid Fast includes a total cholesterol of less 200. HDL cholesterol should be greater than 15. LDL cholesterol should be less than 150, or 100 in some patients. Triglycerides should be less than 250. The reduction, or fast, is to reduce the risk of developing coronary artery disease.

Liquid Fast
A fast evidenced by abstaining from solid food but allowing for liquids. Most fasters drink water during their fasts; however, some also drink fruit juices. A few would include coffee, tea and/or milk as acceptable beverages during a liquid fast.

Media Fast
A fast that involves abstaining from exposure to the media, especially television viewing. This may be a variation of the Disciple's Fast to break addiction and bondage, or the Elijah Fast to overcome habits.

Ministry Fast
Fasting focusing upon the initiation of a new ministry. This may be done privately or in concert with others.

National Fast
Fasting that is performed by the whole nation or a significant segment of that nation (e.g., Christians within a nation), usually at a time of perceived crisis on a national scale. In the Old Testament, national fasts were called during times of war (see Judg. 20:26; 2 Chron. 20:3); when facing widespread pestilence (see Joel 1:13); when the security of the Jews was threatened in the Persian Empire (see Esther 4:16); and when confronted by the threat of imminent divine judgment (see Jon. 3:5).

Partial Fast
A limited fast consisting of abstaining from certain foods for a prolonged period of time (e.g., abstaining from meats during Lent) or abstaining from all foods for a portion of the day (e.g., abstaining from eating before 3:00 P.M.).

Power Fast
Fasting to increase awareness of spiritual warfare and to release God's power to accomplish victory in power encounters.

Purpose of Fasting
Among the motives for fasting are (1) a desire to mortify personal lusts (see 1 Cor. 9:27); (2) express personal repentance (see Jon. 3:5-10); and (3) strengthen personal prayer (see Acts 10:30).

Results of Fasting
Results that may be realized through fasting include (1) increased spiritual authority, (2) receiving divine affirmation of ministry, (3) obtaining new direction for ministry, (4) gaining new insights during Bible study that become foundational truths for ministry, (5) an enhanced desire to pray, (6) affirmation through "sense of destiny" experiences, (7) new power for spiritual warfare, (8) guidance and liberty for workers in ministry, (9) victory over satanic strongholds, (10) assurance of divine protection, (11) an increased sense of God's presence, (12) a breaking of attitudes and policies hindering progress in a new ministry and (13) times when prayer becomes enhanced as a means of effectively wrestling with issues.

Rotation Fast
A rotation fast consists of eating food from only one food group at a time.

Some have called it the Mayo Clinic Diet because it is used in medical research to determine reaction to certain food groups. The rotation diet has two purposes: medical, to determine a person's allergy or "good addiction" and for cleansing the bodily system.

The medical rotation diet is also called the "diversified rotation diet" to help medical technicians successfully diagnose the food or chemically maladaptive allergic reactions. The obvious goal is to establish control of food intake identifying the causes of physical reactions and their associated addictions. By avoiding these foods or food families, a person may enjoy better health. This kind of rotation diet, and all its scientific restrictions, cannot be successfully done without professional guidance because of the need to monitor combinations of food, possible pesticides in commercial foods, cleansing of the system between food avoidance and so on. The diversified rotation diet is described in terms such as "food avoidance" and "food substance types."

The reason the rotation diet might benefit the average person is that it promotes cleansing. Some have suggested that a person follow this diet for six days, eating only from one food group each day for a week. While taking one food group each day, the other food groups are eliminated for approximately one week. The body's molecular system takes energy from ingested food and eliminates the toxins and poisons—including fats—from the cells. When too much of a certain kind of food and its accompanying toxins are ingested, the cells become overloaded in the limitation process.

The rotation diet helps cleanse the cells by allowing the toxins and poisons from each food group to be eliminated and cleansed during a six-day period. The six food groups—Food Family Pyramid: (1) Grains: cereal, pasta, bread, etc.; (2) Dairy products: milk, cheese, yogurt, etc.; (3) Poultry products: chicken, eggs, etc.; (4) Vegetables: leafy, root, etc.; (5) Meats: red meat, fish; (6) Fruits: nuts, juice, etc.

Saint Benedict Fast

The Saint Benedict Fast was written by Saint Benedict of Italy in the sixth century and was taken from *The Rule of the Master*. The community eats its meal (only one meal a day) at the sixth hour (midday on Thursdays and Sundays) and at the ninth hour (3:00 P.M.) the other days. In Lent, the meal is pushed back until after vespers, a time that also holds for the Wednesdays, Fridays and Saturdays two weeks preceding Lent.

The sick eat three hours earlier at the third hour (9:00 A.M.). Children less than twelve fast only in winter on Wednesdays, Fridays and Saturdays.

Brothers on a journey do not fast in the summer. In winter they fast till evening on Wednesdays, Fridays, and Saturdays.

In Paschal the community meal is eaten at noon.

Taken from *To Love Fasting* by Adalbert le Vogue. Petersham, Maine: Saint Bede's Publications.

Saint Paul Fast

Problem. A fast to solve problems or seek wisdom, usually about a major issue or life-turning direction.

Key Verse. "He was three days without sight, and neither ate nor drank" (Acts 9:9).

Prescription. (1) Set aside a time to fast and listen to the voice of Jesus. (2) Ask and answer self-searching questions. (3) Recognize the unchangeable solitude of truth. (4) Stop all self-effort and yield to God. (5) Pay attention to the physical. (6) Pay attention to the spiritual. (7) Obey what you learn from God. (8) Your answer may be an embryonic seed, not a full-grown tree. (9) God may use others to give you insight/wisdom. (10) People may not understand your Saint Paul's Fast or what God is doing in your life.

Practical aspect. (1) The more weighty your decision, the more often or longer you should follow the Saint Paul's Fast. (2) Plan Bible reading that is unrelated to your decision. (3) Gather all information and bring it to the Saint Paul's Fast. (4) Study and apply principles of decision making to the Saint Paul's Fast. (5) Write and rewrite the decision you need to make to clarify your thinking. (6) Write all facts influencing your decision and review them constantly during the fast. (7) Write out all possible solutions before attempting to make a decision. (8) Make a commitment to fulfill your decision.

Samuel Fast

Problem. Fasting to bring the presence of God to revive a lethargic people, providing renewal for believers and salvation for the unsaved. The Samuel Fast is for both "atmospheric revival," in which people feel the presence of God, and individual revival.

Key Verse. "So they gathered together at Mizpah, drew water and poured it out before the Lord. And there they fasted that day" (1 Sam. 7:6).

Prescription. *Pre-fast*—(1) Recognize your bondage. (2) Renew allegiance to God's presence among His people. (3) God's leaders must be in place. *During the fast*—(4) There must be a corporate gathering. (5) God's people must demonstrate sorrow for sin. (6) God's people must search out hidden sin and separate from it. (7) Corporate confession of sin. (8) Apply the power of the Word of God. (9) God blesses symbols. *Post-fast*—(10) Expect post-fast attacks. (11) Enact a continuous process of fasting, not just a one-time event. (12) Continue deeds that grow out of ongoing fasting. (13) Look for victory signs. (14) Victory is an ongoing process, not just a one-time event. (15) Celebrate with victory symbols.

Synonyms for Fasting

The Scriptures use several expressions to describe the practice of fasting. Two different Hebrew expressions are translated "not eat bread" (see 1 Sam. 28:20; 2 Sam. 12:17). The expression "afflict oneself" describes the fasting of Ahab when confronted with the imminent judgment of God (see 1 Kings 21:29). The most frequently used synonym for fasting is "to afflict one's soul" (see Lev. 16:29).

Spiritual Alertness

Our ability to perceive God's direction in this life is directly related to our ability to sense the inward promptings of the Holy Spirit. Spiritual alertness is God providing a specific activity to assist us in doing His will.

Telephone Fast

A fast that involves abstaining from the use of the telephone. See also Media Fast.

Testimony of a Fasting Schedule

When I have to make an important decision or when I have been asked to deliver an important message, I set aside a 24-hour period of fasting prior to the meeting or the time the decision needs to be made. The 24-hour fast is from evening to evening. The following are the items I include in my day of prayer and fasting.

Evening. Reading large sections of Scripture. I read or scan as many significant sections of Scripture as possible for general content and key ideas related to the subject of my needs.

Marking significant sections for future study. When I find particular sections that are significant to me, I make special notation for the purpose of studying them further the following morning.

Sleep.

Morning. My first job in the morning is to enjoy a time of personal edification from the Psalms and Proverbs. This usually puts me in tune with the Lord.

Studying significant sections. I reread the significant sections marked the previous evening and begin studying each one of them. This involves outlining the section, making special word studies, looking up cross-references and writing out practical applications.

Prayer. I spend a significant amount of time praying through my daily, weekly and monthly prayer lists. I cover all of these items on my day of fasting.

Intercession. The items for which I am fasting become the specific target of intercession. I remember those items each hour. I also remember that God created the evening as the beginning of the day. "The evening and the morning were the first day" (Gen. 1:5).

I realize that the important thoughts in the evening are the beginning of my fast. It is important to begin my fast with strength and to continue into the morning and afternoon hours. It is also important that I begin my fast by praying for the decision or meeting ahead of me. Then I continue to pray for that concern every hour throughout my fast.

Worship and fasting. The New Testament teaches that fasting can become an act of worship, i.e., "giving the worship to God that He deserves." One can include music, poetry, praise and fasting in worship as Anna "served God through prayers and fastings daily" (Luke 2:37). We are not told how she fasted daily to worship God. Also, the Early Church fasted in connection with worship. "They [the Church] ministered [from *leiturgeo*, giving us the word "liturgy"] to the Lord and fasted" (Acts 13:2).

Total Fast
A fast that involves abstaining from both food and water. Although Moses engaged in this kind of fast for 40 days, total fasts are now usually observed from 1 to 3 days.

Violated Fast
The violated fast happens when a person (1) does not keep the spiritual

vow to fast or (2) has broken the physical restraints of the fast (i.e., eating or drinking what he/she promised to abstain from). Sometimes the person absentmindedly eats or drinks. At other times the person intentionally eats or drinks, just as purposely as a person chooses to sin.

Obviously, breaking the fast is not the same as violating the fast, because every fast must reach a terminal point (see Breaking the Fast).

The Bible is silent about principles, illustrations or actions to take when a fast is violated. We must, therefore, draw principles from the general body of doctrine (our principles must be in harmony with and not violate biblical doctrine). Also, we can learn from parallel practices of vow breaking, such as principles of breaking the Nazirite vow.

1. *Nonjudgmental*. Because all sins have been forgiven at calvary (see Ps. 103:12), what you have done is covered by the grace of God.

2. *Nonbenefit*. If you eat or drink and break your vow, you will probably not receive the benefits for which you fasted and prayed. Note what God said of those who broke their Nazirite vows. A Nazirite could not touch a dead body, but, "If anyone dies very suddenly beside him, and he defiles his consecrated head, then he shall shave his head" (Num. 6:9). What benefit did he receive for the days he fasted? "The former days shall be lost, because his separation was defiled" (Num. 6:12)—meaning he received no benefit from his vow.

3. *Harm*. Because fasting is not required, a command was not violated when you ate or drank. However, you may have harmed your personal volition or self-esteem. By eating, you demonstrated a lack of self-discipline or the weakness of your resolve. You will probably want to return and remake your vow to the fast, keeping it this time so you can again build up your self-discipline. Although violating your fast was not a "sin" in itself, you may have weakened your faith. "Whatever is not from faith is sin" (Rom. 14:23).

Widow's Fast

Problem. A fast to provide for the needs of others, especially their humanitarian needs such as food and clothing.

Key Verse. "Is it not to share your bread with the hungry, and that you bring to your house the poor who are cast out; when you see the naked, that you cover him, and not hide yourself from your own flesh?" (Isa. 58:7).

Prescription. (1) Become others oriented by being sensitive to the problems of those you come in contact with or hear about. (2) Recognize how much better off you are than others. (3) Give to help meet the need from resources that would normally be consumed by yourself. (4) Ask for wisdom to determine the extent of your involvement in a specific humanitarian project. (5) Pray for the people for whom you are fasting during your fast. (6) Attempt to identify with the suffering of others during your fast. (7) Consider making significant lifestyle changes enabling you to continue contributing to the humanitarian needs of others.

Practical aspects. (1) Identify the specific humanitarian need and/or project in which you will become involved. (2) Estimate the value of the food you would normally consume in a typical day. (3) Send the money to meet the humanitarian need before you begin fasting. (4) Determine how long you should fast to save the amount you intend to give to this project. (5) Break your fast with a simple meal of basic foods. (6) Look for specific ways to reduce your personal cost of living, enabling you to contribute more to meeting the needs of others.

Working Fast
A fast conducted secretly while maintaining regular work habits. This is usually fasting toward a goal.

≋ 3 ≋

COMMENTS ABOUT FASTING BY CHRISTIAN LEADERS

FASTING HAS GONE ALMOST COMPLETELY OUT OF THE LIFE OF THE ORDI-nary person. Jesus condemned the wrong kind of fasting, but he never meant that fasting should be completely eliminated from life and living. We would do well to practice it in our own way and according to our own need.—*William Barclay*

In my personal life, fasting has been for specific purposes and for a long duration. After three days, there are no hunger pains or desire for food. From twelve to fourteen days later, there seems to be a sense of complete cleanliness and mental clarity. After twenty-one days, there seems to be an outpouring of spiritual power and creativity that is inde-scribable, but that continues until the fast is ended. It seems especially after the third week that one is no longer even remotely interested in the trivial physical world around. One's mind is filled exclusively with pro-found spiritual ideas and truths.

One of the most profound things is that the mind will concentrate for hours on the same subject without once wavering or being distracted. There is no question that there is awesome power in fasting. If the fast is controlled by the Holy Spirit and Jesus is foremost, then it is a beautiful and powerful experience.—*Arthur Blessitt*

Inasmuch as fasting is before God, a practical proof that the thing we ask is to us a matter of true and pressing interest, and inasmuch as in a high degree it strengthens the intensity and power of the prayer, and becomes the unceasing practical expression of a prayer without words, I could believe that it would not be without efficacy, especially as the Master's words had reference to a case like the present. I tried it, without telling any one, and in truth the later conflict was extraordinarily lightened by it. I could speak with much greater restfulness and decision. I did not require to be so long present with the sick one; and I felt that I could influence without being present.—*Blumhart*

It would not do to say that preachers study too much. Some of them do not study at all; others do not study enough. Numbers do not study the right way to show themselves workmen approved of God. But our great lack is not in head culture, but in heart culture; not in lack of knowledge, but lack of holiness is our sad and telling defect—not that we know too much, but that we do not meditate on God and His Word and watch and fast and pray enough.—*E. M. Bounds*

Feeling somewhat of the sweetness of communion with God and the constraining force of His love and how admirably it captivates the soul and makes all the desires and affections to center in God, I set apart this day for secret fasting and prayer to God, to direct and bless me with regard to the great work which I have in view of preaching the Gospel and to ask that the Lord would return to me and show me the light of His countenance. I had little life and power in the forenoon. Near the middle of the afternoon God enabled me to wrestle ardently in intercession for my absent friends, but just at night the Lord visited me marvelously in prayer. I think my soul was never in such agony before. I felt no restraint, for the treasures of divine grace were opened to me. I wrestled for absent friends, for the ingathering of souls, for multitudes of poor souls, and for many I thought were the children of God, personally in many places. I was in such agony from sun half an hour high till near dark that I was all over wet with sweat, but yet it seemed to me that I had done nothing; oh, my dear Saviour did sweat blood for poor souls! I longed for more compassion toward them. I felt still in a sweet frame, under a sense of divine love and grace, and went to bed in such a frame, with my heart set on God.—*David Brainerd*

There are indications that New Testament Christians were specially sensitive to the Spirit's communications during fasting.—*F. F. Bruce*

The reason why the Methodists in general do not live in this salvation is, there is too much sleep, too much meat and drink, too little fasting and self-denial, too much conversation with the world, too much preaching and hearing and too little self-examination and prayer.—*William Bramwell*

I am attempting to categorize and define aspects of fasting and praying as an experience leading to church growth. It may be that by exposing these ideas I will get others to learn experientially about fasting and praying and thus stimulate much more church growth. I would desire that....Fasting is a spiritual discipline. It is probably not for everyone. Yet it may be a key to "power theology" needed to break open new works.—*J. Robert Clinton*

I spent Friday in secret fasting, meditation, and prayer for help on the Lord's Day. About the middle of the sermon a man cried out; at the cry my soul ran over. I fell to prayer, nor could we preach any more for cries and tears all over the chapel. We continued in intercessions, and salvation came.—*Thomas Collins*

Fasting is rather widely practiced on our mission fields today. Like every other God-ordained religious practice, fasting can be misused or abused. This will be discussed in later paragraphs. But fasting is still God's chosen way to deepen and strengthen prayer. You will be the poorer spiritually and your prayer life will never be what God wants it to be until you practice the privilege of fasting.—*Wesley L. Duewel*

Who does not know that the fast of the fourth and sixth days of the week are observed by the Christians throughout the world?—*Epiphanius, Bishop of Salamis*

Revival must come to America. Because of this, I have called America to join me in a great fast...I believe that it is biblical for us to call a fast. This is an act of faith. When we call a fast, we challenge people to deprive themselves of one of life's necessities so that they may more effectively pray to God.—*Jerry Falwell*

I was also led into a state of great dissatisfaction with my own want of stability in faith and love....I often felt myself weak in the presence of temptation and needed frequently to hold days of fasting and prayer and to spend much time in overhauling my own religious life in order to retain that communion with God and that hold upon the Divine truth that would enable me efficiently to labor for the promotion of revivals of religion.—*Charles G. Finney*

In my research I have not found a single full-length book written on the subject of fasting from 1861 to 1954, a period of nearly 100 years. What would account such as an almost total disregard of a discipline so frequently mentioned in Scripture and so ardently practiced by Christians throughout the centuries? Two things, at least. First, there has been a reaction, and rightly so, to the excessive ascetic practices of the Middle Ages. Second, there has developed a prevailing philosophy that literally dominates American culture, including American religious culture, that it is a positive virtue to satisfy virtually every human passion....The first thing I learned about myself in experiences of fasting was my passion for good feelings. I was hungry and I did not feel good. All of a sudden I began to realize that I would do almost anything to feel good. Now there is not a thing wrong with feeling good, but that has got to brought to an easy place in our life where it does not control us.—*Richard J. Foster*

If one does fast, let the fasting be done in secret as unto the Father and not to appear before men.—*A. C. Gaebelein*

Our ability to perceive God's direction in life is directly related to our ability to sense the inner promptings of His Spirit. God provides a specific activity to assist us in doing this....Men through whom God has worked greatly have emphasized the significance of prayer with fasting....In an extended fast of over three days, one quickly experiences a great decrease in sensual desires and soon has a great new alertness to spiritual things.—*Bill Gothard*

Voluntary fasting, an age-old practice, has become a therapeutic tool in the control of intractable obesity. Fasting for ten to fourteen days, given access to water, is neither archaic nor barbaric. It is tolerated well by obese men and women, and is a revolutionary and promising approach to the management of obesity.—*Robert B. Greenblatt*

Fasting is not confined to abstinence from eating and drinking. Fasting really means voluntary abstinence for a time from various necessities of life such as food, drink, sleep, rest, association with people and so forth.

The purpose of such abstinence for a longer or shorter period of time is to loosen to some degree the ties which bind us to the world or material things and our surroundings as a whole, in order that we may concentrate all our spiritual powers upon the unseen and eternal things.

To strive in prayer means in the final analysis to take up the battle against all the inner and outward hindrances which would dissociate us from the spirit of prayer.

It is at this point that God has ordained fasting as a means of carrying on the struggle against the subtle and dangerous hindrances which confront us in prayer.—*O. Hallesby*

The Scriptures bid us fast, the Church says now.—*George Herbert*

Fastings and vigils without a special object in view are time run to waste. They are made to minister to a sort of self-gratification, instead of being turned to good account.—*David Livingstone*

As men and women are beginning to consider the days and times through which we are passing with a new seriousness, and as many are beginning to look for revival and reawakening, the question of fasting has become more and more important.—*D. Martyn Lloyd-Jones*

The New Testament often links prayer with fasting. Abstinence from food can be a valuable aid in spiritual exercises. From the human side, it promotes clarity, concentration and keenness. From the divine stand-point, it seems the Lord is especially willing to answer prayer when we put that prayer before our necessary food.—*William MacDonald*

Our temptation is certainly not to fast too much, but of never check-ing our indulgence of appetite in any degree or on any occasion. We would be much healthier and stronger if we sometimes reduced our meals and rested our organs of nutrition.—*F. B. Meyer*

If you say I will fast when God lays it on me, you never will. You are too cold and indifferent. Take the yoke upon you.—*Dwight L. Moody*

Learn from these men that the work which the Holy Ghost commands must call us to new fasting and prayer, to new separation from the spir-it and the pleasures of the world, to new consecration to God and to His fellowship. Those men gave themselves up to fasting and prayer, and if in all our ordinary Christian work there were more prayer there would be more blessing in our own inner life.—*Andrew Murray*

Every time I fasted I established a new spiritual dimension in my life and had new spiritual authority with people.—*George Pitt*

As a Boomer, I have been conditioned to enjoy the best the world has to offer. Fasting speaks boldly to consumerism, one of my generational core values. To set aside what I want to encourage personal spiritual growth is what it means to deny myself and take up my cross daily in the nineties. I suspect it would be difficult for me to rise to the challenge of discipleship and live a consistently Christian lifestyle without practicing the discipline of fasting.—*Douglas Porter*

Every Christian, I think, should occasionally fast and pray, waiting before God until he gets the victory that he needs....Many an experience could I tell of victories and blessings following prayer and fasting. But the one dearest to my heart occurred in 1921....I have seen more people saved in one service than that, but, oh, what a blessing that was to me as a young preacher just starting out! I know that real fasting and prayer and humiliation of mind as we wait on God will get the blessing God wants to give us!—*John R. Rice*

I would suggest that you fast one day a week. However, this would be altered by the burdens that come, the leadership of the Spirit, and the spiritual needs you may face. Many times one needs to go on a semi-fast or maybe a fruit fast or natural food fast for a week just to tone up his physical system and give his body a chance to clean house. If I were to feel a sore throat coming on, I may fast three or four days. If I have an affliction of some sort that comes unannounced, I will fast and pray and read my Bible until it's gone and have God's people, of course, to pray for me and pray with me.—*Lester Roloff*

One obvious value of fasting lies in the fact that its discipline helps us keep the body in its place. It is a practical acknowledgment of the supremacy of the spiritual. But in addition to this reflex value, fasting has direct benefits in relation to prayer as well. Many who practice it from right motives and in order to give themselves more unreservedly to prayer testify that the mind becomes unusually clear and vigorous. There are a noticeable spiritual quickening and increased power of concentration on the things of the spirit.—*J. Oswald Sanders*

After fasting for a number of years, God began to speak to my heart in regard to the power of soul winning. It seemed that the Lord was impressing me that I would never have the God-given anointing to reach the worst of sinners until I could fast for 40 days and read the Bible through at least once. This I did and since that day my life has never been the same. God helped us to win people to Christ that we had on our prayer list for 20 years or more.

I never enter a fast that is an extended fast of 14, 21, or 28 days without first knowing it is the will of God. The greatest Bible Conferences and revivals that I experience today occur when I do not eat one bite of food but just drink water from the time I get on the plane until I get back on the plane to return home.

Fasting will make a difference in winning souls to Christ.—*J. Harold Smith*

Properly speaking, fasting is not so much a duty enjoined by revelation as it is the natural expression of certain religious feelings and desires. There is but one special fast ordained in the Old Testament, and there is none at all ordained in the New. Yet one cannot fail to see that the exercise is, nevertheless, quite in accordance with the whole tenor of a true religious life in all ages; and that, if it is not expressly command-ed, it is only because nature itself teaches us in certain circumstances thus to afflict the soul.—*W. C. Smith*

We should fast when we are concerned for God's work. I believe the greatest thing a church could have is a staff, deacons, and leaders who fast and pray—not when the church burns down, but in order to get the church on fire. A lot of dead churches would catch fire if the people in places of leadership would set aside a period of time for fasting and prayer....Fasting brings about a supernatural work in our lives. God will not entrust supernatural power to those whose lives are not under total control....The Christian who would have the supernatural power of God must be under the total control of the Holy Spirit.—*Charles Stanley*

On the morning of our fast day, the Holy Spirit seemed so to fill sev-eral of us, that each felt (as we found in private conversation afterwards) that we could not bear any more and live.—*Mrs. Howard Taylor*

There are those who think that fasting belongs to the old dispensa-tion; but when we look at Acts 14:23 and Acts 13:2-3, we find that it was practiced by the earnest men of the apostolic day. If we would pray with power, we should pray with fasting. This, of course, does not mean that we should fast every time we pray; but there are times of emergency or special crisis in work or in our individual lives, when men of downright earnestness will withdraw themselves even from the gratification of natural appetites that would be perfectly proper under other circum-stances, that they may give themselves wholly to prayer. There is a peculiar power in such prayer. Every great crisis in life and work should be met that way. There is nothing pleasing to God in our giving up in a purely Pharisaic and legal way things which are pleasant, but there is power in that downright earnestness and determination to obtain in prayer the things of which we sorely feel our need, that leads us to put away everything, even things in themselves most right and necessary, that we may set our faces to find God, and obtain blessings from Him.— *R. A. Torrey*

Although there are many different kinds of fasts, the most common, and the one I recommend for starting, is to abstain from food, but not drink, for a given period of time. So far as drink is concerned, all agree that water is basic. Some add coffee or tea, some add fruit juices. All also agree that something like a milk shake goes too far, and is not in the spirit of fasting. Whatever, the fast involves an intentional practice of self-denial, and this spiritual discipline has been known through the centuries as a means for opening ourselves to God and drawing closer to Him....To the degree that fasting becomes more of a norm in our day-to-day Christian life as individuals and congregations, we will become more effective in spiritual warfare.—*C. Peter Wagner*

Fasting is important—more important, perhaps, than many of us have supposed, as I trust this book will reveal. For all that, it is not a major biblical doctrine, a foundation stone of the faith, or a panacea for every spiritual ill. Nevertheless, when exercised with a pure heart and a right motive, fasting may provide us with a key to unlock doors where other keys have failed; a window opening up new horizons in the unseen world; a spiritual weapon of God's providing, "mighty, to the pulling down of strongholds." May God use this book to awaken many of His people to all the spiritual possibilities latent in the fast that God has chosen.—*Arthur Wallis*

Fasting today is neither commanded nor forbidden, and is beneficial only if practiced under the guidance of the Holy Spirit.—*John F. Walvoord*

A pastor can call for a day of prayer and fasting in his church. Every time I have done this as a pastor we saw unusual results. We usually had it on a Wednesday and closed out with midweek prayer meeting. I would ask the people not to tell me whether or not they were fasting. We would have a special prayer meeting at the church around ten in the morning for those who could come. Some would stay through lunchtime. Sometimes we would break up at noon for the wives who had lunches to prepare or children coming home. An afternoon prayer meeting might be called to be closed out with the evening prayer meeting. Usually a fast would begin in the morning and go to the next morning. That's where the word "breakfast" comes from—it means to "break a fast." There have been times when I fasted only one or two meals in a day because of circumstances.—*C. Sumner Wemp*

First, let it be done unto the Lord, with our eye singly fixed on Him. Let our intention herein be this, and this alone, to glorify our Father which is in heaven; to express our sorrow and shame for our manifold transgressions of His holy law; to wait for an increase of purifying grace, drawing our affections to things above; to add seriousness and earnestness to our prayers; to avert the wrath of God; and to obtain all the great and precious promises which He hath made to us in Jesus Christ....Let us beware of fancying we *merit* anything of God by our fasting. We cannot be too often warned of this; inasmuch as a desire to "establish our own righteousness", to procure salvation of debt and not of grace, is so deeply rooted in all our hearts. Fasting is only a way which God hath ordained, wherein we wait for His unmerited mercy; and wherein, without any deserve of ourselves, He hath promised freely to give us His blessing.— *John Wesley*

It is not wrong to fast, if we do it in the right way and with the right motive. Jesus fasted (Matt. 4:3); so did the members of the early church (Acts 13:2). Fasting helps to discipline the appetites of the body (Luke 21:34) and keep our spiritual priorities straight. But fasting must never become an opportunity for temptation (1 Cor. 7:7). Simply to deprive ourselves of a natural benefit (such as food or sleep) is not *of itself* fasting. We must devote ourselves to God and worship Him. Unless there is the devotion of heart (see Zech. 7) there is no lasting benefit.—*Warren W. Wiersbe*

HOW TO KEEP A
FASTING JOURNAL

THROUGHOUT HISTORY, GREAT CHRISTIAN LEADERS HAVE KEPT PERSONAL journals to record observations about their Christian lives and ministries. These leaders used their journals to record God-given insights and expressions of their personal struggles. Their journals were rarely meant to be published; however, they have helped many Christians today work through similar struggles. The journals of David Brainerd, John Wesley and others are inspiring records of personal experiences with God that help people today in their own unique experiences with Him.

Recently, many Christians have begun the discipline of journaling as a tool for personal growth. At the beginning or conclusion of each day, they take time to record the events and lessons learned during the previous 24 hours. Over a period of several weeks or months, their daily entries provide a means of reviewing God's work in their lives. Often a spiritual journal records the progress of a particular goal or the application and benefit of a new discipline or biblical truth.

Some Christians are reluctant to keep journals because they do not perceive themselves as writers. They feel threatened by their poor spelling and grammar or undeveloped writing styles. Spiritual journals are personal; therefore, a great deal of liberty can be exercised in writing them.

Journals can serve as personal history books, recording even telephone calls and meetings. They can also serve as recorded expressions of daily prayer and personal feelings. Journals can become personal friends—enabling people to write as they would talk to good friends sharing today's events and tomorrow's anticipations.

The benefits of journaling are numerous. First, journaling helps to slow down and refocus fast-paced people. Second, it gives people opportunities to get in touch with and record their feelings. Third, it provides a means of recording important lessons God is daily teaching. Over time, journals may record the significant growth in people's lives that might otherwise go unnoticed and/or unmeasured. Also, journals provide records of God's answers to prayers and other good gifts received from the Father.

How to Start Writing During Your Fast

The most difficult step in any new discipline is often the first step. For many people, taking time to write a journal entry the first day is a hurdle that keeps them from using this tool in their Christian lives. If you do not presently keep a spiritual journal, decide to keep one during your fast. You may find that journaling is a beneficial discipline you want to maintain throughout the rest of your life. Also, by keeping a journal of your fast days as you work through *Fasting for Spiritual Breakthrough*, you will have an accurate record of your feelings as you develop the discipline of fasting, and a reference for the special insights you received from God during your fast.

As you begin journaling on your fast days, remember that you are writing for yourself. This gives you some liberty. You may wish to purchase a special notebook or diary to use as your journal. Or you may choose to write on separate sheets of paper and bind them together later. Your home computer can become your journal. Some people have used a cassette tape recorder as a personal journal, usually to be transcribed to paper later.

Begin by recording the date you start your fast. Then write about the lessons you have recently learned, the circumstances you have encountered, the feelings you have experienced and any other special concerns you may have. Some people find it easier to name their journals, and write to their journals as they might intimately converse with their closest friends.

Your journal should include a variety of entries. Some days your journal entry may represent a personal testimony. Other days it will include insights from that day's Scripture reading, a sermon you heard, an article you read or a Bible study you attended. Often your journaling will reflect your daily prayer requests, or praise to God for answered prayer.

Record the insights you receive from God during your fast. Before you begin writing, take time to consider things that happened on your fast day and the lessons you have learned. Some of these insights will be significant and obvious, and you will have little difficulty recognizing and recording them. At other times, God may use subtle means to reveal Himself to you and to share important lessons you need to learn.

Those involved in the ministry of writing quickly learn the importance of research in the writing process. Before an article or book is written, much time is spent by the writer studying the subject and learning the content that will eventually be part of the article or book. Journaling is also aided by prayer and meditation. If you have difficulty writing a journal entry, it may be because you have not invested enough time with God. During your fast, take extra time to read the Scriptures, pray and study. As you do this, you will gain insights you will want to record in your journal.

How to Maintain Your Journal After Your Fast

After your fast, take time to review your journal entries. As you recall the insights you gained during your fast, thank God for revealing Himself to you and giving you a tool for recording these insights. When you begin to experience the value of having a record of your spiritual experiences during a fast, the value of maintaining a daily spiritual journal all the time will soon become apparent.

How many of last month's insights from the Lord have you already forgotten? Fortunately, some of those insights may be marked in books or the margin of your Bible so they can be reviewed again and again. Unfortunately, some may be lost forever. Someone has said, "A short pencil is better than a long memory." By taking time each day to record your insights in your journal, you can preserve the important lessons

God is teaching you. Then your journal will provide a way for you to periodically review God's work in and through your life.

Many people recognize the value of journaling and begin with good intentions, but within a month or two they find they have abandoned this discipline. Keeping a spiritual journal can quickly become another duty for which there is limited time. In his leader's guide to the popular discipleship course *Experiencing God*, Claude King lists 10 questions designed to help people recognize God's work in their lives.[1] If you have difficulty finding things to record in your journal, you may wish to use this list to guide you as you write.

1. What has God revealed to you about Himself?
2. What has God revealed to you about His purposes?
3. What has God revealed to you about His ways?
4. What has God done in your life or through your life that has caused you to experience His presence?
5. What Scripture has God used to speak to you about Himself, His purposes or His ways?
6. What particular person or concern has God given you a burden to pray for? What has He guided you to pray for in this situation?
7. What has God done through circumstances that has given you a sense of His timing or direction concerning any aspect of His will?
8. What word of guidance or truth do you sense God has spoken to you through another believer?
9. What adjustment is God leading you to make in your life?
10. What acts of obedience have you accomplished this week? What further steps of obedience do you know God is wanting you to take?

Not everyone who keeps a journal makes daily entries. Your schedule may cause you to miss a day or two each week. Occasionally, you may find yourself making both morning and evening entries in your journal. Don't quit in frustration if you miss a day. Begin again the next day and keep writing. Just as you stumbled the first few times you began walking, so you may experience ups and downs as you develop the discipline of journaling.

A NINE-WEEK PLAN FOR JOURNALING

Make your study of *Fasting for Spiritual Breakthrough* more meaningful by maintaining a weekly spiritual journal of your personal fasts for the next nine weeks. Doctors generally agree that most people can fast one day a week without any negative side effects. Some argue that specific health benefits are associated with a weekly one-day fast. If you have a specific medical problem or are currently taking medication, consult with your family physician before fasting.

In this book you have been introduced to nine functions of fasting. For the next nine weeks, determine to fast one day each week, and to focus on one discipline of fasting in each fast. Follow the guidelines suggested in each chapter as you prepare for that particular fast. On your fast day, take time to review the chapter and read any significant Scriptures associated with that fast. During the nine-week period, you may want to commit to memory Isaiah 58, a key passage about fasting, or memorize other verses listed in appendix 5. Use your fast day to learn and reinforce the principles of that fast.

At the conclusion of your fast, take time to make a journal entry recording the experiences and insights you encountered during your fast. You may wish to use the 10 questions previously listed to help you reflect on what God is doing in your life. Begin writing with the statement, "I have just concluded (name of the specific fast). During my fast...." Then record the events and insights associated with your fast. Take time to describe what you did on your fast day and what God taught you. Use your journal to record any commitments made as a result of the lessons you have learned.

Shortly after you have concluded your ninth daily fast and recorded your journal entry, set aside time to read your journal entries. Do you see a pattern or trend in what God has been teaching you? Is there something specific you need to do in obedience to what you have been learning? Journaling provides a beneficial look back over several weeks and exposes the big lessons God is attempting to teach you. What has God been teaching you as you practice the discipline of fasting? Your answer to these and other questions will help you recognize God at work in your life.

Perhaps God has used your fast to teach you lessons that can be an encouragement to others. Share with others in your small group or with your prayer partner how God has been working with you during your fasts. Ask your close Christian friends to hold you accountable for keeping the commitments you believe God would have you make.

May God use your spiritual journal to accomplish His goals in your life.

Note
1. Henry T. Blackaby and Claude V. King, *Experiencing God* (Nashville: Broadman Press, 1994).

≡ 5 ≡

BIBLICAL
REFERENCES
TO FASTING

GENERAL GUIDELINES
FOR FASTING

Spirit of Fasting

Is it a fast that I have chosen, a day for a man to afflict his soul? Is it to bow down his head like a bulrush, and to spread out sackcloth and ashes? Would you call this a fast, and an acceptable day to the Lord? Is this not the fast that I have chosen: to loose the bonds of wickedness, to undo the heavy burdens, to let the oppressed go free, and that you break every yoke? Is it not to share your bread with the hungry, and that you bring to your house the poor who are cast out; when you see the naked, that you cover him, and not hide yourself from your own flesh? (Isa. 58:5-7).

Fasting to God

Say to all the people of the land, and to the priests: "When you fasted and mourned in the fifth and seventh months during those seventy years, did you really fast for Me—for Me? When you eat and when you drink, do you not eat and drink for yourselves?" (Zech. 7:5,6).

But you, when you fast, anoint your head and wash your face, so that you do not appear to men to be fasting, but to your Father who is in the secret place; and your Father who sees in secret will reward you openly (Matt. 6:17,18).

PURPOSE OF FASTING

To Chasten the Soul
When I wept and chastened my soul with fasting, that became my reproach (Ps. 69:10).

To Humble the Soul
Then I proclaimed a fast there at the river of Ahava, that we might humble ourselves before our God, to seek from Him the right way for us and our little ones and all our possessions (Ezra 8:21).

But as for me, when they were sick, my clothing was sackcloth; I humbled myself with fasting; and my prayer would return to my own heart (Ps. 35:13).

To Seek the Lord
And Jehoshaphat feared, and set himself to seek the Lord, and proclaimed a fast throughout all Judah. So Judah gathered together to ask help from the Lord; and from all the cities of Judah they came to seek the Lord (2 Chron. 20:3,4).

To Prepare for Spiritual Warfare
However, this kind does not go out except by prayer and fasting (Matt. 17:21).

WHEN TO FAST

When Facing the Judgment of God
So it was, when Ahab heard those words, that he tore his

clothes and put sackcloth on his body, and fasted and lay in sackcloth, and went about mourning (1 Kings 21:27).

Consecrate a fast, call a sacred assembly; gather the elders and all the inhabitants of the land into the house of the Lord your God, and cry out to the Lord (Joel 1:14).

"Now, therefore," says the Lord, "Turn to me with all your heart, with fasting, with weeping, and with mourning." So rend your heart, and not your garments; return to the Lord your God, for He is gracious and merciful, slow to anger, and of great kindness; and He relents from doing harm (Joel 2:12).

And Jonah began to enter the city on the first day's walk. Then he cried out and said, "Yet forty days, and Nineveh shall be overthrown!" So the people of Nineveh believed God, proclaimed a fast, and put on sackcloth, from the greatest to the least of them (Jon. 3:4,5).

During Periods of National Mourning

Now when the inhabitants of Jabesh Gilead heard what the Philistines had done to Saul, all the valiant men arose and traveled all night, and took the body of Saul and the bodies of his sons from the wall of Beth Shan; and they came to Jabesh and burned them there. Then they took their bones and buried them under the tamarisk tree at Jabesh, and fasted seven days (1 Sam. 31:11-13).

And they mourned and wept and fasted until evening for Saul and for Jonathan his son, for the people of the Lord and for the house of Israel, because they had fallen by the sword (2 Sam. 1:12).

And when all the people came to persuade David to eat food while it was still day, David took an oath, saying, "God do so to me, and more also, if I taste bread or anything else till the sun goes down!" (2 Sam. 3:35).

And when all Jabesh Gilead heard all that the Philistines had done to Saul, all the valiant men arose and took the body of Saul and the bodies of his sons; and they brought them to Jabesh, and buried their bones under the tamarisk tree at Jabesh, and fasted seven days (1 Chron. 10:11,12).

When Communion with Christ Is Broken

And Jesus said to them, "Can the friends of the bridegroom mourn as long as the bridegroom is with them? But the days will come when the bridegroom will be taken away from them, and then they will fast" (Matt. 9:15).

And Jesus said to them, "Can the friends of the bridegroom fast while the bridegroom is with them? As long as they have the bridegroom with them they cannot fast. But the days will come when the bridegroom will be taken away from them, and then they will fast in those days" (Mark 2:19,20).

And He said to them, "Can you make the friends of the bridegroom fast while the bridegroom is with them? But the days will come when the bridegroom will be taken away from them; then they will fast in those days" (Luke 5:34,35).

When Concerned for the Welfare of Others

But as for me, when they were sick, my clothing was sackcloth; I humbled myself with fasting; and my prayer would return to my own heart (Ps. 35:13).

When Challenged by Personal Concerns

Then Nathan departed to his house. And the Lord struck the child that Uriah's wife bore to David, and it became ill. David therefore pleaded with God for the child, and David fasted and went in and lay all night on the ground. So the elders of his house arose and went to him, to raise him up from the ground. But he would not, nor did he eat food with them (2 Sam. 12:15-17).

Then his servants said to him, "What is this that you have done? You fasted and wept for the child while he was alive, but when the child died, you arose and ate food." And he said, "While the child was still alive, I fasted and wept; for I said, 'Who can tell whether the Lord will be gracious to me, that the child may live?' But now he is dead; why should I fast? Can I bring him back again? I shall go to him, but he shall not return to me" (2 Sam. 12:21-23).

When Facing Danger

Then some came and told Jehoshaphat, saying, "A great multitude is coming against you from beyond the sea, from Syria; and they are in Hazazon Tamar" (which is En Gedi). And Jehoshaphat feared, and set himself to seek the Lord, and proclaimed a fast throughout all Judah (2 Chron. 20:2,3).

Then I proclaimed a fast there at the river of Ahava, that we might humble ourselves before our God, to seek from Him the right way for us and our little ones and all our possessions. For I was ashamed to request of the king an escort of soldiers and horsemen to help us against the enemy on the road, because we had spoken to the king, saying, "The hand of our God is upon all those for good who seek Him, but His power and His wrath are against those who forsake Him." So we fasted and entreated our God for this, and He answered our prayer (Ezra 8:21-23).

Then Esther told them to reply to Mordecai: "Go, gather all the Jews who are present in Shushan, and fast for me; neither eat nor drink for three days, night or day. My maids and I will fast likewise. And so I will go to the king, which is against the law; and if I perish, I perish!" (Esther 4:15,16).

When Engaged in Spiritual Warfare

However, this kind does not go out except by prayer and fasting (Matt. 17:21).

So He said to them, "This kind can come out by nothing but prayer and fasting" (Mark 9:29).

When Ordaining Ministers of the Gospel

As they ministered to the Lord and fasted, the Holy Spirit said, "Now separate to Me Barnabas and Saul for the work to which I have called them." Then, having fasted and prayed, and laid hands on them, they sent them away (Acts 13:2,3).

So when they had appointed elders in every church, and prayed with fasting, they commended them to the Lord in whom they had believed (Acts 14:23).

Fasting Accompanied by...

Abstinence from Sexual Relationships

Do not deprive one another except with consent for a time, that you may give yourselves to fasting and prayer; and come together again so that Satan does not tempt you because of your lack of self-control (1 Cor. 7:5).

Confession of Sin

So they gathered together at Mizpah, drew water, and poured it out before the Lord. And they fasted that day, and said there, "We have sinned against the Lord." And Samuel judged the children of Israel at Mizpah (1 Sam. 7:6).

Now on the twenty-fourth day of this month the children of Israel were assembled with fasting, in sackcloth, and with dust on their heads. Then those of Israelite lineage separated themselves from all foreigners; and they stood and confessed their sins and the iniquities of their fathers. And they stood up in their place and read from the Book of the Law of the Lord their God for one-fourth of the day; and for another fourth they confessed and worshipped the Lord their God (Neh. 9:1-3).

Humiliation

And I fell down before the Lord, as at the first, forty days and forty nights; I neither ate bread nor drank water, because of all your sin which you committed in doing wickedly in the sight of the Lord, to provoke Him to anger (Deut. 9:18).

But as for me, when they were sick, my clothing was sackcloth; I humbled myself with fasting; and my prayer would return to my own heart (Ps. 35:13).

When I wept and chastened my soul with fasting, that became my reproach (Ps. 69:10).

So it was, when Ahab heard those words, that he tore his clothes and put sackcloth on his body, and fasted and lay in sackcloth, and went about mourning (1 Kings 21:27).

Now on the twenty-fourth day of this month the children of Israel were assembled with fasting, in sackcloth, and with dust on their heads (Neh. 9:1).

Lamenting

And Mordecai sent letters to all the Jews, to the one hundred and twenty-seven provinces of the kingdom of Ahasuerus, with words of peace and truth, to confirm these days of Purim at their appointed time, as Mordecai the Jew and Queen Esther had prescribed for them, and as they had decreed for themselves and their descendants concerning matters of their fasting and lamenting (Esther 9:30,31).

Mourning

And they mourned and wept and fasted until evening for Saul and for Jonathan his son, for the people of the Lord and for the house of Israel, because they had fallen by the sword (2 Sam. 1:12).

So it was, when Ahab heard those words, that he tore his clothes and put sackcloth on his body, and fasted and lay in sackcloth, and went about mourning (1 Kings 21:27).

And in every province where the king's command and decree arrived, there was great mourning among the Jews, with fasting, weeping, and wailing; and many lay in sackcloth and ashes (Esther 4:3).

So it was, when I heard these words, that I sat down and wept, and mourned for many days; I was fasting and praying before the God of heaven (Neh. 1:4).

"Now, therefore," says the Lord, "Turn to me with all your heart, with fasting, with weeping, and with mourning" (Joel 2:12).

Then Ezra rose up from before the house of God, and went into the chamber of Jehohanan the son of Eliashib; and when he came there, he ate no bread and drank no water, for he mourned because of the guilt of those from the captivity (Ezra 10:6).

Personal Demeanor

But you, when you fast, anoint your head and wash your face (Matt. 6:17).

Prayer

So we fasted and entreated our God for this, and He answered our prayer (Ezra 8:23).

So it was, when I heard these words, that I sat down and wept, and mourned for many days; I was fasting and praying before the God of heaven (Neh. 1:4).

But as for me, when they were sick, my clothing was sackcloth; I humbled myself with fasting; and my prayer would return to my own heart (Ps. 35:13).

Then I set my face toward the Lord God to make request by prayer and supplications, with fasting, sackcloth, and ashes (Dan. 9:3).

Then they said to Him, "Why do the disciples of John fast often and make prayers, and likewise those of the Pharisees, but Yours eat and drink?" (Luke 5:33).

Reading the Scriptures

Now on the twenty-fourth day of this month the children of Israel were assembled with fasting, in sackcloth, and with dust on their heads. Then those of Israelite lineage separated themselves from all foreigners; and they stood and confessed their sins and the iniquities of their fathers. And they stood up in their place and read from the Book of the Law of the Lord their God for one-fourth of the day; and for another fourth they confessed and worshipped the Lord their God (Neh. 9:1-3).

You go, therefore, and read from the scroll which you have written at my instruction, the words of the Lord, in the hearing of the people in the Lord's house on the day of fasting. And you shall also read them in the hearing of all Judah who come from their cities (Jer. 36:6).

Then Baruch read from the book the words of Jeremiah in the house of the Lord, in the chamber of Gemariah the son of Shaphan the scribe, in the upper court at the entry of the New Gate of the Lord's house, in the hearing of all the people (Jer. 36:10).

Weeping

And they mourned and wept and fasted until evening for

Saul and for Jonathan his son, for the people of the Lord and for the house of Israel, because they had fallen by the sword (2 Sam. 1:12).

So it was, when I heard these words, that I sat down and wept, and mourned for many days; I was fasting and praying before the God of heaven (Neh. 1:4).

And in every province where the king's command and decree arrived, there was great mourning among the Jews, with fasting, weeping, and wailing; and many lay in sackcloth and ashes (Esther 4:3).

When I wept and chastened my soul with fasting, that became my reproach (Ps. 69:10).

"Now, therefore," says the Lord, "Turn to me with all your heart, with fasting, with weeping, and with mourning" (Joel 2:12).

Worship

Now on the twenty-fourth day of this month the children of Israel were assembled with fasting, in sackcloth, and with dust on their heads. Then those of Israelite lineage separated themselves from all foreigners; and they stood and confessed their sins and the iniquities of their fathers. And they stood up in their place and read from the Book of the Law of the Lord their God for one-fourth of the day; and for another fourth they confessed and worshipped the Lord their God (Neh. 9:1-3).

PROMISED BLESSINGS ASSOCIATED WITH FASTING

Answered Prayer, Insight and Restoration

Then you shall call, and the Lord will answer; you shall cry, and He will say, "Here I am." If you take away the yoke from your midst, the pointing of the finger, and speaking wickedness, if you extend your soul to the hungry and satisfy the afflicted soul, then your light shall dawn in the darkness, and your darkness shall be as the noonday. The Lord will guide you continually, and satisfy your soul in drought, and strengthen your bones; you shall be like a watered garden, and like a spring of water, whose waters do not fail. Those from among you shall build the old waste places; you shall raise up the foundations of many generations; and you shall be called the Repairer of the Breach, the Restorer of Streets to Dwell In (Isa. 58:9-12).

Joy, Gladness and Cheerfulness

Thus says the Lord of hosts: "The fast of the fourth month, the fast of the fifth, the fast of the seventh, and the fast of the tenth, shall be joy and gladness and cheerful feasts for the house of Judah. Therefore love truth and peace" (Zech. 8:19).

Rewarded by God the Father

But you, when you fast, anoint your head and wash your face, so that you do not appear to men to be fasting, but to your Father who is in the secret place; and your Father who sees in secret will reward you openly (Matt. 6:17,18).

Spiritual Power over Demons

However, this kind does not go out except by prayer and fasting (Matt. 17:21).

So He said to them, "This kind can come out by nothing but prayer and fasting" (Mark 9:29).

Effects of Fasting

And the word of the Lord came to Elijah the Tishbite, saying, "See how Ahab has humbled himself before Me? Because he has humbled himself before Me, I will not bring the calamity in his days. In the days of his son I will bring the calamity on his house (1 Kings 21:28,29).

My knees are weak through fasting, and my flesh is feeble from lack of fatness (Ps. 109:24).

Now Jesus called His disciples to Himself and said, "I have compassion on the multitude, because they have now continued with Me three days and have nothing to eat. And I do not want to send them away hungry, lest they faint on the way" (Matt. 15:32).

I have compassion on the multitude, because they have now continued with Me three days and have nothing to eat. And if I send them away hungry to their own houses, they will faint on the way; for some of them have come from afar (Mark 8:2,3).

PROCLAMATIONS OF FASTS

Yom Kippur (Day of Atonement)
Also the tenth day of this seventh month shall be the Day of Atonement. It shall be a holy convocation for you; you shall afflict your souls, and offer an offering made by fire to the Lord (Lev. 23:27).

By Saul
And the men of Israel were distressed that day, for Saul had placed the people under oath, saying, "Cursed is the man who eats any food until evening, before I have taken vengeance on my enemies." So none of the people tasted food (1 Sam. 14:24).

By Jehoshaphat
And Jehoshaphat feared, and set himself to seek the Lord, and proclaimed a fast throughout all Judah (2 Chron. 20:3).

By Joel
Blow the trumpet in Zion, consecrate a fast, call a sacred assembly (Joel 2:15).

By the King of Nineveh
So the people of Nineveh believed God, proclaimed a fast, and put on sackcloth, from the greatest to the least of them. Then word came to the king of Nineveh; and he arose from his throne and laid aside his robe, covered himself with sackcloth and sat in ashes. And he caused it to be proclaimed and published throughout Nineveh by the decree of the king and his nobles, saying, "Let neither man nor beast, herd nor flock, taste anything; do not let them eat, or drink water. But let

man and beast be covered with sackcloth, and cry mightily to God; yes, let every one turn from his evil way and from the violence that is in his hands. Who can tell if God will turn and relent, and turn away from His fierce anger, so that we may not perish?" (Jonah 3:5-9).

By Jehoiakim

Now it came to pass in the fifth year of Jehoiakim the son of Josiah, king of Judah, in the ninth month, that they proclaimed a fast before the Lord to all the people in Jerusalem, and to all the people who came from the cities of Judah to Jerusalem (Jer. 36:9).

By Ezra

Then I proclaimed a fast there at the river of Ahava, that we might humble ourselves before our God, to seek from Him the right way for us and our little ones and all our possessions. For I was ashamed to request of the king an escort of soldiers and horsemen to help us against the enemy on the road because we had spoken to the king, saying, "The hand of our God is upon all those for good who seek Him, but His power and His wrath are against those who forsake Him." So we fasted and entreated our God for this, and He answered our prayer (Ezra 8:21-23).

By Esther

Then Esther told them to reply to Mordecai: "Go, gather all the Jews who are present in Shushan, and fast for me; neither eat nor drink for three days, night or day. My maids and I will fast likewise. And so I will go to the king, which is against the law; and if I perish, I perish!" (Esther 4:15,16).

For Purim

And Mordecai sent letters to all the Jews, to the one hundred and twenty-seven provinces of the kingdom of Ahasuerus, with words of peace and truth, to confirm these days of Purim at their appointed time, as Mordecai the Jew and Queen Esther had prescribed for them, and as they had decreed for themselves and their descendants concerning matters of their fasting and lamenting (Esther 9:30,31).

DURATION OF FASTS

Part of a Day

Now the king went to his palace and spent the night fasting; and no musicians were brought before him. Also his sleep went from him (Dan. 6:18).

One Day

Also the tenth day of this seventh month shall be the Day of Atonement. It shall be a holy convocation for you; you shall afflict your souls, and offer an offering made by fire to the Lord (Lev. 23:27).

So they gathered together at Mizpah, drew water, and poured it out before the Lord. And they fasted that day, and said there, "We have sinned against the Lord." And Samuel judged the children of Israel at Mizpah (1 Sam. 7:6).

And the men of Israel were distressed that day, for Saul had placed the people under oath, saying, "Cursed is the man who eats any food until evening, before I have taken vengeance on my enemies." So none of the people tasted food (1 Sam. 14:24).

You go, therefore, and read from the scroll which you have written at my instruction, the words of the Lord, in the hearing of the people in the Lord's house on the day of fasting. And you shall also read them in the hearing of all Judah who come from their cities (Jer. 36:6).

Now on the twenty-fourth day of this month the children of Israel were assembled with fasting, in sackcloth, and with dust on their heads (Neh. 9:1).

Three Days

And they gave him a piece of a cake of figs and two clusters of raisins. So when he had eaten, his strength came back to him; for he had eaten no bread nor drunk water for three days and three nights (1 Sam. 30:12).

Now Jesus called His disciples to Himself and said, "I have compassion on the multitude, because they have now continued with Me three days and have nothing to eat. And I do not want to send them away hungry, lest they faint on the way" (Matt. 15:32).

I have compassion on the multitude, because they have now continued with Me three days and have nothing to eat. And if I send them away hungry to their own houses, they will faint on the way; for some of them have come from afar (Mark 8:2,3).

And he was three days without sight, and neither ate nor drank (Acts 9:9).

Seven Days

Now when the inhabitants of Jabesh Gilead heard what the Philistines had done to Saul, all the valiant men arose and traveled all night, and took the body of Saul and the bodies of his sons from the wall of Beth Shan; and they came to Jabesh and burned them there. Then they took their bones and buried them under the tamarisk tree at Jabesh, and fasted seven days (1 Sam. 31:11-13).

And when all Jabesh Gilead heard all that the Philistines had done to Saul, all the valiant men arose and took the body of Saul and the bodies of his sons; and they brought them to Jabesh, and buried their bones under the tamarisk tree at Jabesh, and fasted seven days (1 Chron. 10:11,12).

Then Nathan departed to his house. And the Lord struck the child that Uriah's wife bore to David, and it became ill. David therefore pleaded with God for the child, and David fasted and went in and lay all night on the ground. So the elders of his house arose and went to him, to raise him up from the ground. But he would not, nor did he eat food with them. Then on the seventh day it came to pass that the child died....Then his servants said to him, "What is this that you have done? You fasted and wept for the child while he was alive, but when the child died, you arose and ate food." And he said, "While the child was still alive, I fasted and wept; for I said, 'Who can tell whether the Lord will be gracious to me, that the child may live?' But now he is dead; why should I fast? Can I bring him back again? I shall go to him, but he shall not return to me" (2 Sam. 12:15-18, 21-23).

Fourteen Days

And as day was about to dawn, Paul implored them all to take food, saying, "Today is the fourteenth day you have waited and continued without food, and eaten nothing" (Acts 27:33).

Three Weeks

In those days I, Daniel, was mourning three full weeks. I ate no pleasant food, no meat or wine came into my mouth, nor did I anoint myself at all, till three whole weeks were fulfilled (Dan. 10:2,3).

Forty Days

So he was there with the Lord forty days and forty nights; he neither ate bread nor drank water. And He wrote on the tablets the words of the covenant, the Ten Commandments (Exod. 34:28).

When I went up into the mountain to receive the tablets of stone, the tablets of the covenant which the Lord made with you, then I stayed on the mountain forty days and forty nights. I neither ate bread nor drank water (Deut. 9:9).

And I fell down before the Lord, as at the first, forty days and forty nights; I neither ate bread nor drank water, because of all your sin which you committed in doing wickedly in the sight of the Lord, to provoke Him to anger (Deut. 9:18).

So he arose, and ate and drank; and he went in the strength of that food forty days and forty nights as far as Horeb, the mountain of God (1 Kings 19:8).

Then Jesus was led up by the Spirit into the wilderness to be tempted by the devil. And when He had fasted forty days and forty nights, afterward He was hungry (Matt. 4:1,2).

Then Jesus, being filled with the Holy Spirit, returned from the Jordan and was led by the Spirit into the wilderness, being tempted for forty days by the devil. And in those days

He ate nothing, and afterward, when they had ended, He was hungry (Luke 4:1,2).

ABUSES OF FASTING

By Hypocrites
"'Why have we fasted,' they say, 'and You have not seen? Why have we afflicted our souls, and You take no notice?'" "In fact, in the day of your fast you find pleasure, and exploit all your laborers. Indeed you fast for strife and debate, and to strike with the fist of wickedness. You will not fast as you do this day, to make your voice heard on high" (Isa. 58:3,4).

Then the Lord said to me, "Do not pray for this people, for their good. When they fast, I will not hear their cry; and when they offer burnt offering and grain offering, I will not accept them. But I will consume them by the sword, by the famine, and by the pestilence" (Jer. 14:11,12).

Moreover, when you fast, do not be like the hypocrites, with a sad countenance. For they disfigure their faces that they may appear to men to be fasting. Assuredly, I say to you, they have their reward (Matt. 6:16).

By the Pharisees
The Pharisee stood and prayed thus with himself, "God, I thank You that I am not like other men—extortioners, unjust, adulterers, or even as this tax collector. I fast twice a week; I give tithes of all that I possess" (Luke 18:11,12).

By Queen Jezebel
She wrote in letters, saying, "Proclaim a fast, and seat Naboth with high honor among the people; and seat two men, scoundrels, before him to bear witness against him, saying, 'You have blasphemed God and the king.' Then take him out, and stone him, that he may die" (1 Kings 21:9,10).

By the Leaders of Jezreel
So the men of his city, the elders and nobles who were inhab-

itants of his city, did as Jezebel had said to them, as it was written in the letters which she had sent to them. They proclaimed a fast, and seated Naboth with high honor among the people. And two men, scoundrels, came in and sat before him; and the scoundrels witnessed against him, against Naboth, in the presence of the people, saying, "Naboth has blasphemed God and the king!" Then they took him outside the city and stoned him with stones, so that he died (1 Kings 21:11-13).

By False Teachers

Now the Spirit expressly says that in latter times some will depart from the faith, giving heed to deceiving spirits and doctrines of demons, speaking lies in hypocrisy, having their own conscience seared with a hot iron, forbidding to marry, and commanding to abstain from foods which God created to be received with thanksgiving by those who believe and know the truth (1 Tim. 4:1-3).

EXAMPLES OF CORPORATE FASTING

Israel, Before the Battle Against Benjamin

Then all the children of Israel, that is, all the people, went up and came to the house of God and wept. They sat there before the Lord and fasted that day until evening; and they offered burnt offerings and peace offerings before the Lord (Judg. 20:26).

Israel, at Mizpah

So they gathered together at Mizpah, drew water, and poured it out before the Lord. And they fasted that day, and said there, "We have sinned against the Lord." And Samuel judged the children of Israel at Mizpah (1 Sam. 7:6).

Saul's Army

And the men of Israel were distressed that day, for Saul had placed the people under oath, saying, "Cursed is the man who eats any food until evening, before I have taken vengeance on my enemies." So none of the people tasted food (1 Sam. 14:24).

Men of Jabesh Gilead

Now when the inhabitants of Jabesh Gilead heard what the Philistines had done to Saul, all the valiant men arose and traveled all night, and took the body of Saul and the bodies of his sons from the wall of Beth Shan; and they came to Jabesh and burned them there. Then they took their bones and buried them under the tamarisk tree at Jabesh, and fasted seven days (1 Sam. 31:11-13).

And when all Jabesh Gilead heard all that the Philistines had done to Saul, all the valiant men arose and took the body of Saul and the bodies of his sons; and they brought them to Jabesh, and buried their bones under the tamarisk tree at Jabesh, and fasted seven days (1 Chron. 10:11,12).

Mighty Men of David

And they mourned and wept and fasted until evening for Saul and for Jonathan his son, for the people of the Lord and for the house of Israel, because they had fallen by the sword (2 Sam. 1:12).

Judah

And Jehoshaphat feared, and set himself to seek the Lord, and proclaimed a fast throughout all Judah. So Judah gathered together to ask help from the Lord; and from all the cities of Judah they came to seek the Lord (2 Chron. 20:3,4).

People of Nineveh

So the people of Nineveh believed God, proclaimed a fast, and put on sackcloth, from the greatest to the least of them. Then word came to the king of Nineveh; and he arose from his throne and laid aside his robe, covered himself with sackcloth and sat in ashes. And he caused it to be proclaimed and published throughout Nineveh by the decree of the king and his nobles, saying, "Let neither man nor beast, herd nor flock, taste anything; do not let them eat, or drink water. But let man and beast be covered with sackcloth, and cry mightily to

God; yes, let every one turn from his evil way and from the violence that is in his hands. Who can tell if God will turn and relent, and turn away from His fierce anger, so that we may not perish?" (Jon. 3:5-9).

People of Judah (During the Reign of Jehoiakim)
Now it came to pass in the fifth year of Jehoiakim the son of Josiah, king of Judah, in the ninth month, that they proclaimed a fast before the Lord to all the people in Jerusalem, and to all the people who came from the cities of Judah to Jerusalem. Then Baruch read from the book the words of Jeremiah in the house of the Lord, in the chamber of Gemariah the son of Shaphan the scribe, in the upper court at the entry of the New Gate of the Lord's house, in the hearing of all the people (Jer. 36:9,10).

Remnant Returning After the Captivity
Then I proclaimed a fast there at the river of Ahava, that we might humble ourselves before God, to seek from Him the right way for us and our little ones and all our possessions. For I was ashamed to request of the king an escort of soldiers and horsemen to help us against the enemy on the road, because we had spoken to the king, saying, "The hand of our God is upon those for good who seek Him, but His power and His wrath are against those who forsake Him." So we fasted and entreated our God for this, and He answered our prayer (Ezra 8:21-23).

Remnant in Jerusalem After the Captivity
Now on the twenty-fourth day of this month the children of Israel were assembled with fasting, in sackcloth, and with dust on their heads (Neh. 9:1).

Jews During the Reign of Ahasuerus
And in every province where the king's command and decree arrived, there was great mourning among the Jews, with fasting, weeping, and wailing; and many lay in sackcloth and ashes (Esther 4:3).

Then Esther told them to reply to Mordecai: "Go, gather all the Jews who are present in Shushan, and fast for me; neither eat nor drink for three days, night or day. My maids and I will fast likewise. And so I will go to the king, which is against the law; and if I perish, I perish!" (Esther 4:15,16).

Pharisees

Then the disciples of John came to Him, saying, "Why do we and the Pharisees fast often, but Your disciples do not fast?" (Matt. 9:14).

The disciples of John and of the Pharisees were fasting. Then they came and said to Him, "Why do the disciples of John and of the Pharisees fast, but Your disciples do not fast?" (Mark 2:18).

Then they said to Him, "Why do the disciples of John fast often and make prayers, and likewise those of the Pharisees, but Yours eat and drink?" (Luke 5:33).

Disciples of John the Baptist

Then the disciples of John came to Him, saying, "Why do we and the Pharisees fast often, but Your disciples do not fast?" (Matt. 9:14).

The disciples of John and of the Pharisees were fasting. Then they came and said to Him, "Why do the disciples of John and of the Pharisees fast, but Your disciples do not fast?" (Mark 2:18).

Then they said to Him, "Why do the disciples of John fast often and make prayers, and likewise those of the Pharisees, but Yours eat and drink?" (Luke 5:33).

Multitudes Following Jesus

Now Jesus called His disciples to Himself and said, "I have compassion on the multitude, because they have now continued with Me three days and have nothing to eat. And I do not want to send them away hungry, lest they faint on the way" (Matt. 15:32).

I have compassion on the multitude, because they have now continued with Me three days and have nothing to eat.

And if I send them away hungry to their own houses, they will faint on the way; for some of them have come from afar (Mark 8:2,3).

Leaders of the Church at Antioch

Now in the church that was at Antioch there were certain prophets and teachers: Barnabas, Simeon who was called Niger, Lucius of Cyrene, Manaen who had been brought up with Herod the tetrarch, and Saul. As they ministered to the Lord and fasted, the Holy Spirit said, "Now separate to Me Barnabas and Saul for the work to which I have called them." Then, having fasted and prayed, and laid hands on them, they sent them away (Acts 13:1-3).

Jews Committed to Killing Paul

And when it was day, some of the Jews banded together and bound themselves under an oath, saying that they would neither eat nor drink till they had killed Paul. Now there were more than forty who had formed this conspiracy (Acts 23:12,13).

Crew and Passengers on the Ship of Adramyttium

And as day was about to dawn, Paul implored them all to take food, saying, "Today is the fourteenth day you have waited and continued without food, and eaten nothing" (Acts 27:33).

EXAMPLES OF INDIVIDUALS FASTING

Ahab

So Ahab went into his house sullen and displeased because of the word which Naboth the Jezreelite had spoken to him; for he had said, "I will not give you the inheritance of my fathers." And he lay down on his bed, and turned away his face, and would eat no food. But Jezebel his wife came to him, and said to him, "Why is your spirit so sullen that you eat no food?" (1 Kings 21:4,5).

So it was, when Ahab heard those words, that he tore his

clothes and put sackcloth on his body, and fasted and lay in sackcloth, and went about mourning (1 Kings 21:27).

Anna

Now there was one, Anna, a prophetess, the daughter of Phanuel, of the tribe of Asher. She was of a great age, and had lived with a husband seven years from her virginity; and this woman was a widow of about eighty-four years, who did not depart from the temple, but served God with fastings and prayers night and day (Luke 2:36,37).

Cornelius

So Cornelius said, "Four days ago I was fasting until this hour; and at the ninth hour I prayed in my house, and behold, a man stood before me in bright clothing, and said, 'Cornelius, your prayer has been heard, and your alms are remembered in the sight of God'" (Acts 10:30,31).

Daniel

Then I set my face toward the Lord God to make request by prayer and supplications, with fasting, sackcloth, and ashes (Dan. 9:3).

In those days I, Daniel, was mourning three full weeks. I ate no pleasant food, no meat or wine came into my mouth, nor did I anoint myself at all, till three whole weeks were fulfilled (Dan. 10:2,3).

Darius

Now the king went to his palace and spent the night fasting; and no musicians were brought before him. Also his sleep went from him (Dan. 6:18).

David

But as for me, when they were sick, my clothing was sackcloth; I humbled myself with fasting; and my prayer would return to my own heart (Ps. 35:13).

When I wept and chastened my soul with fasting, that became my reproach (Ps. 69:10).

And when all the people came to persuade David to eat food while it was still day, David took an oath, saying, "God do so to me, and more also, if I taste bread or anything else till the sun goes down!" (2 Sam. 3:35).

Then Nathan departed to his house. And the Lord struck the child that Uriah's wife bore to David, and it became very ill. David therefore pleaded with God for the child, and David fasted and went in and lay all night on the ground. So the elders of his house arose and went to him, to raise him up from the ground. But he would not, nor did he eat food with them (2 Sam. 12:15-17).

My knees are weak through fasting, and my flesh is feeble from lack of fatness (Ps. 109:24).

An Egyptian Servant of an Amalekite

And they gave him a piece of cake of figs and two clusters of raisins. So when he had eaten, his strength came back to him; for he had eaten no bread nor drunk water for three days and three nights (1 Sam. 30:12).

Elijah

So he arose, and ate and drank; and he went in the strength of that food forty days and forty nights as far as Horeb, the mountain of God (1 Kings 19:8).

Esther

Then Esther told them to reply to Mordecai: "Go, gather all the Jews who are present in Shushan, and fast for me; neither eat nor drink for three days, night or day. My maids and I will fast likewise. And so I will go to the king, which is against the law; and if I perish, I perish!" (Esther 4:15,16).

Ezra

At the evening sacrifice I arose from my fasting; and having torn my garment and my robe, I fell on my knees and spread out my hands to the Lord my God (Ezra 9:5).

Then Ezra rose up from before the house of God, and went into the chamber of Jehohanan the son of Eliashib; and when he came there, he ate no bread and drank no water, for he mourned because of the guilt of those from the captivity (Ezra 10:6).

Hannah

So it was, year by year, when she went up to the house of the Lord, that she provoked her; therefore she wept and did not eat. Then Elkanah her husband said to her, "Hannah, why do you weep? Why do you not eat? And why is your heart grieved? Am I not better to you than ten sons?" (1 Sam. 1:7,8).

Jesus

Then Jesus was led up by the Spirit into the wilderness to be tempted by the devil. And when He had fasted forty days and forty nights, afterward He was hungry (Matt. 4:1,2).

Then Jesus, being filled with the Holy Spirit, returned from the Jordan and was led by the Spirit into the wilderness, being tempted for forty days by the devil. And in those days He ate nothing, and afterward, when they had ended, He was hungry (Luke 4:1,2).

John the Baptist

For John came neither eating nor drinking, and they say, "He has a demon" (Matt. 11:18).

For John the Baptist came neither eating bread nor drinking wine, and you say, "He has a demon" (Luke 7:33).

Jonathan

So Jonathan arose from the table in fierce anger, and ate no food the second day of the month, for he was grieved for David, because his father had treated him shamefully (1 Sam. 20:34).

Moses

So he was there with the Lord forty days and forty nights; he neither ate bread nor drank water. And He wrote on the tablets the words of the covenant, the Ten Commandments (Exod. 34:28).

When I went up into the mountain to receive the tablets of stone, the tablets of the covenant which the Lord made with you, then I stayed on the mountain forty days and forty nights. I neither ate bread nor drank water (Deut. 9:9).

And I fell down before the Lord, as at the first, forty days and forty nights; I neither ate bread nor drank water, because of all your sin which you committed in doing wickedly in the sight of the Lord, to provoke Him to anger (Deut. 9:18).

Nehemiah

So it was, when I heard these words, that I sat down and wept, and mourned for many days; I was fasting and praying before the God of heaven (Neh. 1:4).

Paul

And he was three days without sight, and neither ate nor drank (Acts 9:9).

In stripes, in imprisonments, in tumults, in labors, in sleeplessness, in fastings (2 Cor. 6:5).

In weariness and toil, in sleeplessness often, in hunger and thirst, in fastings often, in cold and nakedness (2 Cor. 11:27).

Saul

Immediately Saul fell full length on the ground, and was dreadfully afraid because of the words of Samuel. And there was no strength in him, for he had eaten no food all day or all night (1 Sam. 28:20).

Uriah

And Uriah said to David, "The ark and Israel and Judah are dwelling in tents, and my lord Joab and the servants of my lord are encamped in the open fields. Shall I then go to my house to eat and drink, and to lie with my wife? As you live, and as your soul lives, I will not do this thing" (2 Sam. 11:11).

SPECIALIZED FASTS (RESTRICTED DIETS)

No Cereals or Grains (Feast of Firstfruits)

You shall eat neither bread nor parched grain nor fresh grain until the same day that you have brought an offering to your

God; it shall be a statute forever throughout your generations in all your dwellings (Lev. 23:14).

No Grapes or Grape Products (Nazirite Vow)

He shall separate himself from wine and similar drink; he shall drink neither vinegar made from wine nor vinegar made from similar drink; neither shall he drink any grape juice, nor eat fresh grapes or raisins. All the days of his separation he shall eat nothing that is produced from the grapevine, from seed to skin (Num. 6:3,4).

Vegetarian Dishes Only (Daniel in Babylon)

"Please test your servants for ten days, and let them give us vegetables to eat and water to drink. Then let our appearance be examined before you, and the appearance of the young men who eat the portion of the king's delicacies; and as you see fit, so deal with your servants." So he consented with them in this matter, and tested them ten days. And at the end of ten days their features appeared better and fatter in flesh than all the young men who ate the portion of the king's delicacies. Thus the steward took away their portion of delicacies and the wine that they were to drink, and gave them vegetables (Dan. 1:12-16).

Abstaining from Questionable Foods

Do not destroy the work of God for the sake of food. All things indeed are pure, but it is evil for the man who eats with offense. It is good neither to eat meat nor drink wine nor do anything by which your brother stumbles or is offended or is made weak (Rom. 14:20,21).

Therefore, if food makes my brother stumble, I will never again eat meat, lest I make my brother stumble (1 Cor. 8:13).

ANNOTATED
BIBLIOGRAPHY

Anderson, Andy. *Fasting Changed My Life*. (Foreword by Jack R. Taylor.) Nashville: Broadman Press, 1977. A testimonial of the author's experience of fasting. Also includes testimonials of other Christian leaders.

Beall, James Lee. *The Adventure of Fasting*. Grand Rapids: Fleming H. Revell Co., 1974. A general book about fasting.

Bragg, Paul C. *The Miracle of Fasting*. Santa Ana, Calif.: Health Science, 1976. A popular discussion about fasting from a medical and health perspective. Advocates regular fasting for health reasons.

Bright, Bill. *The Coming Revival: America's Call to Fast, Pray and Seek God's Face*. Orlando: New Life Publications, the publishing ministry of Campus Crusade for Christ, 1995. Recounts the author's 40-day fast and exhorts others to fast and pray for revival in America.

Bright, Bill. *Seven Basic Steps to Successful Fasting and Prayer*. Orlando: New Life Publications, the publishing ministry of Campus Crusade for Christ, 1995. Tells how to prepare spiritually for fasting.

Buckinger, Otto H. F. *Everything You Want to Know About Fasting*. New York: Pyramid Books, 1972. A popular discussion about fasting from a medical and health perspective. Advocates regular fasting for health reasons.

Cott, Allan. *Fasting: The Ultimate Diet*. New York: Bantam Books, 1975. A popular discussion from a medical perspective about fasting as an effective approach to significant weight loss.

Duewel, Wesley L. *Touch the World Through Prayer*. (Foreword by Bill and Vonette Bright.) Grand Rapids: Francis Asbury Press, 1986. A practical manual focusing on various aspects of the ministry of prayer. Includes a chapter about fasting as a means of deepening one's prayer ministry.

Falwell, Jerry. *Fasting: What the Bible Teaches*. Wheaton, Ill.: Tyndale House Publishers, Inc., 1981. A study of biblical teaching about fasting centered on a call for a national fast to galvanize a return to traditional moral values in American politics and social policy.

Greenblatt, Robert B. *Search the Scriptures: Modern Medicine and Biblical Personages*. (Foreword by Henry King Stanford.) Carnforth Lancs, England: The Parthenon Press, 1985. An interpretation of selected biblical events viewed through modern medical knowledge. Includes a brief chapter about fasting.

Grooms, J. O. *Soul-Winner's Fast*. Lynchburg, Va.: Treasure Path to Soul Winning, Inc., 1979. A six-month topical Scripture memory program based on 120 verses addressing various issues of fasting.

Kirban, Salem. *How to Keep Healthy and Happy by Fasting*. Huntingdon, Pa.: Salem Kirban, 1971. A popular discussion of fasting for both health and spiritual reasons, with an emphasis on a weekly one-day fast for better health.

Lloyd-Jones, D. Martyn. *Studies in the Sermon on the Mount*. Grand Rapids: Wm. B. Eerdmans Publishing Company, 1971. A classic study of the Sermon on the Mount (Matt. 5—7) by a leading British expositor. Includes a sermon about fasting based on Matthew 6:16-18.

Murray, Andrew. *With Christ in the School of Prayer: Thoughts on Our Training for the Ministry of Intercession*. Grand Rapids: Fleming H. Revell Co., 1953. A classic study on prayer by a respected Christian leader in the last century. Includes a chapter about fasting.

Porter, Douglas. *Investing in the Harvest*. Lynchburg, Va.: Church Growth Institute, 1991. A stewardship campaign that incorporates a 40-hour fast. Includes a tract offering practical guidelines to be observed in a weekend fast.

Prince, Derek. *Shaping History Through Prayer and Fasting*. Grand Rapids: Fleming H. Revell Co., 1973. An exhortation to fast to change in the United States.

Rice, John R. *Prayer: Asking and Receiving*. Introduction by Oswald J. Smith. Murfreesboro, Tenn.: Sword of the Lord Publishers, 1942. A comprehensive study about prayer by a leading evangelist/revivalist in the middle of this century. Includes a chapter about fasting.

Sanders, J. Oswald. *Prayer Power Unlimited.* Chicago: Moody Press, 1977. A study of various aspects of personal prayer. Includes a chapter titled, "Should Christians Fast?"

Shelton, Herbert M. *Fasting Can Save Your Life.* Chicago: Natural Hygiene Press, 1978. A popular discussion about fasting from a medical and health perspective. Advocates regular fasting to benefit health.

Towns, Elmer L. *Spiritual Factors of Church Growth.* Lynchburg, Va: Church Growth Institute, 1992. A comprehensive study of various spiritual factors that influence church growth. Includes a chapter/lecture about fasting.

Wagner, C. Peter. *Warfare Prayer: How to Seek God's Power and Protection in the Battle to Build His Kingdom.* Ventura, Calif.: Regal Books, 1992. An introductory study about the role of prayer in spiritual warfare. Includes a brief discussion about how to begin the discipline of fasting.

Wallis, Arthur. *God's Chosen Fast.* Fort Washington, Pa.: Christian Literature Crusade, 1969. A study of the primary biblical texts addressing fasting and its benefits in the Christian life.

Wemp, C. Sumner. *How on Earth Can I Be Spiritual?* Nashville: Thomas Nelson Inc., 1978. A popular study of various aspects of the spirit-filled life from a noncharismatic perspective. Includes a chapter about fasting.